DARKSIDERS II

CONTENTS

Introduction

Thank you for purchasing Prima's Official Game Guide to *Darksiders II*. This book has been carefully crafted to enhance your experience as you aid the Pale Rider in his epic quest to restore the balance of power in the realms.

HOW TO USE THIS BOOK

The information in this guide is presented in several chapters.

Exploration and Combat

The Pale Rider's journey takes him to many perilous and decrepit lands, and it's important to learn how to navigate these treacherous worlds. From the basics of traversing terrain, to the fundamentals of combat, this chapter provides a thorough overview of all aspects of gameplay.

Skills and Combos

Death's aptitude for destruction knows no bounds. This chapter provides a closer look at the Pale Rider's many skills and attacks, presenting all of this vital information in quick-reference tables. Refer to this chapter to discover the ever-increasing perks that each skill bestows on the Horseman as you level him up, along with the many violent attack combos that the Reaper can unleash against his foes.

Walkthrough

Restoring the balance of power in the realms is an arduous task, even for one such as Death. In this chapter you will find labeled maps of every area that the Horseman must explore. These maps will help you navigate through the many lands Death must journey to. Pitfalls and puzzles abound, so whenever you become stuck or lost, rely on this step-by-step walkthrough for solutions. You can also follow the walkthrough dilligently as you play, to ensure that you don't miss anything.

WALKTHROUGH MAP LEGEND

ICON	NAME		ICON	NAME		ICON	NAME		ICON	NAME
1	Room/Area			Secret Chest			Stone of Mystics			Relic of Khagoth
A	To/From (showing movement between maps)			Dungeon Map			Stone of Power			Soul Arbiter's Scroll
	Merchant			Skeleton Key			Stone of Resistance			
	Trainer			Boatman Coin			Relic of Etu-Goth			
	Tome			Book of the Dead Page			Relic of Renagoth			

Side Quests and Areas

Many side ventures can be undertaken while Death carries out his primary quest. Each of these optional asides is fully exposed in this chapter, providing you with a convenient place to turn whenever you feel the urge to stray from the beaten path. Here, you'll discover how to accept and fulfill every side quest, and you'll also find out what rewards each quest offers upon completion. Step-by-step walkthroughs are provided for every major side dungeon, ensuring that no secrets can escape your grasp.

Appendix

This guide concludes with several pages of quick-reference checklists designed to help you easily track down every item of interest in *Darksiders II*. Simply mark off each trinket as you obtain it, and you'll never miss a thing!

Exploration and Combat

Exploration and Combat

The Reaper knows many moves and abilities. Here, we review how to control Death and manage his myriad of skills. This chapter covers all of the basics; see the next chapter, "Skills and Combos," for a more in-depth look at the Pale Rider's special skills and attack combos.

CONTROLS

Because *Darksiders II* is a multi-platform title, this guide uses the following terms in reference to controller commands:

COMMAND	XBOX	PS3
Jump button	Ⓐ	✕
Action button	Ⓑ	●
Attack button	Ⓧ	■
Secondary Attack button	Ⓨ	▲

COMMAND	XBOX	PS3
Evade trigger	RB	R1
Skill trigger	LB	L1
Special Item trigger	RT	R2
Focus trigger	LT	L2

COMMAND	XBOX	PS3
Aim button	R3	R3
Pause button	START	START
Chronicle button	BACK	SELECT

EXPLORING

In *Darksiders II*, Death spends much of his time exploring ancient temples and ruins. Let's examine the many ways in which the Pale Rider can traverse his unusual surroundings.

Wall-Run

By running and jumping onto smooth walls, Death can scamper upward or sideways across short distances. This maneuver is known as a wall-run.

Vaulting

Death will automatically vault off of small wooden pegs during wall-runs, using them to preserve his momentum and extend his run along the wall.

Rounding Corners

During horizontal wall-runs, Death can round corners by jumping when he nears them. The Rider then continues to run along the adjacent wall.

Wall Bounce

When positioned between two narrow walls, Death can jump between them to extend a vertical or horizontal wall-run. This

allows the Reaper to reach greater heights, or to traverse long, narrow passages that have no floor.

Finding Purchase

Death will eventually fall if he doesn't grab onto something during a wall-run. Let's take a look at objects that the Horseman can cling to.

Hand Holds

The most common objects that Death can grab are hand holds. These distinct grips allow the Rider to find purchase and keep from falling.

Death can shimmy between hand holds, jump from them, and even perform wall-runs from them. Consider the environment carefully whenever hand holds are present, as the Rider's surroundings will often provide clues about where you might need to go.

> **NOTE**
> Press the Action button to drop down from any object that Death is hanging from.

Growth

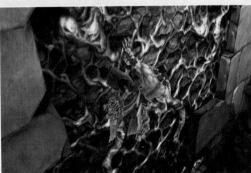

The Pale Rider can scale the distinct growth that sprawls across walls. Death has complete freedom of movement while traversing growth, and can even climb onto the ceiling if the growth spreads to it. Like hand holds, Death can also jump and perform wall-runs from this scalable substance.

Posts

Wooden posts offer Death purchase as well. The Rider can circle around these narrow objects, climb up or slide down them, and jump upward or away from them, potentially initiating a wall-run. Some posts are affixed to walls, while others are free-standing.

180 Leap

Death can perform a special backward leap while clinging onto any object. Simply press and hold the Focus trigger to make the Rider turn and lean, and then press the Jump button to make Death leap directly away from the surface or object he's grabbing onto. This useful maneuver is called a 180 leap, and is handy when you need to make precise backward jumps.

Crossing Beams

The Reaper can stand atop horizontal beams, as well as jump and initiate wall-runs from them. Tap the jump button while moving forward to skip across rows of beams.

Swimming

Death can dive underwater to explore the murky depths of any aquatic surroundings. Use the Secondary Attack button to dive, the Jump button to rise, and the Evade trigger to make Death zip forward with a burst of speed. The Rider can also initiate wall-runs while treading along the water's surface—this lets him scale walls to reach higher ledges and hand holds.

Object Interaction

The Pale Rider can interact with a wide variety of objects. The vast majority of these interactions are performed by simply approaching the object and pressing the Action button. Such interactions include pushing switches, pulling levers, opening chests and doors, and speaking with entities that the Rider encounters.

> **NOTE**
>
> Occasionally, further action is required after you press the Action button to initiate an interaction with an object. Examples include turning a crank or dragging a movable object around. It's usually obvious, and the walkthrough will detail how any special interactions are performed.

Other objects can be activated simply by moving Death into contact with them. For example, the Rider can activate pressure plates by standing atop them. Pressure levers that stick out from walls can be triggered by maneuvering Death on top of them as well. Whenever you see an unusual object that Death can't activate through the use of the Action button, try standing atop it, or look for some other type of trigger in the environment. When all else fails, consult the walkthrough.

Using the Map

The map is an invaluable resource that keeps you on course as you explore *Darksiders II*'s vast locales. Regularly press the Chronicle button to call up your map—it'll help you keep your bearings. The onscreen mini-map helps as well. Whenever you're stuck or lost, consult the Chronicle map to determine which areas you've yet to explore.

> **TIP**
>
> By visiting the pause menu options, you can choose whether to have your mini-map rotate, or to lock it in place.

> **NOTE**
>
> As you explore your environment, treasure chests will appear on the in-game maps. Some chests aren't easy to reach, even though you know where they're located. Consult the walkthrough for help in finding them, along with any other items of interest.

The Dungeon Map

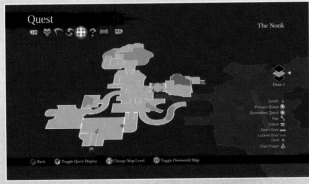

Every major dungeon in *Darksiders II* contains a special item known as the Dungeon Map. Once you find the ornate chest within each dungeon that contains this item, your Chronicle will be updated with a complete map of the current dungeon. Refer to the walkthrough to discover where each Dungeon Map lies.

Fast Travel

Darksiders II features a convenient fast travel mechanic that allows Death to travel instantly to any area he's previously discovered. Simply call up the World Map through the Chronicle, highlight the desired destination, and press the Attack button to fast travel there. If you're currently exploring a dungeon, a waypoint marker will be left at your current position—this allows you to fast travel back to the exact point where you left the dungeon.

Summoning Despair

While roaming through spacious areas, you'll often be able to summon and ride Death's fearsome steed, Despair. Whenever Despair's icon appears onscreen, summon Despair by pressing the Skill and Evade triggers simultaneously. Banish Despair in the same fashion to return to normal exploration.

While riding Despair, press the Attack button to lash out with Death's scythe. The Special Item trigger allows you to use your currently equipped item, such as Redemption, from horseback.

Press the Evade trigger to make Despair charge forward with a boost of speed. Each charge drains one pip of Despair's stamina, which slowly regenerates over time.

The Pale Rider's journey is fraught with danger, and Death is commonly drawn into furious combat—often with little warning. To better prepare yourself, let's review the basics of battle in *Darksiders II*.

Death and Dying

Death's health is measured by a green meter at the screen's top-left corner. Hostile attacks that strike the Rider will drain some of his health. If Death's health is completely drained, then his soul is lost, forcing you to restart at a previous checkpoint.

Death can carry a maximum of five health potions. Purchase more potions from merchants when his stock runs low, or destroy clutter in the environment to potentially find some. Don't hesitate to use the fast-travel mechanic to return to merchants and replenish your supplies.

> ### NOTE
> Some gear can cause Death's health to slowly regenerate over time. Other gear can cause the Reaper to regain health when he slays enemies. Keep these traits in mind when you decide which pieces of armor to equip.

Use the Rider's great agility to avoid attacks. Equip pieces of armor to reduce the damage he suffers when struck. When matters become dire, down a health potion to bring Death back from the brink. Each potion restores Death to full health, but it takes a few seconds for his health meter to fill, so don't wait too long to drink one.

Creature Classes

Every monster that Death encounters falls into one of five general categories, as detailed here:

Fodder: These lowly foes pose little threat to the Reaper, and are easily slain.

Soldier: The most common enemy class. Dangerous only in groups; easily handled individually.

Elite: These unique enemies possess some form of special talent, such as summoning or reviving other enemies. They're not particularly strong or resilient, though.

Brute: These monstrous foes pose a great threat to the Horseman. Their attacks are powerful, and they can withstand plenty of punishment before they fall.

Boss: Many dungeons feature at least one boss enemy, commonly encountered at the dungeon's end. Many bosses are unique and must be combated using special skills, or by exploiting the environment to the Rider's advantage.

> **TIP**
> Consult the walkthrough to find sidebars and boss battle sections that provide combat strategies for each and every foe that the Reaper encounters.

Focusing

Hold the Focus trigger to lock Death's aim onto the nearest adversary. While focused, Death will move in relation to his current target, and the targeted enemy's name and health will appear above its head. Focus on enemies during battle to avoid sensory overload. Use the right stick to switch Death's aim to other enemies without breaking focus.

> **TIP**
> After knocking down an enemy, switch Death's focus to another foe to avoid being struck by other swarming hostiles.

> **NOTE**
> When lots of enemies swarm the Reaper, it can sometimes be better not to focus.

Evading

Dodging enemy attacks is paramount, especially when faced with larger, more powerful foes. Make liberal use of the Evade trigger to dart out of harm's way and set up counterattacks. Tap the Evade trigger while standing still to make Death perform a long backflip—a great way to escape from swarms of smaller minions.

Scythe Attacks and Combos

The Pale Rider's primary weapons are his twin scythes, which he wields with practiced lethality. Simply press the Attack button in rapid succession to unleash a basic yet blistering attack combo that is ideal for most combat situations. See the next chapter, "Skills and Combos," to discover many more vicious attacks.

> **NOTE**
> After Death gains Reaper Form, every enemy he slays with his scythes will grant him a small amount of Reaper Energy. See the following "Reaper Form" section for further details.

Secondary Weapons

Death can find and equip an assortment of secondary weapons that can be used either by themselves or in conjunction with his primary scythes. While there are many different types of secondary weapons, they all fall into one of two basic categories: melee or heavy.

✦ Melee secondary weapons inflict modest damage with each hit, and can be used to unleash combos with great speed and ferocity.

✦ Heavy secondary weapons inflict tremendous damage with each hit, but are slow and somewhat cumbersome to wield.

> **NOTE**
>
> See the next chapter, "Skills and Combos," for an in-depth look at each type of secondary weapon, including the various combos they can perform.

Executions

Death has a small chance to instantly slay any enemy with a dramatic execution move. Whenever you see the Action button icon appear above a foe, press the Action button to finish them off with a flourish. Death is immune to damage while executing an enemy, so sit back and enjoy the show.

> **NOTE**
>
> Death's chances of performing executions can be increased, allowing him to execute enemies more often. See the following "Death's Attributes" section for details.

Skills

Death isn't limited to simply attacking his enemies—the Pale Rider can also unleash an array of powerful skills to facilitate his foes' demise.

Skills Radial

Press down on the directional pad to pause the action and call up the Skills Radial. This special menu lets you unleash skills, drink potions, or switch out the special item that Death has equipped. You can assign any of these functions to various buttons on the controller by highlighting the desired function, holding the Skill trigger, and then pressing the desired button. You may then quickly perform actions such as drinking potions or unleashing specific skills in the heat of battle by simply pressing the Skill trigger in conjunction with the buttons you've mapped out.

> **NOTE**
>
> Skills require Wrath to perform. The Wrath meter is located below Death's health meter in the screen's top-left corner. Wrath slowly builds as Death attacks his enemies, and can be quickly replenished by drinking a Wrath potion. The Reaper may carry up to five Wrath potions at a time.

Damage Types

Damage comes in many forms in *Darksiders II*. While every weapon will inflict normal damage, certain weapons can also inflict one or more types of additional damage, adding to their lethality.

Arcane: This type of enhanced damage occurs when Death calls upon his Reaper Form. Certain attack combos will also cause Death to briefly unleash his Reaper Form during the combo, inflicting extra Arcane damage. See the next chapter, "Skills and Combos," for further details.

Fire: Some weapons can set enemies ablaze, dealing extra damage. This can inflict steady damage over time.

Ice: Certain weapons have a chilling effect that freezes enemies for extra damage. This can slow enemies for a few seconds, making them easier to outmaneuver.

Lightning: Some weapons may zap foes for added lightning damage. This can temporarily stun enemies, leaving them highly vulnerable.

Piercing: Certain weapons can pierce through enemy defenses, dealing significant amounts of additional damage. This kind of damage can be highly effective against armored enemies.

Critical Hits

The Horseman has a small chance to score critical hits when attacking enemies. These masterful blows inflict far more damage than normal attacks. Critical hits can make a big difference in battle, dramatically reducing a powerful enemy's health with a single blow. Certain weapons and gear can increase Death's chance to score critical hits—see the following "Death's Attributes" section for more info.

Reaper Form

As Death gains experience and levels up, he'll eventually gain the ability to unleash his Reaper Form at will. This powerful ability causes the Rider to reveal his true form and lay waste to foes with devastating Arcane attacks. Reaper Form can simplify challenging battles, but it doesn't last long and takes effort to recharge. It's therefore best to use it only when necessary.

> **NOTE**
>
> To activate Reaper Form, Death's Reaper Energy must be full. Generate Reaper Energy by slaying enemies with Death's scythes. A special item known as the Grim Talisman can help the Horseman fill his Reaper Energy with greater haste—obtain this item by completing the "Shaman's Craft" side quest for Muria at Tri-Stone.

LEVELING UP

Death gains Experience Points (XP) by slaying enemies and completing quests. Amass enough XP to fill the meter above Death's health bar and the Reaper will advance to the next level. Every time Death gains a level, he earns one Skill Point. These precious points can be spent at the Chronicle to enhance Death's current skills, or to acquire entirely new ones.

Call up the Chronicle and cycle to the Skills tab to view Death's twin talent trees: Harbinger and Necromancer. Highlight any skill for a detailed description, and choose which one you'd like to upgrade or unlock. Study the skill trees carefully and choose wisely because certain skills need to be unlocked before you can acquire others. You may put Skill Points into any skill that's not grayed out.

> **TIP**
>
> Purchase a Respec from demonic merchant Vulgrim, and Death will be able to re-choose all of his skills. This comes in handy later in the adventure, when Death's enemies become incredibly powerful.

> **NOTE**
>
> See the next chapter, "Skills and Combos," for an in-depth look at all of Death's skills.

EQUIPPING GEAR

As the Pale Rider defeats enemies, opens chests, and destroys clutter, he'll regularly discover new weapons and pieces of gear that he can equip to enhance his combat prowess. Simply approach any bit of gear you discover and pick it up to add it to Death's inventory. You can also choose to equip gear right away if you like, without having to call up the Chronicle. However, you may wish to visit the Chronicle and check the Inventory tab for a more detailed analysis of Death's current gear.

> **NOTE**
>
> Most gear will increase Death's attributes in a variety of ways. See the following "Death's Attributes" section for more info.

Possessed Weapons

A handful of incredibly rare possessed weapons can be found within the realms. Immensely powerful in their own right, these special weapons can become even more deadly at the Reaper's hand. By "feeding" unwanted gear to a possessed weapon, Death can boost its innate stats to greater and greater heights. In this manner, entirely new benefits can be added to such weapons.

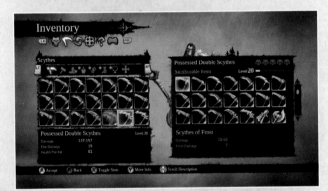

Possessed weapons can give the Reaper a dramatic advantage in combat, so keep an eye out for them. It's easy to tell when you've discovered a possessed weapon—their names always feature the prefix "possessed". Once you've discovered a possessed weapon, work at increasing its power by feeding it other weapons. Simply select the possessed weapon in your inventory and choose the Upgrade option to begin feeding it other weapons.

Here are some things to keep in mind regarding possessed weapons:

+ Each possessed weapon can be "leveled up" five times by filling its XP bar five times.

+ When fed to a possessed weapon, high-level weapons will grant lots of XP; low level weapons will grant less XP.

+ Each time a possessed weapon levels up, you may be able to upgrade it with new attributes that benefit Death. These attribute bonuses are determined by the weapons you choose to feed to the possessed weapon. For example, feeding a possessed weapon lots of weapons with the Health Regen attribute will increase your chances of bestowing the Health Regen attribute to the possessed weapon when it levels up. Keep this in mind when feeding your possessed weapons.

Special Items and Abilities

Death must utilize a number of special items over the course of his great quest. After discovering one of these items, equip it through the Skills Radial or by visiting the Chronicle.

Redemption

The first special item that Death acquires is his pistol, Redemption. This handy sidearm can be used to pick off smaller enemies and detonate remote Shadowbombs. Once Death acquires the Lure Stone as part of the "Sticks and Stones" side quest, he can also use Redemption to draw in the energy of Stonebites that are scattered around the realms. Redemption has a large clip of bullets and automatically reloads over time.

TIP

Use the right stick to enter aiming mode and line up the perfect shot with Redemption, or focus on enemies during the heat of battle to ensure that Redemption's rounds find their mark.

Deathgrip

The Deathgrip is a versatile tool that Death obtains near the end of his journeys in the Forge Lands. When used, the Deathgrip fires out a ghostly hand that grasps faraway objects. This allows Death to tractor in distant items and lighter enemies, or grapple and zip toward heavier objects and foes. Use the Deathgrip to snatch out-of-reach Shadowbombs, swing from hoops, stun lesser enemies, and quickly zip toward larger enemies after dodging their attacks.

TIP

Look for objects that glow with a purple hue in the environment, and try Deathgripping them to see what happens.

Interdiction

For a short time during his travels through the Kingdom of the Dead, Death gains the use of a special power known as Interdiction. This ability enables the Horseman to summon and issue orders to the Dead Lords that he subjugates in service to the Lord of Bones.

After subjugating a Dead Lord, use Interdiction at any Summoning Circle to call the Dead Lord forth. Enter aiming mode afterward to target special environmental objects, such as levers and pressure plates, and then use Interdiction again to order the Dead Lord to trigger the object. This allows Death to progress through areas he otherwise couldn't.

> **NOTE**
>
> Dead Lords will also assist Death in battle. Simply summon them again if they happen to be defeated by your enemies.

> **TIP**
>
> After ordering a Dead Lord to trigger a pressure plate, you're able to Deathgrip the Dead Lord and zip to his position. This comes in handy at several points in the adventure.

Soul Splitter

After Death completes a difficult task for the Lord of Bones, his Interdiction ability is replaced with the Soul Splitter ability. This power allows Death to split his soul into two mirror images, leaving his physical form behind. The Soul Splitter helps Death solve an array of mind-bending puzzles, and it lets him navigate areas he couldn't normally traverse. Hold the Action button to switch between Death's two souls as you use them to explore his surroundings in new ways. Don't stray too far from Death's physical form, however, or the Soul Splitter will deactivate and Death will revert back to his normal form.

Voidwalker

Near the end of the adventure, Death acquires a special tool that allows him to activate the blue warp portals found around the realms. Simply fire the Voidwalker at a warp portal to open it, and then look for another nearby portal to open. Pass through one open portal to emerge from the other. Only two portals can be open at any one time.

> **TIP**
>
> Hold the Special Item trigger to charge up a Voidwalker blast, and then release it to fire and open a charged portal. The Pale Rider rockets out of charged portals at high velocity, allowing him to access areas that would otherwise be out of reach.

Phasewalker

The Phasewalker is an enhanced version of the Voidwalker. With this unique tool, Death can open green time portals in addition to blue warp portals. Simply fire the Phasewalker at a time portal, and then step through to travel between the present and the past. This comes into play primarily during Death's journey through the demonic realm of Shadow's Edge.

DEATH'S ATTRIBUTES

The Reaper's might and battle prowess are determined by a number of important attributes. Many of these attribute scores increase as the Horseman levels up; others can only be increased by equipping gear that provides stat boosts. Call up the Chronicle to view Death's attribute scores, and press the Attack button to cycle through his various stats.

Let's review each of the Reaper's attributes:

Health: The greater Death's health, the more damage he can withstand.

Wrath: More Wrath means that Death can unleash more skills in quick succession.

Strength: This stat affects how much damage Death can inflict with his weapons. The higher his strength, the greater the damage.

Defense: This attribute helps to determine how much damage Death will suffer from physical attacks. The higher Death's defense, the less damage he'll sustain when struck.

Arcane: This stat affects how much damage Death can inflict with his Arcane attacks. Arcane attacks occur when Death unleashes his Reaper Form.

Resistance: This attribute helps to determine how much damage Death will suffer from magical and elemental attacks. The higher Death's resistance, the less damage he'll suffer from non-physical attacks.

Primary Weapon: This stat relates to how much damage Death can inflict with each strike from his scythes.

Secondary Weapon: This stat relates to how much damage Death can inflict with each blow from his current secondary weapon.

Primary Weapon Damage Per Second: This stat is an average value that shows how much damage Death will inflict per second with a weapon.

Critical Chance: This attribute shows the percentage chance that Death has to score a critical hit against his enemies. The default value is 3 percent.

Critical Damage: This stat shows the percentage multiplier that's applied to Death's normal damage when he scores a critical hit. The default value is 100 percent, meaning that Death will inflict double damage when critical hits are scored.

Health Regen: This attribute determines how much health Death will regenerate per second. Death does not regenerate health over time unless he equips an item that provides this benefit.

Wrath Regen: This stat determines how much Wrath Death will regenerate per second. Death does not regenerate Wrath over time unless he equips an item that provides this advantage.

Arcane Critical Chance: This attribute shows the percentage chance that Death has to score a critical hit against his enemies while unleashing Reaper Form. The default value is 3 percent.

Arcane Critical Damage: This stat shows the percentage multiplier that's applied to Death's normal damage when he scores a critical hit during the use of Reaper Form. The default value is 100 percent, meaning that Death will inflict double damage when Arcane critical hits are scored.

Execution Chance: This attribute determines the percentage chance that Death has to instantly execute his enemies. The default value is 10 percent, giving Death a one in ten chance to execute foes.

Skills and Combos

Skills and Combos

We've covered the basics; now let's dig a little deeper into Death's many different abilities. This chapter details all of the Horseman's various skills and attack combos, providing a thorough breakdown that will help you obliterate all who would seek to challenge you.

SKILLS

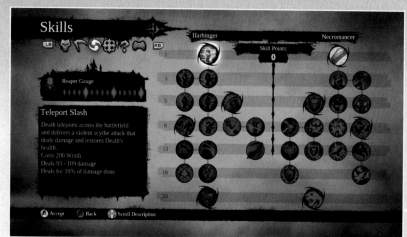

Every time Death levels up, he earns one Skill Point. These precious points are used to purchase and master powerful skills that make the Reaper even more dangerous. There are two major skill trees: Harbinger and Necromancer.

> ### TIP
>
> Not thrilled with the skills you've chosen? Visit the demonic merchant, Vulgrim, and he'll sell you a Respec for a modest fee. You'll then be able to reassign Death's skill points as you see fit.

Harbinger Tree

The Harbinger skill tree focuses on dealing direct damage to Death's enemies and strengthening the might of his standard attacks. This skill tree features several "sub-trees" that enhance the effectiveness of the Harbinger tree's three primary skills: Teleport Slash, Harvest, and Unstoppable.

Teleport Slash Sub-Tree

Teleport Slash is an excellent skill in which Death darts forward to deliver a lethal scythe attack. This skill also has several other advantages: it heals Death by a small degree, and can also help him slip past foes to avoid their attacks. Teleport Slash can be enhanced in a variety of ways by purchasing other skills within its sub-tree. Unending Fury and Death Blossom rank among the best—the former allows Death to quickly generate Wrath so that Teleport Slash can be used more often, while the latter greatly increases the power of Teleport Slash, turning it into a devastating anti-group skill.

ICON	SKILL	LEVEL	PREREQ.	DESCRIPTION	LEVEL 1 STATS	LEVEL 2 STATS	LEVEL 3 STATS
	Teleport Slash	1	None	Death teleports across the battlefield and delivers a violent scythe attack that deals damage and restores Death's health.	Costs 200 Wrath Deals 99-117 damage Heals for 10% of damage done	Costs 200 Wrath Deals 111-130 damage Heals for 12% of damage done	Costs 200 Wrath Deals 122-144 damage Heals for 15% of damage done
	Immolation	3	Teleport Slash	All enemies struck by Teleport Slash have a chance to be set ablaze.	Deals 102 damage every 0.5 seconds Lasts 5 seconds 25% chance to set on fire	Deals 153 damage every 0.5 seconds Lasts 6 seconds 25% chance to set on fire	Deals 179 damage every 0.5 seconds Lasts 7 seconds 25% chance to set on fire
	Inescapable	3	Teleport Slash Immolation	All enemies struck by Teleport Slash have a chance to be slowed by Frost.	Slows by 20% Lasts 2 seconds 25% chance to slow	Slows by 25% Lasts 3 seconds 25% chance to slow	Slows by 30% Lasts 4 seconds 25% chance to slow
	Unending Fury	5	Teleport Slash Immolation	Wrath generation is increased for a short time after performing Teleport Slash.	Increases Wrath Generation by 40% Lasts 10 seconds	Increases Wrath Generation by 45% Lasts 10 seconds	Increases Wrath Generation by 50% Lasts 10 seconds
	Rage of the Grave	5	Teleport Slash Inescapable	Increases the Critical Hit Chance on Teleport Slash attacks.	Teleport Slash gains 10% increased Critical Strike Chance	Teleport Slash gains 15% increased Critical Strike Chance	Teleport Slash gains 20% increased Critical Strike Chance
	Death Blossom	8	Teleport Slash Immolation Unending Fury	Hitting enemies with Teleport Slash also causes an explosion, damaging nearby foes.	Deals 684 damage	Deals 1027 damage	Deals 1370 damage

Harvest Sub-Tree

Harvest is a fantastic anti-group skill that summons Death's Reaper Form for a brief instant to level surrounding enemies with a swirling scythe attack. Even if Harvest doesn't wipe out Death's foes, it will push them back and give the Horseman a chance to flee or follow up with another attack. The skills that fall under Harvest's sub-tree can increase Death's damage output or generate Reaper Energy, allowing the Rider to pour on the punishment while easily defeating entire mobs of foes.

ICON	SKILL	LEVEL	PREREQ.	DESCRIPTION	LEVEL 1 STATS	LEVEL 2 STATS	LEVEL 3 STATS
	Harvest	5	None	Death's true incarnation appears, unleashing a spinning scythe attack that devastates surrounding foes.	Costs 200 Wrath Deals 1210 damage	Costs 200 Wrath Deals 1478 damage	Costs 200 Wrath Deals 1747 damage
	Reaping	8	Harvest	Reaping increases the chance of scoring a critical hit on enemies struck by Harvest.	Harvest gains a 15% increased Critical Strike Chance	Harvest gains a 20% increased Critical Strike Chance	Harvest gains a 25% increased Critical Strike Chance
	Trauma	8	Harvest Reaping	Enemies struck by Harvest increase the damage dealt by all of Death's attacks for a short time.	Increases damage by 10% per enemy hit.	Increases damage by 15% per enemy hit.	Increases damage by 20% per enemy hit.
	Red Harvest	12	Harvest Reaping Trauma	Enemies struck by Harvest grant Reaper Energy.	Adds 8 Reaper Energy per enemy hit	Adds 10 Reaper Energy per enemy hit	Adds 12 Reaper Energy per enemy hit

Skills

Moves and Combos

INTRODUCTION

EXPLORATION AND COMBAT

SKILLS AND COMBOS

WALKTHROUGH

SIDE QUESTS AND AREAS

APPENDIX

BEHIND THE SCENES

Unstoppable Sub-Tree

For the true carnage addict, there is Unstoppable. This skill greatly increases Death's Strength attribute for a short time, allowing the Reaper to devastate those who would seek to thwart him. Unstoppable can be made even more lethal by upgrading its sub-tree skills, which can increase Death's ability to inflict critical hits, along with enhancing his critical damage. Upgrade Unstoppable with Call of the Grave, and you'll be able to keep the mayhem going for longer periods of time.

ICON	SKILL	LEVEL	PREREQ.	DESCRIPTION	LEVEL 1 STATS	LEVEL 2 STATS	LEVEL 3 STATS
	Unstoppable	8	None	Death's unearthly strength is increased for a short time.	Costs 300 Wrath Increases Strength by 30 while active Lasts 8 seconds	Costs 300 Wrath Increases Strength by 40 while active Lasts 8 seconds	Costs 300 Wrath Increases Strength by 50 while active Lasts 8 seconds
	Inevitability	12	Unstoppable	While Unstoppable is active, Death is more likely to deal a Critical Strike.	10% increased Critical Strike Chance	15% increased Critical Strike Chance	20% increased Critical Strike Chance
	Empowerment	12	Unstoppable Inevitability	Death's Critical Strikes deal additional damage while Unstoppable is active.	Increases Critical Strike Damage by 20%	Increases Critical Strike Damage by 30%	Increases Critical Strike Damage by 40%
	Killing Blow	16	Unstoppable Inevitability	While Unstoppable is active, Death has a chance to deal a second strike with each attack.	5% chance of a second strike	10% chance of a second strike	15% chance of a second strike
	Call of the Grave	16	Unstoppable Inevitability Empowerment	The duration of Death's Unstoppable ability is increased.	Increases Unstoppable duration by 3 seconds	Increases Unstoppable duration by 4 seconds	Increases Unstoppable duration by 5 seconds

Final Harbinger Skill: Reaper Storm

When Death advances to Level 20, he'll have the option to unlock the Harbinger Tree's final skill, Reaper Storm. Think of this as an even more lethal version of Harvest—one that can last for up to 8 seconds of anti-group annihilation. Unleash Reaper Storm in the midst of mobs whenever possible, for the initial blast inflicts tremendous damage.

ICON	SKILL	LEVEL	PREREQ.	DESCRIPTION	LEVEL 1 STATS	LEVEL 2 STATS	LEVEL 3 STATS
	Reaper Storm	20	None	Death's form rips apart into a tornado of debris and fragments of ancient bone, laying waste to those caught in the maelstrom.	Costs 400 Wrath Lasts 4 seconds Deals 80 damage every 0.2 seconds Storm blasts deal 1204 damage	Costs 400 Wrath Lasts 6 seconds Deals 120 damage every 0.2 seconds Storm blasts deal 1606 damage	Costs 400 Wrath Lasts 8 seconds Deals 160 damage every 0.2 seconds Storm blasts deal 2008 damage

Necromancer Tree

The Necromancer skill tree focuses on bolstering Death's defenses and summoning lesser minions to his aid. Like the Harbinger tree, this one features several "sub-trees" that enhance the effectiveness of its three primary skills: Exhume, Aegis Guard, and Murder.

Exhume Sub-Tree

Exhume is a versatile skill that allows Death to summon a pair of aggressive Ghouls that hunger for combat. The primary benefit of these bloodthirsty minions is to distract and harass Death's enemies, taking the heat off of the Reaper and allowing Death to flank his foes. Max out Undying and not only will the Ghouls last longer, but you'll also gain a third Ghoul. Corpse Explosion is also excellent—purchase it to turn your Ghouls into lethal time bombs that obliterate nearby enemies when slain.

ICON	SKILL	LEVEL	PREREQ.	DESCRIPTION	LEVEL 1 STATS	LEVEL 2 STATS	LEVEL 3 STATS
	Exhume	1	None	Death summons bloodthirsty Ghouls from beyond the grave to fight alongside him.	Costs 300 Wrath Ghouls deal 26 damage per attack Ghouls summoned: 2	Costs 300 Wrath Ghouls deal 40 damage per attack Ghouls summoned: 2	Costs 300 Wrath Ghouls deal 53 damage per attack Ghouls summoned: 2
	Undying	3	Exhume	Increases the health of the summoned Ghouls.	Increases Ghoul health by 451	Increases Ghoul health by 632	Increases Ghoul health by 813 Additional Ghouls Summoned: 1
	Enervation	3	Exhume Undying	Damage dealt by the Ghouls is awarded as Wrath to Death.	Restores 1 Wrath per Ghoul attack	Restores 3 Wrath per Ghoul attack	Restores 4 Wrath per Ghoul attack
	Fiery Souls	5	Exhume Undying	Ghouls deal additional fire damage to surrounding enemies.	Adds 13 Fire damage Fire aura deals 16 Fire damage every 0.5 seconds	Adds 20 Fire damage Fire aura deals 32 Fire damage every 0.5 seconds	Adds 20 Fire damage Fire aura deals 32 Fire damage every 0.5 seconds Exhume gains 5% Arcane Critical Strike Chance
	Death's Allure	5	Exhume Undying Enervation	Death's enemies are driven to attack the summoned Ghouls.	—	Increases radius by 50%	Increases radius by 100%
	Corpse Explosion	5	Exhume Undying Fiery Souls	Summoned Ghouls explode when killed or when the ability ends, damaging and knocking back nearby enemies.	Explosion deals 402 damage	Explosion deals 562 damage	Explosion deals 723 damage

Aegis Guard Sub-Tree

When it comes to increasing Death's defense, nothing does the job better than Aegis Guard. This lifesaving skill greatly boosts Death's Defense and Resistance attributes, making him extremely difficult to kill for a brief time. Aegis Guard can also punish Death's adversaries through sub-tree skills such as Reflect and Grounding, and can greatly increase the effectiveness of Death's Arcane attacks through Grave Defense and Enraged Guardian, all while ensuring that the Reaper remains in the fray.

ICON	SKILL	LEVEL	PREREQ.	DESCRIPTION	LEVEL 1 STATS	LEVEL 2 STATS	LEVEL 3 STATS
	Aegis Guard	5	None	Death surrounds himself with a necromantic shield, significantly increasing his Defense and Resistance.	Costs 300 Wrath Adds 321 Defense while active Adds 321 Resistance while active Lasts 8 seconds	Costs 300 Wrath Adds 642 Defense while active Adds 642 Resistance while active Lasts 8 seconds	Costs 300 Wrath Adds 963 Defense while active Adds 963 Resistance while active Lasts 8 seconds
	Grave Defense	8	Aegis Guard	Aegis Guard enhances Death's Arcane attribute while the ability is active.	20 Arcane	25 Arcane	30 Arcane
	Reflect	8	Aegis Guard Grave Defense	Death's Aegis Guard reflects a portion of any damage dealt to Death back at its source.	Reflects 10% of damage done to Death.	Reflects 15% of damage done to Death.	Reflects 20% of damage done to Death.
	Grounding	12	Aegis Guard Grave Defense	Threads of lightning arc from death while Aegis Guard is active, damaging nearby enemies.	Strikes 1 enemy every 0.5 to 1 seconds Deals 176 Lightning damage	Strikes 2 enemies every 0.5 to 1 seconds Deals 268 Lightning damage	Strikes 3 enemies every 0.5 to 1 seconds Deals 321 Lightning damage
	Enraged Guardian	12	Aegis Guard Grave Defense Reflect	The arcane power of Aegis Guard increases Death's Arcane Critical Chance while active.	10% increased Arcane Critical Chance	15% increased Arcane Critical Chance	20% increased Arcane Critical Chance
	Death Guard	16	Aegis Guard Grave Defense Reflect Enraged Guardian	Death's Aegis Guard lasts longer and requires less effort to summon.	Reduces Wrath cost by 10% Lasts 3 additional seconds	Reduces Wrath cost by 15% Lasts 4 additional seconds	Reduces Wrath cost by 20%

Skills
Moves and Combos

INTRODUCTION
EXPLORATION AND COMBAT
SKILLS AND COMBOS
WALKTHROUGH
SIDE QUESTS AND AREAS
APPENDIX
BEHIND THE SCENES

Murder Sub-Tree

Murder is a unique skill that summons one or more flocks of otherworldly crows to harass and distract Death's enemies. Coupled with Exhume, Murder can be a fantastic way to keep swarming hostiles from singling Death out. Murder can be upgraded in various ways; it can help restore Death's health, restore his Reaper Energy, or freeze his foes cold in their tracks.

ICON	SKILL	LEVEL	PREREQ.	DESCRIPTION	LEVEL 1 STATS	LEVEL 2 STATS	LEVEL 3 STATS
	Murder	8	None	A murder of crows emerges from the ether, called down by Death to attack his foes.	Costs 300 Wrath Flocks deal 20 damage Summons 1 flock	Costs 300 Wrath Flocks deal 160 damage Summons 2 flocks	Costs 300 Wrath Flocks deal 201 damage Summons 3 flocks
	Bless	12	Murder	Death's crows restore their master's health by attacking his enemies.	Restores 27 health per hit	Restores 41 health per hit	Restores 54 health per hit
	Heralds of Death	16	Murder Bless	The summoned crows restore Reaper Energy to Death with every strike.	Hits add 3 Reaper Energy	Hits add 5 Reaper Energy	Hits add 7 Reaper Energy
	Ice Crows	16	Murder Bless	Death's crows, imbued with the chill of the Abyssal Plains, deal ice damage to all enemies they strike.	Deals 40 Ice damage	Deals 80 Ice damage	Deals 80 Ice damage 2% chance to freeze

Final Necromancer Skill: Frenzy

The Necromancer Tree's final skill is designed to pour all of Death's Wrath into one single, devastating attack. The more Wrath Death possesses when unleashing Frenzy, the more powerful the skill will be. Chug a Wrath potion after using Frenzy, and then unleash the skill again. Repeat as needed until none are left to challenge you.

ICON	SKILL	LEVEL	PREREQ.	DESCRIPTION	LEVEL 1 STATS	LEVEL 2 STATS	LEVEL 3 STATS
	Frenzy	20	None	Death channels his Wrath reserves to attack his enemies. Frenzy increases in power depending on the amount of Wrath available.	Costs 100 Wrath per projectile Deals 160 damage per projectile	Costs 100 Wrath per projectile Deals 201 damage per projectile	Costs 100 Wrath per projectile Deals 241 damage per projectile

Skill Pairings

Try combining the following skills in order to achieve effective skill synergies:

Convenient Healing: Teleport Slash (maxed out) + Harvest (with Trauma) + Murder (with Bless)

Endless Wrath: Teleport Slash (with Unending Fury) + Exhume (with Enervation) + Frenzy

Anti-Group: Exhume (with Undying maxed out) + Harvest (maxed out) + Murder (maxed out, with Ice Crows) + Reaper Storm

Crushing Criticals: Teleport Slash (with Rage of the Grave) + Unstoppable (with Inevitability and Empowerment)

Chilling Out: Teleport Slash (with Inescapable) + Murder (with Ice Crows maxed out)

Burning Vengeance: Teleport Slash (with Immolation) + Exhume (with Fiery Souls)

Fear the Reaper: Harvest (with Red Harvest) + Aegis Guard (with Grave Defense and Enraged Guardian) + Murder (with Heralds of Death)

MOVES AND COMBOS

Here we review the many different combat moves and attack combos that are available to Death. Some of these are known to the Pale Rider from the start of his adventure, while others must be taught to Death by special trainers found in the realms. These trainers are Thane and Draven, located at Tri-Stone and the *Eternal Throne*, respectively.

Scythe Combos

Until Death acquires a secondary weapon, he's limited to the use of his scythes. As you'll see in the following table, the Reaper is capable of dispensing plenty of mayhem with these trademark tools. Scythes have the advantage of being quick to wield. Longer scythe combos will cause Death's true incarnation to briefly appear, delivering powerful blows that deal extra Arcane damage. Once Death can access his Reaper Form ability, every enemy he slays with his scythes will generate a small amount of Reaper Energy for him. This is the most straightforward way to build Reaper Energy, making scythe kills particularly important after Reaper Form has been unlocked.

NOTE

See the "Exploration and Combat" section of this guide for details about Reaper Form and the various forms of combat damage that can be dealt.

SCYTHE ATTACKS

MOVE	COMMANDS (XBOX)	COMMANDS (PS3)	TRAINER	TRAINER'S MOVELIST NAME
Cross Slash	✗	■	—	—
Return Slash	✗, ✗	■, ■	—	—
Double Slash	✗, ✗, ✗	■, ■, ■	—	—
Twin Humanities	✗, ✗, ✗, ✗	■, ■, ■, ■	—	—
Razor Slash	✗, delay, ✗	■, delay, ■	Thane	Razor Combo
Razor Wheel	✗, delay, ✗, ✗	■, delay, ■, ■	—	—
Razor Strike	✗, delay, ✗, ✗, ✗	■, delay, ■, ■, ■	—	—
Harvester Spiral	✗, ✗, delay, ✗	■, ■, delay, ■	Thane	Whirlwind Combo
Harvester Whirlwind	✗, ✗, delay, ✗, ✗	■, ■, delay, ■, ■	—	—
Harvester Blade	✗, ✗, delay, ✗, ✗, ✗	■, ■, delay, ■, ■, ■	—	—
Harvester Slam	✗, ✗, ✗, delay, ✗	■, ■, ■, delay, ■	Thane	Harvester Slam
Twin Cannon	(LT + BACK) + ✗	(L2 + BACK) + ■	Thane	Twin Cannon
Harvester Revenge	✗ during Forward Evade	■ during Forward Evade	Thane	Harvester Revenge
Crossover: Side Saw	✗ after any basic 4 attack	■ after any basic i attack	—	—
Crossover Special: Buzz Saw	✗ after any Crossover	■ after any Crossover	—	—
Twin Humanities	✗ after any Crossover Special	■ after any Crossover Special	—	—
Sky Slash	(Air) ✗	(Air) ■	—	—
Sky Cross	(Air) ✗, ✗	(Air) ■, ■	—	—
Sky Smash	(Air) ✗, ✗, ✗	(Air) ■, ■, ■	—	—
Hellraiser	(Air) ✗, ✗, delay, ✗	(Air) ■, ■, delay, ■	Thane	Hellraiser
Flip Saw	(Air) ++✗ or ✗ during Quick Fall	(Air) R1+■ or ■ during Quick Fall	Draven	Flip Saw

Melee Weapon Combos

Melee weapons are light, easy to wield, and blistering in their combos. The short attack range of these secondary weapons favors single-target combat. There are four basic types of melee weapons: bucklers, claws, gauntlets, and tonfas. The following table reveals the various combos that can be performed with melee weapons.

MELEE ATTACKS

MOVE	COMMANDS (XBOX)	COMMANDS (PS3)	TRAINER	TRAINER'S MOVELIST NAME
Wild Swing	Y	▲	—	—
Killer Intent	Y,Y	▲,▲	—	—
Triple Threat	Y,Y,Y	▲,▲,▲	—	—
Blackout	Y,Y,Y,Y	▲,▲,▲,▲	—	—
Tremor Smash	(LT + BACK) + Y	(L2 + BACK) + ▲	Thane	Tremor Smash Series
Earthbreaker	during Tremor Smash — mash Y (up to 5 times)	during Tremor Smash — mash ▲ (up to 5 times)	—	—
Power Geyser	automatic finisher after 5 Earthbreakers	automatic finisher after 5 Earthbreakers	—	—
Godfist	Y during Forward Evade	▲ during Forward Evade	Thane	Godfist
Rising Upper	Y during Godfist	▲ during Godfist	Draven	Rising Upper
Crossover: Frenzy	Y after any basic X attack	▲ after any basic ■ attack	—	—
Crossover Special: Wildstorm	Y after any Crossover	▲ after any Crossover	—	—
Blackout	Y after Crossover Special	▲ after Crossover Special	—	—
Double Cross	(Air) Y	(Air) ▲	—	—
Return Strike	(Air) Y,Y	(Air) ▲,▲	—	—
Gut Check	(Air) Y,Y,Y	(Air) ▲,▲,▲	—	—
Vital Edge	(Air) Y,Y,Y,Y	(Air) ▲,▲,▲,▲	—	—
Berserker Fury	Claws: hold Y (release to strike)	Claws: hold ▲ (release to strike)	—	—
Super Berserker Fury	Claws: hold Y (timed release)	Claws: hold ▲ (timed release)	Draven	Claw Training
Berserker Dive	Claws: (Air) hold Y (release to strike)	Claws: (Air) hold ▲ (release to strike)	—	—
Super Berserker Dive	Claws: (Air) hold Y (timed release)	Claws: (Air) hold ▲ (timed release)	Draven	Claw Training
Wind Blade	Tonfa: hold Y (release to strike)	Tonfa: hold ▲ (release to strike)	—	—
Super Wind Blade	Tonfa: hold Y (timed release)	Tonfa: hold ▲ (timed release)	Draven	Tonfa Training
Wind Strike	Tonfa: (Air) hold Y (release to strike)	Tonfa: (Air) hold ▲ (release to strike)	—	—
Super Wind Strike	Tonfa: (Air) hold Y (timed release)	Tonfa: (Air) hold ▲ (timed release)	Draven	Tonfa Training
Sidewinder	Gauntlet: hold Y (release to strike)	Gauntlet: hold ▲ (release to strike)	—	—
Super Sidewinder	Gauntlet: hold Y (timed release)	Gauntlet: hold ▲ (timed release)	Draven	Gauntlet Training
Seismic Hammer	Gauntlet: (Air) hold Y (release to strike)	Gauntlet: (Air) hold ▲ (release to strike)	—	—
Super Seismic Hammer	Gauntlet: (Air) hold Y (timed release)	Gauntlet: (Air) hold ▲ (timed release)	Draven	Gauntlet Training
Fortress Stance	Buckler: hold Y	Buckler: hold ▲	—	—
Fortress Blast	Buckler: hold Y (release to strike)	Buckler: hold ▲ (release to strike)	—	—
Super Fortress Blast	Buckler: hold Y (timed release)	Buckler: hold ▲ (timed release)	Draven	Buckler Training
Fortress Drift	Buckler: (Air) hold Y	Buckler: (Air) hold ▲	—	—
Fortress Smash	Buckler: (Air) hold Y (release to strike)	Buckler: (Air) hold ▲ (release to strike)	—	—
Super Fortress Smash	Buckler: (Air) hold Y (timed release)	Buckler: (Air) hold ▲ (timed release)	Draven	Buckler Training

Prima Official Game Guide   www.primagames.com

Heavy Weapon Combos

Heavy weapons are incredibly large, making them somewhat slow and cumbersome to wield. However, their wide reach and devastating attack power make them quite versatile. These weapons are capable of both beating back swarming foes and dealing great damage to a single target. There are four basic types of heavy weapons: axes, hammers, maces, and glaives.

TIP

Heavy weapons are best used to extend Death's scythe combos, lending them weight and anti-group effectiveness. Open up with a few scythe strikes, and then switch to a heavy weapon mid-combo to lend greater speed and potency to your attack.

HEAVY ATTACKS

MOVE	COMMANDS (XBOX)	COMMANDS (PS3)	TRAINER	TRAINER'S MOVELIST NAME
Heavy Slash	Y	▲	—	—
Heavy Double Cross	Y, Y	▲, ▲	—	—
Crushing Blows—Power Slam	Y, Y, Y	▲, ▲, ▲	—	—
Gravel Wizard	(LT + BACK) + hold Y (release to strike)	(L2 + BACK) + hold ▲ (release to strike)	Thane	Gravel Wizard
Painbringer	Y during Front Evade/Dash	▲ during Front Evade/Dash	Thane	Painbringer
Widowmaker	timed Y during impact of Heavy Power Attacks	timed ▲ during impact of Heavy Power Attacks	Draven	Widowmaker
Riftbreaker	timed Y during impact of Heavy Power Attacks	timed ▲ during impact of Heavy Power Attacks	Draven	Riftbreaker
Crossover: Cyclone	Y after any basic X attack	▲ after any basic p attack	—	—
Crossover Special: Hilt Strike	Y after any Crossover	▲ after any Crossover	—	—
Power Slam	Y after Crossover Special	▲ after Crossover Special	—	—
Falling Star	(Air) Y	(Air) ▲	—	—
Rock Breaker	Hammer: hold Y (release to strike)	Hammer: hold ▲ (release to strike)	—	—
Super Rock Breaker	Hammer: hold Y (timed release)	Hammer: hold ▲ (timed release)	Draven	Hammer Training
Rock Crusher	Hammer: (Air) hold Y (release to strike)	Hammer: (Air) hold ▲ (release to strike)	—	—
Super Rock Crusher	Hammer: (Air) hold Y (timed release)	Hammer: (Air) hold ▲ (timed release)	Draven	Hammer Training
Grand Slam	Mace: hold Y (release to strike)	Mace: hold ▲ (release to strike)	—	—
Super Grand Slam	Mace: hold Y (timed release)	Mace: hold ▲ (timed release)	Draven	Mace Training
Moonshot	Mace: (Air) hold Y (release to strike)	Mace: (Air) hold ▲ (release to strike)	—	—
Super Moonshot	Mace: (Air) hold Y (timed release)	Mace: (Air) hold ▲ (timed release)	Draven	Mace Training
Tempest	Axe: hold ↗ (release to strike)	Axe: hold ▲ (release to strike)	—	—
Super Tempest	Axe: hold ↗ (timed release)	Axe: hold ▲ (timed release)	Draven	Axe Training
Tornado	Axe: (Air) hold Y (release to strike)	Axe: (Air) hold ▲ (release to strike)	—	—
Super Tornado	Axe: (Air) hold Y (timed release)	Axe: (Air) hold ▲ (timed release)	Draven	Axe Training
Knight Spear	Glaive: hold Y (release to strike)	Glaive: hold ▲ (release to strike)	—	—
Super Knight Spear	Glaive: hold Y (timed release)	Glaive: hold ▲ (timed release)	Draven	Glaive Training
Dragonslayer	Glaive: (Air) hold Y (release to strike)	Glaive: (Air) hold ▲ (release to strike)	—	—
Super Dragonslayer	Glaive: (Air) hold Y (timed release)	Glaive: (Air) hold ▲ (timed release)	Draven	Glaive Training

Skills

Moves and Combos

INTRODUCTION

EXPLORATION AND COMBAT

SKILLS AND COMBOS

WALKTHROUGH

SIDE QUESTS AND AREAS

APPENDIX

BEHIND THE SCENES

Mixed Weapon Combos

Death is a practiced combatant, able to switch between his scythes and secondary weapons in mid-combo with violent results. Don't simply attack with only his scythes or only his secondary weapons; mix things up to perform longer and more lethal combinations.

🔎 TIP

Consider the stats of the Rider's currently equipped weaponry and look to finish enemies off with the weapon that will grant him the greatest benefit for the kill. Scythes always reward Death with Reaper Energy when they land the fateful blows, while secondary weapons may be able to restore the Reaper's health or Wrath as they rack up kills. Consult the Inventory menu of the Chronicle to see the stats and attributes of Death's arms.

Other Moves

Death can unleash a handful of special moves that do not require the use of his weaponry. Reaper Form is one example, and the highly effective Evade Counter is another. The following table details the Reaper's non-weapon-based moves.

OTHER MOVES

MOVE	REQUIREMENT	COMMANDS (XBOX)	COMMANDS (PS3)	TRAINER	TRAINER'S MOVELIST NAME
Razor Kick	—	❌+Ⓐ or Ⓐ during most attacks	p+u or u during most attacks	—	—
Meteor Strike	—	(Air) RB	(Air) R1	Thane	Meteor Strike
Reaper Counter	Level 5	timed + against incoming attacks	timed R against incoming attacks	—	—
Reaper Form	Level 10	LB + RT	L1 + R2	—	—

Walkthrough

The Keeper of Secrets

The Veil

Our story begins in a chilling, desolate place. Through frozen winds and swirling snow, a Pale Rider storms toward his destiny. What need could have driven this lone Horseman to such a cold and inhospitable realm? What dark, guarded secrets might lie at the top of the keep that looms on the horizon? Whatever the Rider's purpose, it is certain to be one of grave import—for this grim Horseman is one of the Four...

THE VEIL

The Crowfather's keep lies just ahead, seemingly frozen in time amidst a swirling snowstorm. Ride Death's fearsome steed, Despair, forth into the blinding blizzard.

TIP
Hasten your journey by pressing the Evade trigger to make Despair charge forward with a burst of speed. Each charge costs one pip of Despair's stamina, shown in the upper-right corner of the screen. Despair's stamina slowly regenerates while galloping at a normal gait.

NOTE
Should you accidentally banish Despair, simultaneously press the Ability and Evade triggers to summon Death's steed once more.

Despair vanishes into oblivion when you arrive at the keep's shattered steps. Death's stallion can carry you no farther, so approach the stone wall ahead on foot. Press the Jump button to leap at the wall, and Death will run up the wall and grab the hand hold above.

Cold Welcome

The entrance to the Crowfather's keep lies just ahead, but the path is not safe. A trio of ice skeletons burst from their frozen molds and storm forward with hostile intent.

Lay waste to these frigid minions by rapidly pressing the Attack button to unleash fluid combos with Death's twin scythes. Tap the Evade trigger to perform an acrobatic dodge that helps Death avoid being struck.

ENEMY: ICE SKELETON

Class: Soldier

These chilling undead warriors attack relentlessly, but mindlessly. Evade to avoid becoming surrounded as you cut them down with swift combos.

Collect any loot that the ice skeletons may have dropped, and be sure to equip any gear you discover. Then join up with Death's faithful companion, a crow named Dust, who has perched near the keep's front entrance. Step inside and begin exploring the frigid fortress.

⟡ **NOTE**

Dust often perches near places of importance. Pay attention to the wily crow; he'll help keep you on track. Click in the left thumbstick to send Dust flying toward your next objective.

Crumbling Keep

This stronghold is losing its battle against time, and it's not long before you encounter your first obstacle: a long pit. Run and jump at the left wall, and Death will run along it, crossing the expanse in a fluid maneuver known as a wall-run.

Hidden Treasure

Before wall-running across the next pit, attack the ice block in the left wall. Shatter the ice to loose another ice skeleton, then do battle and slay the fiend. Afterward, explore the short passage that the ice skeleton was blocking to discover a treasure chest which contains random plunder.

Wall-run along the right wall to clear the second pit. Death automatically grabs the far hand hold; shimmy around the corner and jump up.

Attack and defeat two more frozen ice skeletons beyond the second pit. These fiends won't bother you unless you strike first, but every kill is worth experience points (XP), so it's wise to battle as many foes as possible, particularly in the early stages of the Rider's quest.

Precarious Pillars

Leap onto the broken post that hangs over the next yawning abyss. Like ledges, Death will automatically grab these objects.

Tilt the Movement stick to the left to make Death circle around the post. Once Death's back is facing the next post ahead, hold the Focus trigger to make the Rider turn and lean in preparation to jump. While still holding the Focus trigger, press the Jump button to leap to the second post in a maneuver called the 180 leap. Perform additional 180 leaps until you reach the far ledge.

Ice Skeleton Ambush

Beware: the ice skeletons in the following passage will burst from their frozen molds and attack as you draw near. The confines of this space make this a dangerous ambush. Evade often to preserve Death's health as you land attacks where and when you can.

TIP

If you've found a secondary weapon you can extend Death's attack combos by mixing up your use of the Attack and Secondary Attack buttons. See the "Moves and Abilities" chapter for an in-depth look at all of Death's combos and combat abilities.

When the ice skeletons are no more, scamper up the nearby wall and scale the hand holds to reach a post. Wall-run to the right to reach another post and continue your ascent. Press the Action button to drop from the third post and land on a higher path.

Ambushed Again

Cut down more ice skeletons that burst to life. Use evasive tactics to avoid damage, and strike only when it's safe.

After the battle, look for a unique patch of growth running up the nearby wall. Jump at this growth to make Death grab it, and then climb up the wall. Continue climbing the growth along the ceiling, making your way to a higher passage. Press the Action button when you reach the end of the growth to drop to solid ground.

Smash up more frozen ice skeletons if you wish, then scale another stretch of growth to climb the wall that follows. Wall-run up to a hand hold, and then wall-run to the left to reach a spacious area where you encounter a monstrous foe.

Icebound Guardian

This enormous ice skeleton seeks to bring Death's journey to an early end. Only a fool would tackle a monster of this size head on—and the Pale Rider is far from foolish!

Hold the Focus trigger to target the Icebound Giant throughout the battle. Watch the monster's movements and Evade when you see it reach back in preparation to smash Death with its giant fists or feet, then counter with swift combinations. Pour on the damage at every opportunity, but always be ready to dodge out of harm's way.

> **TIP**
>
> If you're close to the Icebound Giant, try jumping to avoid the shockwave caused by its foot stomps.
>
> Consume health potions whenever Death's health becomes dangerously low. If the Rider falls in combat, he'll be restored at the nearest checkpoint—albeit with only a fraction of his health.

ENEMY: ICEBOUND GIANT

Class: Brute

The Icebound Giant is the first brute-class enemy that Death encounters. Its attacks are slow and predictable, yet devastating. Evading this giant's blows is of paramount concern—inflicting damage is secondary. Find your timing and settle in for a lengthy clash.

Venturing Onward

A nearby passage opens after the Icebound Giant has been felled. Enter and cross a long chasm by wall-running along the left wall. Death automatically vaults the short wooden peg that sticks out from the wall, using it to preserve his momentum and extend his wall-run across the long pit.

Ancient Elevator

A large switch catches the eye in the quiet chamber that follows. Approach the switch and press the Action button to grab and shove it inward. This causes the floor to rise like a lift, delivering Death to an even higher portion of the keep.

The lift becomes stuck during the ascent—you'll have to find another way to the top. Run up the nearby wall and scale the hand holds, and then round the corner and drop down to solid ground.

Climbing Higher

You soon encounter a dead-end. To progress, jump at either the left or right wall, and then jump again after Death reaches the height of his vertical wall-run. This causes Death to leap over to the opposite wall and scamper up even higher. Continue leaping between the two parallel walls until you reach a high ledge.

The next segment requires skillful timing. First, wall-run and vault from a peg on your way to some growth. Scale the growth and perform a vertical wall-run, vaulting from another peg to reach more growth above.

Slay another group of ice skeletons that swarm you on the snowy ledge, and then enter the ominous cave.

Ice Cave Antics

When you reach the end of the second patch of growth, wall-run to the right and grab a post. Climb to the top and let the camera pan upward to reveal another post directly overhead. Hold up on the Movement stick to ready Death for an upward jump, then leap up to the short post.

Circle around the short post so that Death's back faces the nearby post to the right. Hold the Focus trigger and jump across with a 180 leap. Circle around the pillar and climb up, and then wall-run over to a snowy ledge.

Delve into the cave and wall-run to reach some growth. Climb down and to the right, and then wall-run again to reach a long hand hold. Shimmy around the corner and jump across the gap to the right before dropping down to the ledge below.

Navigate the snowy trail until you reach a series of wooden beams that jut out from the left wall. Jump onto the first beam. Then, simply hold forward on the Movement Stick and keep tapping the Jump button to hop across each beam in the series. Death will leap out and grab the growth on the wall at the end of the run.

Apex Ascent

Jump a short gap to reach another beam, and then perform a vertical wall-run, vaulting from a peg to reach a hand hold. Climb up to find the passage that leads to the keep's final area.

Scale the growth and wall-run to the post on the right. Keep climbing and jump the gap to reach the broken post's top half.

Hold the Focus trigger and jump to perform a 180 leap over to the next hanging post.

Perform additional 180 leaps to reach the final post in the series, and then perform a 180 leap toward the foreground to land on a wooden beam.

Keeper of Secrets

At last, the Pale Rider has reached the keep's summit, where a tortured soul known as the Crowfather awaits. The dialogue does not go well, for the Reaper refuses to relieve the Crowfather of his terrible burden—an amulet filled with writhing souls. Within moments, an epic battle begins.

BOSS BATTLE: WAR'S SHADE

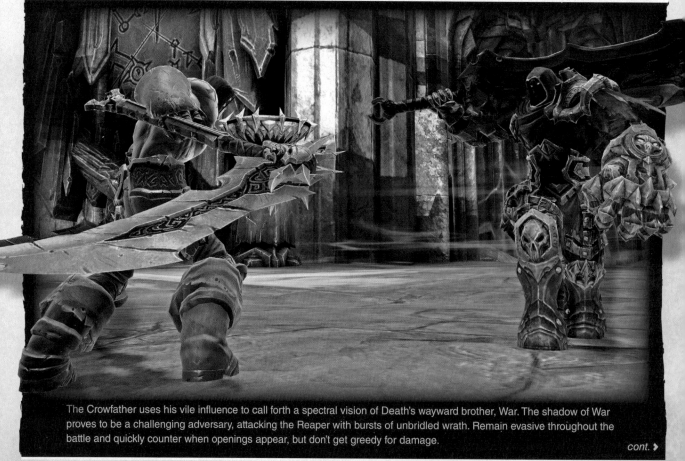

The Crowfather uses his vile influence to call forth a spectral vision of Death's wayward brother, War. The shadow of War proves to be a challenging adversary, attacking the Reaper with bursts of unbridled wrath. Remain evasive throughout the battle and quickly counter when openings appear, but don't get greedy for damage.

cont. ▸

War commonly attacks by unleashing a fluid trio of heavy sword strikes. Evade to the left or right to dodge each attack in the sequence, and try to land a few counter-strikes of your own between War's comparatively slow blows.

When War begins to block, immediately Evade and jump to avoid his imminent special ability in which massive yellow swords stab up from the ground all around him.

You can inflict the most damage against War after avoiding his third sword strike. Beware the long line of impact damage that lashes out from this final blow, however.

When you lock swords with War, quickly press the onscreen button to overpower him.

The Crowfather's trickery ends after War's shadow falls. Approach the battered old man and press the Action button to seal his fate. Unfortunately, this violent act seals Death's fate as well...

INTRODUCTION

EXPLORATION
AND COMBAT

SKILLS AND
COMBOS

WALKTHROUGH

SIDE QUESTS
AND AREAS

APPENDIX

BEHIND THE
SCENES

The Fire of the Mountain

Tree of Life

The Forge Lands

The Shattered Forge

Shadow Gorge

The Fjord

BEFORE DRAWING HIS FINAL BREATH, THE VILE CROWFATHER USES THE LAST OF HIS POWER TO TRANSPORT DEATH TO A DISTANT AND TROUBLED LAND. THE PALE RIDER AWAKENS TO FIND HIMSELF IN CURIOUS SURROUNDINGS WITH A BURLY, BEARDED GIANT TOWERING OVER HIM, GENTLY INSPECTING A WOUND THAT THE HORSEMAN INCURRED DURING HIS CLASH WITH THE KEEPER OF SECRETS. WARY OF THIS MYSTERIOUS FIGURE, DEATH QUICKLY RISES TO HIS FEET AND DEMANDS INFORMATION ABOUT THE TREE OF LIFE, WHICH HOLDS THE KEY TO FREEING THE REAPER'S IMPRISONED BROTHER, WAR.

WITH A SAD LAUGH, THE OLD MAN INFORMS THE RIDER THAT HIS WORLD IS DYING—A NEFARIOUS SUBSTANCE KNOWN AS CORRUPTION IS CHOKING THE VERY LIFE OUT OF HIS REALM. HE WARNS DEATH THAT EVEN THE GREAT TREE OF LIFE WILL SOON PERISH IF SOMETHING ISN'T DONE...

The Forge

Tri-Stone

The Crucible

The Foundry

The Drenchfort

The Cauldron

FORGE LANDS

The Forge Lands

Construct Clash

Death's chat with the old giant, Eideard, is cut short by the appearance of several hostile beings known as Construct Warriors. Prove your battle prowess by defeating these foes born of Corruption.

ENEMY: CONSTRUCT WARRIOR

Class: Soldier

These mindless golems attack with slow, heavy blows. Evade when you see them raise an arm to the sky in preparation to strike, and then counter. Avoid becoming surrounded as you hack these troublesome monsters to rubble.

Trek to Tri-Stone

Impressed by the Horseman's skill, Eideard advises that Death seek out the Forge Sister in the nearby village of Tri-Stone. By helping her, the Rider will move closer to reaching the Tree of Life. Question Eideard to learn that he is a Maker—an ancient being whose hands have laid the foundation for many worlds.

Before venturing up the western trail, check behind the large statue to discover a hidden chest.

43

Tri-Stone is the home of the Makers: venerable creators of worlds. This tranquil setting serves as a place where Death can purchase goods and obtain new quests.

1ST FLOOR

> ## NOTE
> See the "How to Use This Book" section at the beginning of the guide for a map icon legend.

Meet the Makers

Run up the west trail from the Forge Lands and pass through a hollow log to reach the village of Tri-Stone. A younger, yet equally burly, Maker named Thane is busy practicing his combat skills in the north plaza. Speak to Thane to learn a bit more about the Corruption that plagues the Makers' land. Thane also offers to teach you new attacks and combos for a modest fee.

☙ TIP

Thane's moves are well worth buying, but we recommend saving your hard-earned gilt for gear and health potions—these are more valuable in the early stages of Death's quest.

☙ CAUTION

Thane offers a side quest called "The Maker Warrior," which asks you to best Thane in single combat. The towering Maker is beyond Death's current skills, however, so it's unwise to attempt this quest until after the Rider has gained a few levels and acquired better gear.

SIDE QUEST ACQUIRED: "THE MAKER WARRIOR"

Destroy the debris that lies around the north plaza; you may discover valuable items.

Practice your attack combos on the surrounding wooden posts as well. You can focus on the posts and maneuver around them just like enemies.

When you've finished honing your combat skills, venture south and turn right, scaling the west stairs and heading for a gazebo. A blind woman is practicing magic here, and she has anticipated Death's arrival. This Maker's name is Muria, and she is a shaman. Muria offers to sell Death a small variety of talismans and potions, and can give the Reaper a bit more insight into the Tree of Life. Muria also bestows upon Death a side quest called "Shaman's Craft"—accept this quest, as you'll naturally complete it while performing your primary endeavors here in the Forge Lands.

☙ TIP

Muria's talismans are quite expensive, but her health potions are a bargain. Stock up in preparation for the trials to come.

SIDE QUEST ACQUIRED: "SHAMAN'S CRAFT"

The Forge Sister

Cut across Tri-Stone's south plaza and climb the east steps to reach another gazebo. This is where the Makers' Forge is located. Speak with the Forge Sister, Alya, to advance your quest and learn more about what you must do to clear the giant nest of Corruption that blocks access to the Tree of Life. Alya asks for the Reaper's help in restarting her forge, and won't agree to sell Death any of her wares until he has proven his worth.

SIDE QUEST ACQUIRED: "THE FIRE OF THE MOUNTAIN"

Ancient Tome

Did you notice this curious device on your way to speak with the Forge Sister? This is known as a Tome, and it allows you to send and receive gifts to/from other *Darksiders II* players. Simply select items in your inventory that you wish to send to friends, or check for any gifts that your friends may have sent you. Receiving gifts is a great way to gain an early advantage!

☙ NOTE

Test out the Tome with Prima's special code, and score a unique secondary weapon! Log onto primagames.com for further instructions.

Speak with Thane

Backtrack to the north plaza and sprint up the curved steps to find both Thane and Eideard waiting near Tri-Stone's north gate. Speak with Thane, and he'll open the gate and allow Death to journey toward the Cauldron, the temple from which the Fire of the Mountain flows. Thane also teaches you a free combat move called Harvester Revenge. Question Thane and Eideard to learn more about the Fire of the Mountain and what it will take to reactivate the Makers's Forge.

◉ TIP

Practice your new move on the nearby training posts before venturing onward.

Leaving Tri-Stone

Ancient ruins lie beyond Tri-Stone's north gate.

Wall-run up the west wall to escape the pool, and then climb a ledge and drop off the edge to return to the entry stairs.

Dive into the central pool and collect a special item called a Boatman Coin that floats beneath the water. A merchant you've yet to encounter has a special interest in these items, so seek them out.

Run up the east wall to reach a short trail that leads to the opposite side of the pool. Proceed north to leave these ruins.

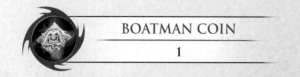

BOATMAN COIN

1

STONEFATHER'S VALE

This wide valley lies north of Tri-Stone and offers plenty of room to roam. Death's menacing steed, Despair, may be summoned here to hasten explorations.

Nest of Evil

Death gets his first glimpse of Corruption here in Stonefather's Vale. A giant nest of the sickening substance blocks the north trail, which leads to the Tree of Life. Clearing this won't be easy.

Vale Valuables

Two items of worth can be found in the vale. Ride west to discover a Boatman Coin near the west gate, and explore the vale's north tip to locate an ancient page from the Book of the Dead. Both items are of value to a merchant who you'll soon meet.

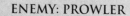

BOATMAN COIN
2

BOOK OF THE DEAD
PAGE 1

ENEMY: PROWLER

Class: Soldier

Prowlers are lesser enemies that Death can dispatch with relatively little trouble. Dangerous only in large groups, the Prowler's speed and ability to leap and strike at Death from range makes it troublesome. Fortunately, Prowler attacks deal relatively little damage, and they can't suffer much of the Reaper's wrath.

> **NOTE**
>
> Did you notice the blue gemstone on the cliff near the Book of the Dead page? This is a Stonebite, but Death can't harvest these special collectibles until he acquires a special item. All Stonebites are shown on the maps for future reference.

Beware: collecting the Book of the Dead page from Stonefather's Vale causes a trio of vicious Prowlers to appear. These savage creatures are agile and often avoid Death's combos, so attack in short bursts and Evade often to keep them from flanking you.

When you've finished exploring Stonefather's Vale, follow the east trail to a cave that leads into the mountains.

THE WEEPING CRAG

The Pale Rider's journey to the Cauldron takes him through this ominous cave.

Crossing the Crag

The Weeping Crag is a small ruin that Death can opt to explore at any time. While there's no need to explore this dismal place, valuable treasure can be found here. Refer to the "Side Quests" chapter of this guide for a complete walkthrough of this optional area.

⟡ CAUTION

Beware: a vicious beast guards the Weeping Crag's greatest treasure, and Death poses little threat to this monster at present. We recommend waiting to explore the Weeping Crag until after you've cleared out the Cauldron.

Merchant of Death

The trail forks beyond the Weeping Crag's drawbridge. Venture north to encounter a demonic peddler named Vulgrim. In addition to offering Death a selection of clandestine goods, Vulgrim also asks that the Pale Rider keep an eye out for lost pages of the Book of the Dead, which have been scattered across the realms. The savvy demon assures the Reaper that his reward for retrieving these precious pages would be substantial.

⟡ NOTE

Vulgrim is the only merchant that accepts Boatman Coins. In addition to a modest amount of gilt, Boatman Coins are required in order to purchase Vulgrim's wares.

⟡ **SIDE QUEST ACQUIRED:** ⟡
THE BOOK OF THE DEAD

This dense forest lies to the east of the Stonefather's Vale, and is wide enough for Death to explore with Despair. Beware the Construct Warriors that patrol this ancient wood.

Northwest Ruin

Veer left as you enter Baneswood and dispatch the dangerous Construct Warriors that lurk near the wood's northwest ruin. You can fight the Constructs from horseback, or you can dismount and battle them on foot.

After clearing out the Constructs, enter the nearby ruin and run up the interior wall, vaulting off a peg to reach a hand hold. Climb up to discover a hidden chest with random loot.

> ### NOTE
> Did you notice the peculiar blue stone on the wall inside the ruin? It's eye-catching, but you won't be able to interact with it for a while yet.

Southwest Ledge

Travel south from the northwest ruin and fight your way up a grassy rise. Spy a Boatman Coin hovering on high and leap from the ledge to snatch it from midair.

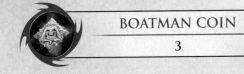

BOATMAN COIN
3

Central Ruin

Next, head for the small decrepit shrine near the center of the wood. Open the chest you discover here for more random plunder.

East Ruin

A statue of a Maker stands in the midst of Baneswood's east ruin. Search behind the statue to discover a Book of the Dead page. This is all you can claim from this forgotten site at present, as a special item is needed to traverse its upper ledges.

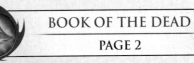

BOOK OF THE DEAD
PAGE 2

Northeast Ruin

Another ruin lies at the wood's northeast corner. Enter the front door and smash the junk upstairs to discover a Boatman Coin and a chest. You can't interact with the curious lump of glowing stones here, and there's little else to accomplish. Head back outside.

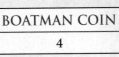

BOATMAN COIN
4

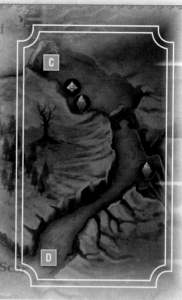

Take the east trail out of Baneswood, heading toward your primary quest objective. Dispatch more Construct Warriors along the way, and explore a short side trail to the right where a chest sits amongst the crumbling remains of a shrine.

Keep moving uphill to the west of the chest, and look for a Boatman Coin hovering on high. Again, leap up and grab it before venturing onward.

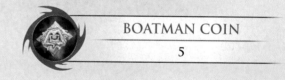

BOATMAN COIN

5

Enclosed Shrine

As you begin to head south along the trail, enter the small stone structure that stands to the left. Locate the hand hold in the shrine's southwest corner and run up the nearby wall, then jump and grab the hand hold to reach an overhead ledge.

Perform a pair of wall-runs to circle around the shrine's ledges and land near a wooden post. Climb the post, then wall-run from the top of it to reach an even higher ledge.

Perform one last wall-run to reach a chest. Claim your loot, then drop to the ground and continue your journey to the Cauldron.

THE CHARRED PASS

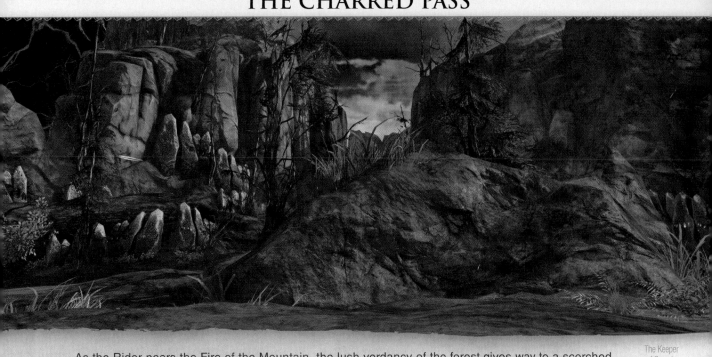

As the Rider nears the Fire of the Mountain, the lush verdancy of the forest gives way to a scorched and barren landscape. The Cauldron can't be far.

Passing Through

Cut down Construct Warriors as you enter the Charred Pass, and explore a large hollow log to discover a hidden Boatman Coin.

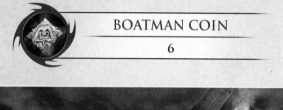

BOATMAN COIN
6

Travel north from the log and slay the Constructs that guard a shallow marsh. After securing the area, scour the rocky north bank to discover a chest.

⊙ **NOTE**

There's no need to venture down the Charred Pass's southern trail. It leads to a side dungeon that Death cannot clear until much later in the adventure.

Dive into the well at the heart of the marsh and swim down to the bottom. Surface in a shallow cave, then scale the smooth wall and 180 leap to a chest. As you swim back out, claim a Boatman Coin that's hidden near the side of the well's broken piping.

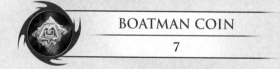

BOATMAN COIN
7

Southwest Ruin

Pause to explore one last ruin before making your way to the Cauldron. Inside, run up the wall and perform a 180 leap from the highest hand hold to reach a wooden beam.

Jump to the next beam, and then leap at the far wall to run up it and reach the hand holds above. Scale the hand holds to reach a chest on a balcony.

Warriors at the Gate

After looting the final ruin, ride hard up the west trail to at last reach the Cauldron's entrance. A burly Maker is battling a host of Construct Warriors near the drawbridge, so join him in dispatching the teeming fiends.

⟡ CAUTION

The vast number of Constructs that attack you here make this a challenging battle. Evade often, and forego focusing on any one enemy to maintain a wider view of the area—this helps you identify and avoid Constructs that try to flank you.

Speak with the Maker, Karn, to learn that Corruption has taken hold in the Cauldron. Grave danger lies within, yet Karn believes that Death might be capable of success. Question Karn to advance Muria's quest.

⟡ SIDE QUEST ADVANCED: "SHAMAN'S CRAFT"

With a swing of his mighty hammer, Karn shatters a thick chain and lowers the Cauldron's drawbridge. Cross the bridge, but sneak along the ledge to the right and raid a hidden chest before entering the temple.

⟡ NOTE

Death has surely leveled up by this point. Be sure to spend his skill points to unlock new skills.

⟡ TIP

Assign Death's skills to action buttons by using the radial skill menu. This lets you quickly activate Death's skills in the heat of combat without having to call up the menu. See the "Moves and Abilities" chapter for complete details and strategies for all of the Pale Rider's skills.

The oppressive heat of the Cauldron washes over Death as he enters this foreboding place. Corruption has taken hold in this once-sacred temple, and it must be confronted to restore the Fire of the Mountain.

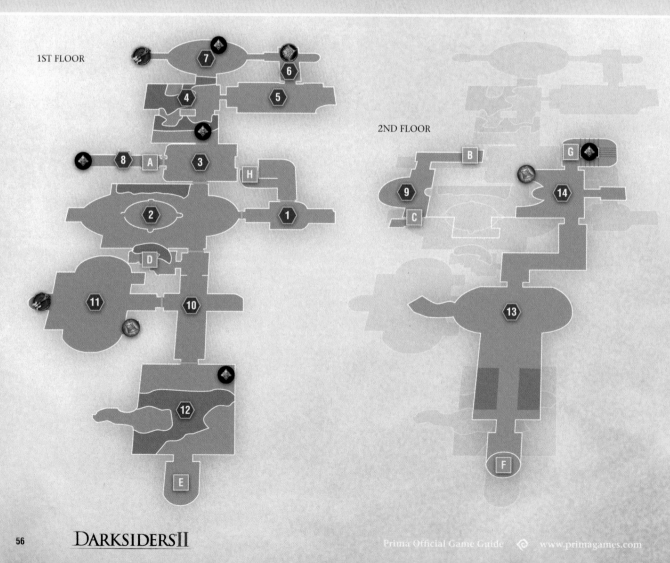

1ST FLOOR

2ND FLOOR

Area 1: Cauldron Entry

Destroy the debris in the Cauldron's first room to discover minor items, and then push the handle on the wall to unbar the west door.

Area 2: Cauldron Chamber

This wide chamber houses the Cauldron, but the massive device has been sealed so the Fire of the Mountain does not flow from the temple as it should. Slay the Construct Warriors to the west, and then open the chest they were guarding. Afterward, head north to discover a curious object called a Shadowbomb pod.

Press the Action button to collect a Shadowbomb from the pod, and then press the Aim button to take aim at the switch on the north wall. Press the Special Item trigger to hurl the Shadowbomb at the switch. The bomb sticks to the switch, then quickly explodes. This activates the switch and unbars the north door.

TIP

Now that you've discovered the Cauldron, you can pause the game and use the map screen to quickly travel back to Tri-Stone via the fast travel mechanic. Stock up on Muria's potions, then fast travel back to the Cauldron and continue your quest. Keep this feature in mind: you can fast travel back to Tri-Stone for potions at any point while exploring the temple, and then quickly return.

Before advancing through the north door, collect another Shadowbomb and run west, circling around the Cauldron itself to locate some yellow Corruption crystals. Stand back and toss the bomb at the crystals—it obliterates them when it explodes, exposing a hidden chest! Proceed through the north door after claiming your valuables.

Area 3: Statue Room

A giant statue of a proud Maker dominates the east side of this room, and a locked door lies to the west. Cut down more Construct Warriors here. Advance through the north door afterward.

Area 4: Broken Floor Chamber

Beware of accidentally falling into boiling lava in this hazardous room. Carefully collect the Boatman Coin from the sloped floor near the lava, then run up the west wall and grab the long hand hold. Shimmy across and perform a 180 leap to reach solid ground. Jump over the next small gap in the floor, and then move to explore the chamber's north half.

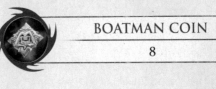

BOATMAN COIN

8

Run up the small south wall and grab a hand hold. Run up the wall again and jump to grab the hanging post behind you.

Circle around the post and perform a 180 leap to reach a series of beams.

Leap across the beams to reach a wall with a hand hold, and then wall-run to reach another hand hold.

Shimmy around the second hand hold and wall-run to reach some growth. Climb down and press the Action button to drop to solid ground.

The growth leads down to a Shadowbomb pod. Collect a bomb and toss it at the distant switch to activate it and unbar the east door.

Area 5: Statue Room 2

Beware: Construct Warriors ambush you in this wide chamber, along with new enemies called Construct Adjuncts. Take advantage of the ample space and Evade often to avoid damage. Proceed through the north door after the battle.

ENEMY: CONSTRUCT ADJUNCT

Class: Soldier

Rather than attacking Death directly, Construct Adjuncts prefer to keep their distance and hurl boulders at the Horseman from afar. Adjuncts can be quite troublesome if allowed to toss fodder at Death during battle, for their attacks are quite accurate and difficult to anticipate when you're distracted by melee foes. It's wise to seek out Adjuncts and slaughter them first whenever they're encountered in mixed groups.

Area 6: Crumbling Corridor

Cut straight across this ruined corridor to discover an ornate chest that contains the Dungeon Map. Now you can see the whole of the Cauldron by consulting your map. Rooms you've yet to explore appear as a darker shade of gray.

Destroy the arena's outlying clutter to potentially score healing potions, along with a Boatman Coin.

DUNGEON MAP

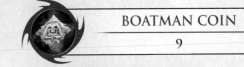

BOATMAN COIN
9

Area 7: Stalker Arena

The crumbling corridor leads to a wide, circular room. Death witnesses a curious sight here: a monstrous beast known as a Stalker is being attacked by a relentless torrent of Construct Warriors. Pause and watch the battle, for the Constructs are doing you a favor in weakening the Stalker.

> **TIP**
> Enter Aiming mode to monitor the Stalker's health from afar.

Open the ornate chest in the room's west alcove to obtain a special item called a Skeleton Key.

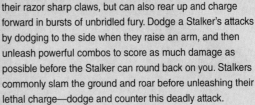

SKELETON KEY

When the Stalker is near death, storm forward and join the fray. Cut down the remaining Constructs, then land the killing blow against the Stalker to advance Muria's side quest.

ENEMY: STALKER

Class: Brute

Stalkers are large, ferocious beasts that possess terrifying speed and agility. They primarily attack by swiping at Death with their razor sharp claws, but can also rear up and charge forward in bursts of unbridled fury. Dodge a Stalker's attacks by dodging to the side when they raise an arm, and then unleash powerful combos to score as much damage as possible before the Stalker can round back on you. Stalkers commonly slam the ground and roar before unleashing their lethal charge—dodge and counter this deadly attack.

With the Skeleton Key in hand, wall-run across the south pit to return to Area 4. Continue moving south to reach Area 3, where more Construct Warriors guard the locked door you noticed before. Dispatch the Constructs and open the door with the Skeleton Key, which vanishes after use.

If you ever feel lost, press and hold the Movement Stick to summon Dust and send the crow flying toward Death's next objective. Dust can help show his master the way forward at any time, so keep this in mind.

Area 8: Orb Room 1

Approach the unusual blue orb in this small room and press the Action button to grab it.

Shimmy to the right and perform a 180 leap to grab a floating Boatman Coin.

Roll the orb over the indentation on the ground to cause a section of nearby wall to rotate, revealing a peg.

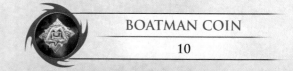

BOATMAN COIN
10

Return to the hand hold and wall-run to the right to reach a balcony. Check behind the large statue here to discover a chest.

Run up the wall and vault from the peg to reach a high hand hold.

Return to the hand hold and wall-run to the left to reach some growth. Climb up to visit the Cauldron's second floor.

Area 9: Cauldron Chamber—West Balcony

You're now on the second floor, overlooking the Cauldron chamber. Raid the chest on the west landing and smash the surrounding jars and debris for minor valuables.

Run up the wall in the south alcove and vault from the peg to reach a hand hold. Before shimmying around the corner, perform a 180 leap to reach a small nook behind you, where a large chest is cleverly hidden.

> **NOTE**
>
> Large chests often contain more valuable plunder than normal-size chests.

Return to the hand hold and shimmy around the corner, then run over to some growth. Climb down and drop to solid ground before heading through the hole in the wall.

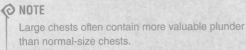

Area 10: Lava Corridor

Push the switch on the wall beyond the hole. This lowers a gate to the south. Advance and slay the Construct Warriors you encounter farther down the corridor. The south door is locked, so proceed through the west door instead.

Area 11: Orb Room 2

Cut down more Constructs in this area, including a few bothersome Adjuncts. Collect a Shadowbomb from a pod in the northern nook afterward, then use it to destroy the nearby Corruption crystals, exposing another blue orb.

Roll the orb south, past the first indentation on the ground, and fit it into the southern-most indentation. This lowers a gate, exposing a second orb. Collect the Book of the Dead Page found near the second orb.

> **TIP**
>
> If you accidentally rolled the orb into the wrong slot, use a Shadowbomb to dislodge it.

BOOK OF THE DEAD
PAGE 3

Grab the second orb and roll it onto either of the two slots near the west stairs. Use a Shadowbomb to dislodge the first orb, and then roll it onto the remaining slot near the stairs. With both orbs in place, the west gate lowers, exposing a chest that contains a Skeleton Key.

SKELETON KEY

Well done! Now return to the outer hall and use the Skeleton Key to unlock the chained door to the south.

First thing's first: smash the debris in this large room's northeast corner to discover a hidden Boatman Coin.

BOATMAN COIN
11

Immediately after raising the cauldron, run up the west wall and grab the hand hold.

Wall-run across the gap in the hand hold, then drop from the end to reach solid ground below.

Next, push the nearby switch to raise the central cauldron. You must use the cauldron to cross the room, but it lowers after a brief time, so make haste.

Make a daring jump and grab the hand hold at the base of the raised cauldron.

Shimmy to the left and jump up to grab the cauldron's higher hand hold. Shimmy around and perform a 180 leap to reach the east ledge.

You made it! Now, use the south alcove's pegs to reach a high hand hold,  and then wall-run to the left. Jump from another peg to reach a higher hand hold, and then shimmy to the left and drop down to the balcony below.

Shadowbomb Action

Next, grab a Shadowbomb from the balcony's pod and take aim. Toss it down at the Corruption crystals in the west alcove below. This clears out a nook that contains a large chest. Carefully drop down to the ground floor and explore the nook to claim your prize.

⬡ **CAUTION**

Looting the large chest causes a small group of Construct Warriors to spawn near the ground-floor switch, which you must use again to raise the central cauldron and maneuver around the chamber.

Return to the upper balcony with the Shadowbomb pod. This time, throw a bomb at the far switch near the north stairs. This raises the central cauldron once more, and you can simply sprint across it to reach the north balcony.

INTRODUCTION

EXPLORATION
AND COMBAT

SKILLS AND
COMBOS

WALKTHROUGH

SIDE QUESTS
AND AREAS

APPENDIX

BEHIND THE
SCENES

A gate rises behind Death as he struts into this circular chamber, trapping the Rider inside. Within moments, a monstrous Construct named Gharn smashes through the far wall. Prepare for battle!

BOSS BATTLE: GHARN

Gharn is surprisingly quick for his size, and can cover a lot of ground with his furious charge attack. Whenever you see the brute raise an arm, be ready to Evade to the side and avoid the forthcoming blow. Quickly close in and utilize combos each time you successfully dodge.

Gharn will periodically fall to one knee during the battle, giving you a chance to pile on the damage. Be ready to flee when the brute begins to recover, though, for Gharn will soon rise and unleash an explosive attack that inflicts tremendous damage if you're caught in the blast.

 TIP

Tap the Evade trigger a few times to backflip away from Gharn before he erupts.

Defeating Gharn unbars the north door, allowing you to advance. In addition, you receive a unique secondary weapon called the Dark Avenger for defeating this worthy foe.

DARK AVENGER

Area 14: Cauldron Chamber—East Balcony

Destroy any clutter in the hallway that leads to this balcony, and loot the chest along the way. Investigate the balcony's east alcove to discover another chest, and then clear out more debris on the balcony's northwest corner to expose another missing page from the Book of the Dead.

BOOK OF THE DEAD
PAGE 4

After pocketing your plunder, grab the central lever and rotate it counterclockwise to lower the giant counterweights in the chamber below. This lifts the lid off of the massive Cauldron, restoring the flow of the Fire of the Mountain to Tri-Stone at last.

Excellent work, Rider! The time has now come to leave this place. Proceed through the north door and descend the winding stairs to return to the ground floor. Jump down the center of the stairwell to claim a Boatman Coin. Crack open the chest that's tucked beneath the stairs as well before you leave.

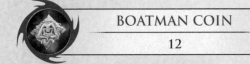

BOATMAN COIN
12

Converse with Karn

Exit the temple and speak with Karn outside. The young Maker is happy that you've accomplished your goal. Speaking with Karn also advances Muria's side quest.

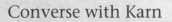

SIDE QUEST ADVANCED: "SHAMAN'S CRAFT"

Return to Tri-Stone

It's a long way back to Tri-Stone, so take advantage of the map's fast travel function if you're in a hurry. Speak with Alya once you arrive to complete the Fire of the Mountain quest and receive an excellent new item—a powerful pistol called Redemption. This is sure to come in handy during the Horseman's travels!

> **TIP**
>
> Alya will now sell you wares crafted at the forge by her brother, Valus. Barter with Alya and sell your unwanted gear to gain coin for more valuable equipment. Armor with high defense is particularly valuable in the early stages of Death's quest.

REDEMPTION

> **TIP**
>
> Shoot five out-of-reach vases around Tri-Stone to make a secret chest appear! Two vases are found alongside the main thoroughfare, another two are found around Muria's platform, and the final vase is found atop a column at Alya's platform.

⟲ Tears of the Mountain

THE FIRE OF THE MOUNTAIN FLOWS AGAIN, BUT THE HORSEMAN'S WORK IS FAR FROM FINISHED. DEATH'S NEXT TASK IS TO RESTORE THE TEARS OF THE MOUNTAIN, ANOTHER VITAL COMPONENT IN HELPING THE MAKERS' FORGE ROAR BACK TO LIFE. NOW ARMED WITH REDEMPTION—A POWERFUL PISTOL THAT ONCE BELONGED TO DEATH'S BROTHER, STRIFE—THE PALE RIDER IS EQUIPPED TO VENTURE TO THE FORSAKEN DRENCHFORT AND RESTORE THE TEARS. WHAT PERIL MIGHT AWAIT THE REAPER IN THE NEW LANDS THAT LIE AHEAD?

STONEFATHER'S VALE

With Redemption at his side, the Pale Rider is now able to open the Vale's west gate and explore the lands beyond.

Breaking the Barrier

Ride west across Stonefather's Vale, heading for a massive stone gate. Karn stands near the gate; speak with the giant to learn a bit about what lies beyond.

> ⟲ TIP
> Grab the Boatman Coin that's tucked behind the nearby tree if you didn't collect it during your first trip through the Vale.

After speaking with Karn, look up at the Shadowbombs that stick out from the top of the gate. Enter Aiming mode and target the bombs, then press the Special Item trigger to fire Redemption and detonate them, clearing the way forward.

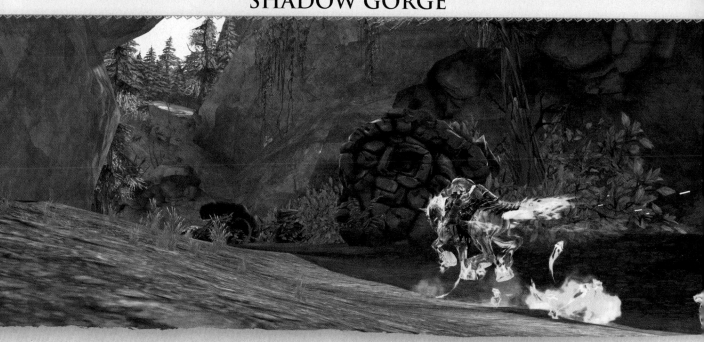

SHADOW GORGE

This ominous gorge lies west of the Stonefather's Vale. Death must brave this dreary passage to reach the Drenchfort, from which the Tears of the Mountain once flowed.

On the Prowl

The path widens as you near a gate, and a couple of Prowlers are on patrol. A Stinger Hive also stands in the distance, churning out vicious little critters called Stingers. Dispatch these minions n horseback if you like, using Redemption in combination with Death's scythes to quickly cut them down. Killing your first Stinger advances Muria's side quest.

SIDE QUEST ADVANCED: SHAMAN'S CRAFT

ENEMY: STINGER

Class: Fodder

Stingers are small flying foes that pose little threat to the Horseman individually, but become somewhat troublesome when encountered in swarms. Stingers can be difficult to strike with melee attacks, so use Death's pistol, Redemption, to shoot down these lowly pests with greater ease. Anti-group attacks and skills, such as Harvest, can quickly eliminate whole swarms of Stingers if you risk letting them close in.

Underwater Plunder

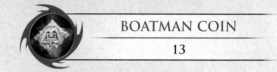

Before investigating the gate and tower to the west, explore the north trail to reach a old, abandoned keep that's fallen to ruin. Search the shallow moat to discover an underwater Boatman Coin amongst the remnants of the collapsed bridge.

BOATMAN COIN
13

> **NOTE**
>
> The abandoned keep, which is called the Shattered Forge, is a side dungeon that pertains to a side quest you've yet to acquire. You can explore it now, or wait until you gain the side quest. See the "Side Quests and Areas" chapter for a complete walkthrough.

Raising the Gate

The Shadow Gorge's west trail is blocked by a massive gate, and you've got to find some way to open it. Locate the Shadowbomb sticking out of the nearby tower's wall, right between two yellow Corruption crystals. Use Redemption to detonate the bomb and destroy the crystals, exposing a peg.

Run up the wall and vault from the peg to reach the balcony above. Before entering the tower, creep along the balcony's lip to claim a Boatman Coin. Ensure Death is in good health, and then enter the tower.

BOATMAN COIN
14

Beware: you're sealed inside this small, crumbling tower the moment you enter, and are swarmed by a host of vicious Stingers. Use Redemption to wipe out these flying pests, and Evade often to present a difficult target.

The battle intensifies after you slaughter the Stingers, and a mob of Savage Prowlers emerge from the central pit. Beware their aggressive attacks, and stay light on your feet while cutting them down with Death's best moves.

The tower unseals after the Savage Prowlers have fallen to the Reaper's wrath. Exit the tower and turn right to claim a Boatman Coin from the west balcony, and then drop down from the tower to land on the opposite side of the gate. Pull a lever to open the gate and you'll never need to cut through the tower again.

BOATMAN COIN
15

ENEMY: SAVAGE PROWLER

Class: Minion

More powerful and aggressive than the standard Prowler, Savage Prowlers retain the same frightening agility and long-range leaping attacks that make their predecessors so troublesome. Savage Prowlers can also charge up a powerful leaping strike that covers a great distance and is best avoided by a lateral dodge. Evade in a circle around Savage Prowlers when you see them glow with ire in preparation for avoiding their forthcoming attack.

INTRODUCTION

EXPLORATION AND COMBAT

SKILLS AND COMBOS

WALKTHROUGH

SIDE QUESTS AND AREAS

APPENDIX

BEHIND THE SCENES

THE FJORD

The landscape opens up beyond the Shadow Gorge's west gate, offering plenty of room for exploration. Summon Despair once more and ride through this gloomy region.

Fiends in the Fjord

Beware: bloodthirsty Prowlers and hulking Stalkers lurk in the lands beyond the tower gate. Remain on Despair and run circles around each fearsome beast as you pick them apart with Redemption and scythe attacks. Battle these fiends on foot only if you wish to unleash Death's combat skills.

Blackroot Banter

Scale the cliff to the west of the tower gate to speak with a curious construct named Blackroot. This being hasn't been taken by Corruption, but is suffering the early effects of starvation. Blackroot feeds on special Stonebites that are scattered about the realms, and gives Death a special item that allows the Reaper to harvest these stones if he's feeling merciful. There's reward in collecting Stonebites for Blackroot, so it's wise to seek them out.

SIDE QUEST ACQUIRED: "STICKS AND STONES"

LURE STONE

After speaking with Blackroot and receiving the Lure Stone, scan the nearby cliff to spy a blue Stonebite up on high. Enter Aiming mode and blast the Stonebite with Redemption to activate the Lure Stone and draw in your first Stonebite, a Stone of Mystics. Only 68 more Stonebites to go!

> ⟡ **TIP**
>
> Stonebites emit a soft, unique ringing sound. Turn up the volume and listen for this tone, then search high and low for Stonebites whenever you hear it.

STONE OF MYSTICS
1

> ⟡ **NOTE**
>
> You've likely noticed several Stonebites during your travels through the Forge Lands thus far. Now that you possess the Lure Stone, you can shoot these special objects with Redemption and draw out the power of each stone. The walkthrough will begin to call out each Stonebite you encounter from this point forward. Refer to the previous area maps, along with the checklists at the end of this guide, to discover the locations of Stonebites found in areas you've previously explored.

STONE OF POWER
1

STONE OF MYSTICS
2 - 9

After chatting with Blackroot, charge Despair off the nearby cliff to claim the floating Boatman Coin.

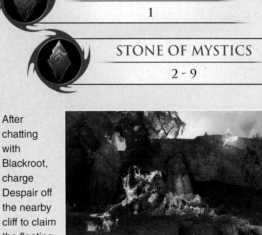

BOATMAN COIN
16

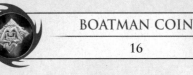

Fjord Harbor

Ride downhill to a dismal lake and notice a collection of Corruption crystals near a ruined pier. Shoot the central Shadowbomb pod to obliterate the Corruption crystals. Dive into the water afterward and swim underneath the pier. Wall-run up and vault a peg to reach the pier's chest.

Dive into the water and explore the lakebed to discover a Boatman Coin near the pier's underwater supports. This is the only item of interest to be found underwater.

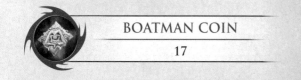

BOATMAN COIN
17

Next, swim east to reach a sizable stone mooring station. Scamper up the wall and explore the interior balcony to discover a chest. You can't reach the Boatman Coin or chest on the mooring station's roof at present—a special item is required to climb up there.

Vulgrim's Hideout

Plunk back into the water and swim south to discover another stone enclosure where the demonic merchant Vulgrim has set up shop. Sell off all unwanted gear to earn coin and free up your inventory, then consider purchasing something from Vulgrim's stock.

After trading with Vulgrim, slip past the wall behind the merchant to find a peg and series of hand holds running up the wall. Vault off of the peg and make your way up the hand holds, and then wall-run from the highest hand hold to reach a ledge with a chest. You can't interact with the curious portals here at present, so return to the ground floor.

Sleeping Giant

Continue swimming south from Vulgrim's hideout to reach a small patch of dry land. This turns out to be a dead-end, yet there's life to be discovered here. Unfortunately, you can't wake the sleeping construct you find without a special item, but simply visiting this site is enough to earn you a new side quest.

╟─── SIDE QUEST ACQUIRED: ───╢
SILENT STONE

East Keep

You've fully explored the harbor, so swim north, all the way back to the Fjord's main trail. Ride east and follow a snaking path to reach the door of a keep that's built into the mountainside. Inside, a pair pressure plates presents a puzzle you currently cannot solve. Raid two chests and shoot the Stonebite on the wall to score a Stone of Power, and then search the west nook to discover a hidden Boatman Coin.

BOATMAN COIN
18

STONE OF POWER
2

When you've finished pillaging the Fjord, follow the east trail toward your primary objective: the Drenchfort. Before you enter a cave, turn around and leap from the nearby cliff to claim a floating Boatman Coin. Enter the cave afterward and blast a Stonebite as you pass through.

STONE OF MYSTICS
10

BOATMAN COIN
19

THE DRENCHFORT

This aquatic stronghold lies east of the Fjord and houses the source of the Tears of the Mountain. The Pale Rider must brave this forgotten temple to restore the flow of the Tears to the Maker's Forge.

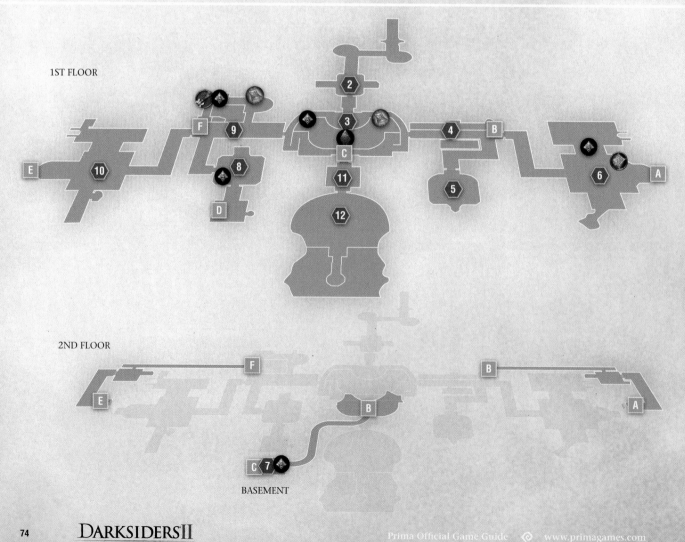

Area 1: Entry Hall

A swarm of Stingers fly out to meet Death as he delves into the Drenchfort's impressive entry hall. Use Redemption and anti-group attacks to wipe out these bothersome buzzers.

◉ TIP

If you would like to, you can fast travel back to Tri-Stone and trade with the Makers before braving the Drenchfort. Stocking up on Muria's potions is always wise before entering a dangerous place!

Area 2: Savage Ambush

A pair of Savage Prowlers roam the small room at the entry hall's end. Unleash the Reaper's fury and slay these foul predators to secure the area before you unbar the south door.

After the battle, scale the west wall's pegs to reach a hand hold, then wall-run to the left to reach a high ledge.

Collect a Shadowbomb from the ledge's pod, toss it at the distant orb, and then shoot it.

The explosion knocks the orb to the ground. Roll it onto the circular indentation to unbar the south door and enter the temple proper.

Area 3: Great Aqueduct

This massive outdoor area features giant stone aqueducts. No water is currently flowing—the Tears of the Mountain are being blocked elsewhere in the Drenchfort.

Next, spy a Stonebite on the south wall and shoot it.

Turn left as you enter and sprint east along the upper balcony. Look for the top of a hand hold on the outside of the balcony, to the left. Slowly walk off the edge here to make Death drop down and grab the hand hold.

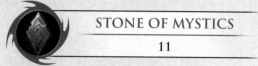

STONE OF MYSTICS
11

Shimmy and wall-run to the right across the series of hand holds that follow. Drop down from the final hand hold to land on a tiny ledge where you find a lost page of the Book of the Dead.

Drop down to the bottom of the area and scale the west wall's pegs and hand holds to return to the upper level. Smash the jars in the corner and do battle with the Savage Prowlers that attack you. Climb the west stairs to return to the north balcony.

BOOK OF THE DEAD
PAGE 5

Leap to the west, onto the central platform, and raid the chest that sits near the large statue.

Stand in the northwest corner of the balcony and peer over the edge where the hand hold is to spy a Boatman Coin on a lower ledge. Carefully drop down and claim this prize.

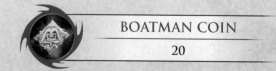

BOATMAN COIN
20

Scale the west wall's pegs again to return to the balcony. Go east this time, cutting down more Savage Prowlers on your way to a pair of pegs that lead up to a hand hold on the east wall. Vault up the pegs and then shimmy to the left, rounding the corner.

Don't wall-run to the next hand hold. Instead, let go after rounding the corner and raid the chest you discover on the landing of the broken east stairs. Fall from the stairs afterward and vault up the east wall's pegs again. This time, wall-run to the left after shimmying around the corner to reach a high east door, and then go through it.

Area 4: East Tear Duct

Venture eastward through this area and explore a ruined room to your right to locate a chest.

Cut down the Stingers that swarm you as you approach the area's east door. Don't enter the door; instead, face north while standing until you can spy a chest across the aqueduct. Leap over, loot the chest, and then use a hand hold to escape the barren channel. Again, ignore the east door and follow the corridor to another door that leads south.

Area 5: Earth Crag Chamber

A chest tantalizes you from the far side of this crumbling chamber, but reaching it won't be easy. A gate suddenly rises to protect the chest, and a number of Stingers swarm you, followed by several Savage Prowlers. Evade often and use anti-group attacks such as Harvest to even the odds.

After the weaker foes have fallen, a monstrous Earth Crag emerges from the floor. These hulking monsters are swift and can quickly close the distance by charging forward. Evade around the room's pillars to prevent the Earth Crag from crashing into you, then quickly counter with Death's most powerful skills and combos.

ENEMY: EARTH CRAG

Class: Brute

These rampaging beasts demand the Reaper's undivided attention. Earth Crags primarily attack by charging forward with frightening speed and ramming the Rider if he doesn't manage to evade. Earth Crags also attack by leaping into the air and crashing back down, sending out a wide shockwave that is best dodged by jumping. Batter Earth Crags with Death's best combos each time you avoid their attacks, but stay mindful of their tactics and always be ready to dodge or jump to avoid their next punishing assault.

Destroy the surrounding debris in search of loot after slaying the Earth Crag, and then raid the south chest to claim some loot. Backtrack to the previous area and proceed through the east door you previously ignored.

Area 6: East Reservoir

All is quiet as the Pale Rider enters this wide chamber. Two orbs must be placed in the room's central slots to lower the east gate.

First, go south and dive into the water. Swim through an underwater hole to reach a secret cave where a large chest containing valuable loot is hidden.

Swim out from the cave and vault up off a peg to escape the water and reach the top of the nearby wall. Turn around and wall-run along the wall to your right, jumping when you reach the corner and vaulting off of the two pegs that follow to extend the run.

Jump again as you near the next corner and you'll run down to the top of the neighboring wall, where a blue orb sits. Roll the orb off the wall, then drop down and maneuver it onto the nearby orb slot. The east gate lowers halfway, but there's still work to do.

The Other Orb

Scale the north wall's hand holds to reach the wall's top, and then run across the arch to snag a Boatman Coin. Keep going to reach an ornate chest that contains the Dungeon Map. Backtrack afterward and drop down from the wall to reach the room's northern half, where a puzzle must be solved in order to free the second orb.

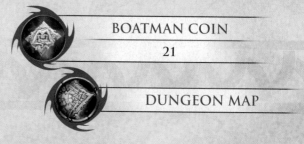

BOATMAN COIN

21

DUNGEON MAP

First, raid the chest that's tucked away in the north alcove. Priorities!

Stand on the nearby pressure plate to lower the gate, and then shoot the Shadowbomb to blast the orb into the main chamber.

Next, use hand holds to scale the southeast wall and reach a nook with a Shadowbomb pod.

Excellent work! Now scale the wall and roll the orb into place. The east gate lowers, allowing you to proceed through the door beyond.

Hallway Hive

Collect a Shadowbomb and use it to destroy the northwest Corruption crystals that are trapping the orb.

A giant pulsating Stinger hive stands in the passage beyond the door. Switch to Aiming mode and shoot down the Stingers that emerge from the hive, then rush forward and attack the hive itself with powerful combos. Don't relent until the hive is destroyed and the Stingers cease to emerge.

Roll the orb close to the south gate which leads to the area's center. Retrieve another Shadowbomb and stick it onto the orb.

The hall leads to a small room that's guarded by a pair of Savage Prowlers. Kill them, and then collect a Shadowbomb from the nearby pod and use it to obliterate the nearby Corruption crystals. Pull the lever that the crystals were covering to at last unblock the Drenchfort's east channel, allowing water to flow through the aqueduct more.

Back to the Aqueduct

After all that hard work, it's time to cool off. Leap into the rushing water and swim down the channel. As you near the end, look for a hand hold to the left and leap up to reach a small ledge where a chest is secreted.

Return to the water and allow the current to carry you all the way to the grate at the channel's far end. Climb out and head through the door to return to the Great Aqueduct area. The Tears are now filling half of the aqueduct, but there's still more to restore.

Dive into the water that now fills the bottom half of the Great Aqueduct and swim through the south tunnel to reach the next area.

Area 7: Tunnel Exit

The tunnel leads to a small, tall chamber. With the east Tears flowing strong, the water level is high enough to let you reach this chamber's hand holds. Claim an underwater Boatman Coin before beginning your ascent.

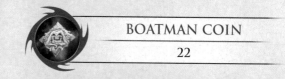

BOATMAN COIN
22

Scale the wall using the hand holds, and then wall-run to the *left* (not the right). Jump as you near the corner and vault off a peg to extend your run. Keep going until you reach a high nook where a chest awaits plundering.

Drop back into the water and scale the wall again. This time, wall-run to the right to reach some climbable growth. Use this to reach the passage above and enter the next area.

Area 8: Savage Ambush

Beware: a swarm of Savage Prowlers fall upon you in this square room, and gates rise up to trap you inside. Try to weaken all of the Prowlers with anti-group attacks before killing too many, as a monstrous Savage Stalker joins the battle once several of the Prowlers go down. Use Death's best abilities to simplify this challenging battle, and smash the surrounding debris in search of healing potions.

TIP
Evade around the room's pillars to give enemies the slip!

ENEMY: SAVAGE STALKER

Class: Brute

Like Savage Prowlers, these hulking beasts attack with greater ferocity than the standard Stalker, often swiping multiple times with their claws in a fluid frenzy. A Savage Stalker's claw combo can't always be avoided with a single dodge, so evade multiple times in a circle and don't allow Death to become trapped by his environment. Unleash the Reaper's most powerful skills to slay these savage brutes before they can cause too much damage.

Things settle down after the Savage Stalker is slain. Collect the Boatman Coin from the room's southwest corner if you haven't already, and then destroy any lingering clutter before advancing through the west door.

BOATMAN COIN
23

Area 9: West Tear Duct

Dispatch a Savage Prowler as you enter this area, and take note of the locked door to the west. Drop down into the barren water channel and head north to reach the area's northern half where the stone water channel has collapsed.

Drop down to the ground and run through the hole in the west wall to reach the area's northwest section, where a number of Savage Prowlers lurk. Slay them all to secure the area and open the ornate chest unhindered. Inside, you discover a Skeleton Key.

SKELETON KEY

You can't reach the high hand holds above the chest at present, so backtrack to the broken channel and use the west wall's hand holds to return to the West Tear Duct's southern half. Use your newfound Skeleton Key to open the locked door and proceed to the next area.

Area 10: West Reservoir

Shoot down some Stingers in the corridor that leads to this sizable area. An orb must be manipulated to reach the area's western half.

Before messing with the orb, run north and open the chest in the northwest nook. Easy money!

Next, scale the north wall's hand holds, and then begin a long wall-run around the room, vaulting from pegs and jumping at corners until you eventually land atop the inside wall near the room's entry. Here, you discover a chest that sits near a patch of oozing black Corruption. Drop down from the wall after claiming your treasure.

Orb Action

Scale the south hand holds to reach a Shadowbomb pod above the entry. Use a bomb to destroy the nearby Corruption crystals.

Drop to the ground and search the nook beyond the crystals to discover another chest.

Run down the south slope and grab the blue orb. Start rolling it up the slope, and then press the Special Item trigger to shove it with extra velocity.

Roll the orb over the slot to lower the nearby west platform.

Collect another Shadowbomb from the pod above the entry, and then carry it over to the platform you've just lowered.

Prima Official Game Guide   www.primagames.com

While standing on the lowered platform, toss the bomb onto the orb, and then shoot it. The platform rises, elevating you to the high west door.

Familiar Flow

Go on the offensive and wipe out the Prowlers and Stinger hive in the hall beyond the west door. Proceed to a small room containing a lever that releases the water.

Pulling the lever does nothing; Corruption crystals are obstructing the dam mechanism. Take aim and blast the Shadowbomb pod that sticks out from the wall near the crystals, eliminating the obstacles. Now you can pull the lever to restore the flow of water through the Drenchfort's west channel.

One Last Lever

You're nearly finished with your business here at the Drenchfort. Drop down into the water and swim east, and then head north to return to the West Tear Duct area's northern half. Water now fills the area; swim across and investigate the broken portion of the aqueduct to discover a Book of the Dead page which was previously unreachable.

Dive underwater and swim through the now-submerged hole in the west wall to reach the area's northwest section, where you previously discovered the Skeleton Key. The high water level now enables you to reach the hand holds here.

Work your way around the hand holds to reach a high passage with a lever. Pull this to raise the final gate and allow the last of water to rush into the Great Aqueduct.

As you backtrack out of the lever passage, leap out to claim a floating Boatman Coin. The east door unbarred when you pulled the last lever, so you can now use it to return to the Great Aqueduct.

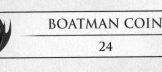

BOATMAN COIN
24

Area 11: Pool Room

With the east and west Tears filling the Great Aqueduct, you're now able to advance to the Drenchfort's final area. Proceed through the Great Aqueduct's south door to visit a chamber that you couldn't have reached without fully restoring the Tears. Simply swim across the central pool and proceed through the south door to reach the final room.

Area 12: Earth Crag Den

All is quiet in this chamber—but not for long. Ensure that Death is in good health, and then grab hold of the orb-like object in the room's center. Press the Special Item trigger to shove the object at the room's peculiar stone mound.

BOSS BATTLE: KARKINOS

The mound turns out to be a monstrous Earth Crag unlike anything Death has seen thus far. Slamming it with the orb-like object causes the creature to roar to life, and it isn't happy!

Karkinos regularly rears back, screams, and then races toward Death with lethal intent. Evade to one side to dodge this linear rush.

Each time you dodge Karkinos's charge, the monster slams into a wall and knocks an orb-like object from the ceiling. These are actually Earth Crag eggs, and in order to damage Karkinos, you must grab and shove an egg at the boss while it's temporarily stunned from ramming the wall.

◈ CAUTION

It doesn't take long for Karkinos to recover after charging into a wall. Hurry and shove an Earth Crag egg at the brute before it rights itself!

Striking Karkinos with a high-velocity Earth Crag egg knocks the boss for a loop. Now's your chance! Race into striking range and unleash Death's most devastating attacks and skills. Target the monster's fleshy underside for maximum damage.

◈ CAUTION

Launching Earth Crag eggs at Karkinos causes the eggs to hatch, unleashing additional enemies!

If Karkinos recovers before you can stun it, the monster will often leap into the air and come crashing back down, sending out a shockwave of lethal magnitude. Jump to avoid the wave, but beware: it will stir all Earth Crag eggs in the room, causing young Earth Crags to emerge! These baby brutes add an unwelcome layer of mayhem to the battle, but they can't suffer much punishment. Eliminate Karkinos's young before turning your attention back to the boss.

◈ NOTE

Slaying Karkinos earns you a unique hammer: the Masher of Karkinos.

MASHER OF KARKINOS

Tears Unleashed

Make a thorough search for loot after killing Karkinos, and then step out onto the sunlit south balcony. Pull the lever there to open the floodgates and send the Drenchfort's torrent of Tears rushing off toward Tri-Stone. Well done!

With the Tears of the Mountain flowing strong, there's only one thing left to do: use the fast travel option to exit this sacred place and hurry back to Tri-Stone.

Forge Restored

When you appear back at Tri-Stone, run south and open the giant doors to enter the Maker's Forge. Speak with the Makers to advance your quest and receive a vital new item: the Maker's Key. This wondrous tool has the power to awaken slumbering constructs!

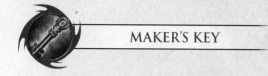

MAKER'S KEY

NOTE

Now that you've obtained the Maker's Key, you can awaken the sleeping Construct you noticed back at the Fjord harbor. You will then be able to complete a side quest that involves tracking down the construct's four missing limbs. See the "Side Quests and Areas" chapter for further details.

HEART STONE TALISMAN

SIDE QUEST COMPLETE: "WANDERING STONE"

Chat with Alya after receiving the Maker's Key to gain a new side quest that involves exploring the Shattered Forge—a ruin you've visited on your way to the Drenchfort. Now is an excellent time to clear this side dungeon—but first, shoot the Stonebite on the back (south) side of the Maker's Forge. Then see the "Side Quests and Areas" section for a complete walkthrough of the Shattered Forge.

STONE OF MYSTICS
12

BOATMAN COIN
25

OMEGA BLADES

BOOK OF THE DEAD
PAGE 7

SIDE QUEST COMPLETE: "THE SHATTERED"

Taming Thane

Now that Death's gear and skills have improved, it's a good time to challenge Thane to a fight. The burly Maker's attacks should seem very predictable—simply evade in a circle and flank Thane whenever he prepares to strike, and then counter-attack. Respect the Maker warrior's might by fighting a strategic battle and you should have little trouble in besting him. Speak with Thane afterward to complete his side quest, and also to gain another which you won't be able to complete until much later in Death's adventures.

NOTE

Now that you've acquired the Maker's Key, you can also advance the "Silent Stone" side quest that you acquired by discovering the giant sleeping construct in the Fjord. This side quest can be easily completed now if you would like to do so. Refer to the "Side Quests" chapter of this guide for further details.

SIDE QUEST COMPLETED: "THE MAKER WARRIOR"

SIDE QUEST ACQUIRED: "FIND AND KILL BHEITHIR"

SIDE QUEST ACQUIRED: "FIND AND KILL GOREWOOD"

SIDE QUEST ACQUIRED: "FIND AND KILL THE DEPOSED KING"

SIDE QUEST ACQUIRED: "FIND AND KILL ACHIDNA"

To Move a Mountain

WITH THEIR LEGENDARY FORGE
BURNING ANEW, THE MAKERS HAVE
MANAGED TO FASHION DEATH A
SPECIAL KEY—ONE THAT WILL BE
INSTRUMENTAL IN COMBATING
CORRUPTION IN THE FORGE LANDS.
NOW THE REAPER MUST RIDE TO A
LONG-FORGOTTEN TEMPLE, WHERE
A MIGHTY CONSTRUCT KNOWN AS
THE WARDEN SLUMBERS. ONLY THIS
ANCIENT BEING HAS THE POWER TO
MEND THE RUINED BRIDGE TO THE
FOUNDRY, WHERE AN EVEN GREATER
CONSTRUCT IS HOUSED...

THE NOOK

Use the fast travel option to quickly return to the Nook—
Baneswood's northeast ruin, which you previously visited
while exploring Baneswood on your trek to the Cauldron.

> ◉ **TIP**
>
> If you didn't bother to visit the Nook before, fast
> travel to the Weeping Crag instead to hasten
> your journey there. Explore Baneswood's
> northeast ruins to locate the Nook.

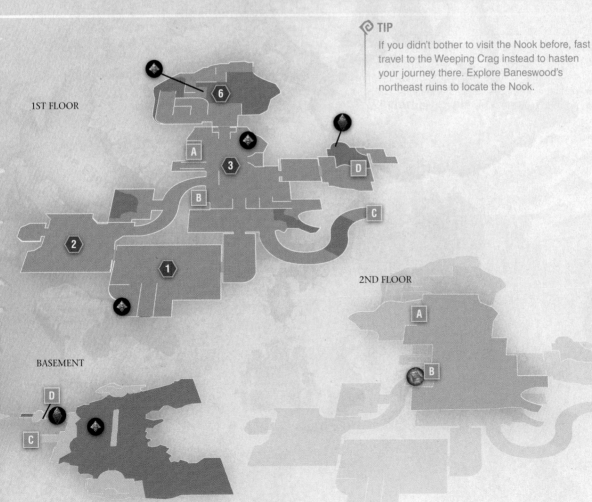

1ST FLOOR

2ND FLOOR

BASEMENT

Area 1: Ruin Entry

Approach the pile of glowing blue rubble in the ruin's first room. Now that you possess the Makers' Key, you can bring this curious heap to life by standing before it and pressing the Action button. The rubble begins to shudder and takes the form of a mighty stone construct known as a Maker Custodian.

Death automatically mounts the Custodian, assuming control. Roll over the nearby indentation to fit the Custodian's locomotive orb into it. The Custodian glows orange, and you automatically enter aiming mode. Press the Special Item trigger to launch a chain from the Custodian, latching onto the glowing target on the west wall.

> **NOTE**
>
> Should Death ever dismount from his Maker Custodian, the being will simply remain inactive until the Rider returns.

With the Custodian's chain extended, press the Action button to dismount from the construct and step onto the chain. Cross the chain and climb the far ledge to reach the high west door, which you couldn't have entered without the Custodian's help.

Area 2: Upper Courtyard

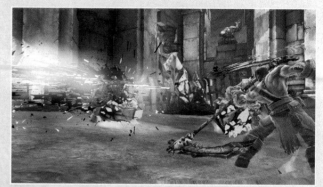

The door leads to an open area with a locked door and some yellow Corruption crystals. Lay waste to the Tainted Construct Warriors that ambush you here.

ENEMY: TAINTED CONSTRUCT WARRIOR

Class: Soldier

These evil constructs have been tainted by Corruption, and attack with greater wrath and tenacity than typical Construct Warriors. Their punishing blows can leave a lingering effect that steadily damages Death over a brief time. Remain evasive and strike hard each time you manage to flank one of these aggressive melee monsters.

When the Warriors are no more, claim a Shadowbomb from the west alcove and use it to obliterate the Corruption crystals. Loot the chest that one patch of crystals was covering, and then scale the northeast wall to enter a room with no floor.

Cross a wooden beam, then leap out and grab the wooden post that hangs from the ceiling.

Circle around the post and perform a 180 leap to reach the row of beams to the north.

Cross the beams and leap from the final one to grab the east wall's hand holds. Shimmy around the corner and then drop down to solid ground.

Descend the stairs that follow to reach the next area.

Area 3: Lower Courtyard

The stairs lead down to another courtyard and serve as just one of many access points to this tranquil site.

Make a thorough sweep for smashable debris. Collect the Boatman Coin that is hidden amongst the northeast clutter. Then, scale the west wall to reach a ledge with two chests, one of which requires a special ability to open that you do not yet possess.

BOATMAN COIN
26

Drop down from the ledge and pull the south lever to lower the nearby gate and unbar the neighboring door. The stairs beyond the door lead up to the ruin's entrance, while the broken stairwell beyond the gate leads down to an optional area where treasure can be found. It doesn't take long to navigate the ruin's basement, so take a moment to explore it. Wall-run along the broken stairwell's right wall to bypass the lava pit.

Area 4: Lava Cavern

The heat is oppressive in this massive underground cavern. You can't fully explore this broiling area without a special item you've yet to acquire, so simply run north and then west to locate the door to the next room.

Area 5: Elevator Chamber

Cut straight across this tall room and climb the short east wall to approach a lava pit. Jump onto the nearby wooden beam.

Leap to the second beam, then run up the north wall to reach a higher row of beams above.

Skip across the high beams and wait on the final one. It turns out to be a lever that lowers under Death's weight. This lowers a gate to the south, causing an orb to roll partway down a ramp.

Drop down and cross the lower beams. Again, wait on the final beam until it lowers. This removes another obstacle, allowing the orb to roll all the way down the ramp.

Leave the lava pit and pull a nearby lever to lower a tall stone elevator. With the elevator lowered, roll the orb onto it.

Now with the orb on the elevator, pull the lever once again. Quickly jump aboard as the elevator begins to rise.

Roll the orb over to the nearby slot that opens the west door. Raid the chamber's chest and then continue through the open door.

After the elevator reaches its full height, grab the orb and shove it to the south, onto the opposite elevator. Shoot the nearby Stonebite afterward.

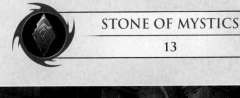

STONE OF MYSTICS

13

Area 3, Revisited

You emerge in a small chamber with a lever and chest. Loot the chest, and then pull the lever to open the nearby gate. Go through to find yourself back in the lower courtyard. Proceed through the north door to continue your journey toward your primary objective.

Area 6: Waterworks

One might suspect that many secrets lie within the Nook's last cavernous area, but there's only one item of interest to be discovered here: an underwater Boatman Coin. Find this prize by following the submerged walkway to a small, flooded room, where the coin is found.

Drop and scale the south wall. Pull the lever above to raise the second elevator and deliver the orb to your level.

BOATMAN COIN

27

Ascend the west stairs and locate a wall with some hand holds. Jump over and climb up to a ledge.

Turn left to spy another hand hold on the wall above. Use it to climb even higher.

Drop down onto some stairs, and then follow the short path to a door leading out to fresh air.

Temple Path

Beyond the ruin, a short trail leads to the door of a massive temple.

> **NOTE**
>
> The colorful door along the trail is eyecatching, but it can't be opened without help from the demonic merchant, Vulgrim. See the "Side Quests and Areas" chapter for further details.

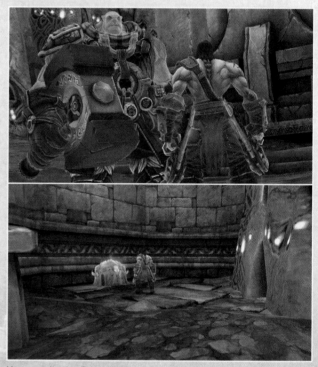

Karn awaits the Reaper outside the temple's door. Speak with the young Maker to advance Muria's side quest if you haven't already. Raid the chest that's tucked away to the left of the temple's stairs before heading inside.

SIDE QUEST ADVANCED: "SHAMAN'S CRAFT"

THE LOST TEMPLE

The Lost Temple

The purpose of this ancient temple's construction is unknown, but one thing is certain: Death will face many trials as he explores this fallen place.

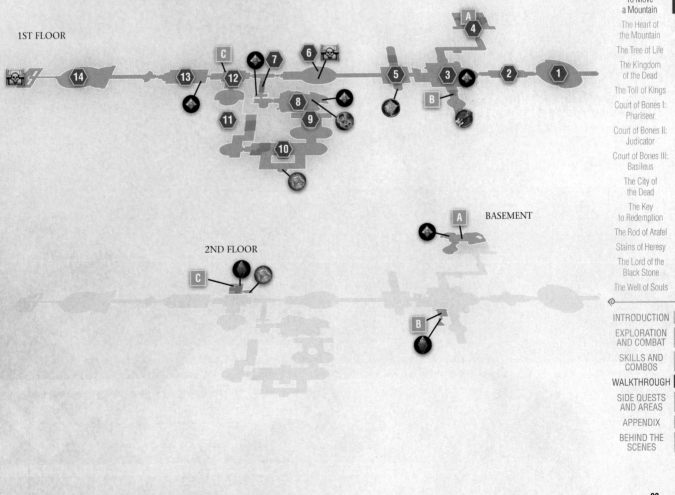

1ST FLOOR

2ND FLOOR

BASEMENT

INTRODUCTION

EXPLORATION
AND COMBAT

SKILLS AND
COMBOS

WALKTHROUGH

SIDE QUESTS
AND AREAS

APPENDIX

BEHIND THE
SCENES

Area 1: Temple Entry

A pack of Prowlers ambush the Reaper in the temple's very first chamber. Show them no mercy, and then search between the south stairs and wall to locate a chest that's tucked away. After collecting your loot, climb the stairs and proceed through the west door.

Area 2: Custodian Corridor

A Maker Custodian rests in the quiet hall beyond the entry stairs. Awaken the construct and ride it as close to the yellow Construction crystals before pressing the Attack button to smash the crystals to bits. It only takes a swing of the Custodian's massive arm. Then, park the Custodian on the orb slot beyond the crystals to unbar the west door. Dismount here and venture onward alone.

Area 3: Great Hall

This wide courtyard features a locked door and a dangerous new enemy.

An ancient sentry known as a Construct Sentinel awakens as you explore this area. The Sentinel has he power to revive fallen constructs. Two Tainted Construct Warriors also appear and attack—defeat them to entice the Sentinel into reviving them, then focus on the Sentinel and blast it with Redemption while its shield is down. The fight won't end until you manage to destroy the Sentinel and finish off any lingering constructs.

ENEMY: CONSTRUCT SENTINEL

Class: Elite

These ugly hovering heads possess the power to revive fallen constructs after the Reaper defeats them. This forces Death to repeatedly fight the same adversaries until all present Sentinels have been destroyed. This is easier said than done, for Construct Sentinels also possess a powerful shield which nullifies all damage. Fortunately, Sentinels must deactivate their shields while reviving fallen constructs, making them temporarily vulnerable. Slaughter lesser constructs, such as Warriors and Adjuncts, to lure a Sentinel into reviving them. Then, quickly focus on the Sentinel and pepper it with Redemption before its shield is restored.

Dispatching the Sentinel advances Muria's side quest. A section of wall also rotates after the battle, exposing a peg. Before vaulting up off of it, destroy the surrounding debris to discover valuable loot, including a Boatman Coin that's hidden amongst the junk near the east door you entered through.

BOATMAN COIN

28

Vault up from the peg to reach a hand hold. Shimmy around the corner, and then drop from the end of the hand hold to land in the hall beyond the north Construction crystals.

Area 4: Sunken Bridge

Sprint through a long corridor filled with Corruption crystals until you reach the north wing of the temple. Dive into the central pond and swim to the northwest corner to discover a Boatman Coin.

BOATMAN COIN
29

After claiming the Boatman Coin, swim south to discover an underwater tunnel that leads to a small cave with a chest. Surface and claim your loot before swimming back out.

Scale the west slope to escape the lake, and then climb the west wall to reach a hand hold. Wall-run to the right, vaulting off a peg on your way to the area's northern half, and face a Tainted Construct Warrior and Adjunct attack.

ENEMY: TAINTED CONSTRUCT ADJUNCT

Class: Minion

The tainted version of the Construct Adjunct attacks more often than the standard Construct Adjunct, and can withstand more of the Reaper's wrath. Tainted Construct Adjuncts maintain their distance and hurl vile ranged projectiles, making them troublesome when encountered alongside Construct Warriors (as they often are). Stay mobile to present a difficult target, and try to single out Adjuncts first, cutting them down to simplify battles.

A Maker Custodian rests in a nearby alcove. Assume control of the brute, and then enter Aiming mode and fire its chain at the Corruption crystals in the distance. The crystals shatter, exposing a lever.

Dismount the Custodian and climb the growth on the west wall. Wall-run to the south, vaulting from a peg on your way to the lever. Pull the lever to raise a bridge up from the water.

Return to the Custodian and climb aboard. Cross the bridge and use the Custodian's devastating attacks to annihilate the army of Constructs that storm forth to thwart you.

Roll your Custodian down the corridor, backtracking toward the Great Hall. Smash more crystals to expose a hole in the wall, then loot the large chest within.

Area 3, Revisited

With the aid of your Maker Custodian, you're able to explore more of the Great Hall. Destroy the south crystals to expose an orb slot, and then park the Custodian on the slot and fire its chain at the far target. Before crossing the chain, drop into the pit below to discover a chest, and don't forget to shoot the Stonebite on the wall.

STONE OF MYSTICS
14

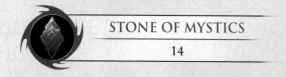

Return to the Custodian and tiptoe across its chain. A puzzle must then be solved to access a chest.

Aim and blast the Shadowbomb pod on the wall to knock down the nearby orb.

Grab the orb and roll it onto the orb slot. This lowers a gate to the south, but also raises another. Defeat the Constructs that ambush you.

Collect a Shadowbomb from the pod near the gate and toss the bomb onto the orb.

Remain near the gate and shoot the bomb to dislodge the orb. This lowers the gate near the chest, letting you claim a Skeleton Key from within.

Climb the nearby wall growth and wall-run toward a peg. Vault up from the peg to bypass the raised gate and escape captivity.

Head north and park the Custodian on another orb slot. Fire its chain across the northern gap and cross it to reach another chest which coughs up random goodies.

⟡ CAUTION

Don't drop into the north pit—there's nothing down there except for a long fall!

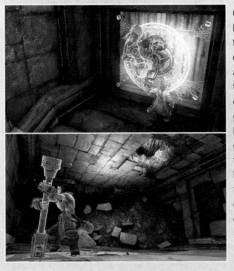

Great work! Now, cross the chain once more and use the key to open the great hall's locked west door. Climb the growth beyond the door to cross the ceiling and reach a neighboring ledge with a lever. Slay the Constructs that ambush you here before pulling the lever to lower a gate that leads to the next area.

Tiptoe back across the chain and assume control of the Custodian once more. Roll west and park the Custodian on the west orb slot to lower the far gate. Dismount and proceed west toward the next area.

Area 5: Corruption Junction

Area 6: Sentinel Checkpoint

Return to the Maker Custodian and ride it west into a small junction filled with Corruption crystals. Clear away the Corruption with the Custodian's mighty blows, then dismount and open the chest in the south nook to claim the Lost Temple's Dungeon Map.

Beware: you become trapped in this wide, circular chamber, forced into a deadly battle against a number of Constructs and Sentinels.

At first, only a few Construct Warriors and Adjuncts appear, backed by a Sentinel.

Defeat these just as you did before, by dispatching the aggressive minions to make the Sentinel lower its shield as it revives them. Inflict as much damage against the Sentinel as possible while its shield is down.

Proceed west after dispatching the Sentinels, then go through the south door. A long pit stretches out before you.

TIP

If possible, use the Unstoppable skill to increase the damage of Death's attacks.

More Construct minions and a second Sentinel appear after the first Sentinel falls. Repeat the same tactics, using Death's skills to simplify the fight.

TIP

Destroy the outlying debris for health and Wrath potions.

Initiate a wall-run, then jump to bounce between the narrow walls, extending your run and clearing the chasm.

You must defeat a total of six individual Sentinels in order to survive this trying encounter. More and more construct underlings appear with each new Sentinel, steadily increasing the challenge factor. Dangerous Construct Champions appear with the final two Sentinels, making matters extremely difficult. Try to preserve your Reaper Form for the dungeon's final battle, but don't hesitate to use it if matters become dire.

NOTE

This is likely the most challenging battle you've faced thus far, so expect to burn through a number of potions during this fight. Consider returning to Tri-Stone via the fast travel mechanic to stock up on potions after the battle.

Turn around when you land and grab the Boatman Coin that's tucked in the corner.

ENEMY: CONSTRUCT CHAMPION

Class: Brute

Champions are towering constructs that are too large for Death to lift and combo in the air (as he can do to Warriors and Adjuncts). Their attacks are slow, but mighty, so be certain to evade whenever they raise an arm in preparation to strike. Hammer Champions from advantageous angles, and pick these powerful enemies apart without becoming too greedy for damage. Like Stalkers, Champions can take plenty of punishment, so steel yourself for a tactical battle.

BOATMAN COIN
30

Jump between the narrow vertical walls near the east waterfall to reach higher ground.

Area 8: Temple Plaza

This tranquil plaza holds a handful of secrets.

After scaling the vertical walls, turn around and wall-run up the south wall to reach a ledge.

Search behind the pillars as you enter to discover a chest.

Open the chest you discover on the ledge, and then wall-run back out to explore the next area.

Collect a Boatman Coin that sits near a large tree.

BOATMAN COIN
31

Raid the chest located near the south door, and then go through to the lower hold.

Area 9: Lower Custodian Hold

Destroy the debris in one corner of this room. Activate the nearby Maker Custodian and roll it over to the south elevator.

Dismount and use the nearby hand hold to reach a wall with a peg that can be vaulted off of to reach an overhead beam. Climb up and leap from the beam to reach another hand hold, and then wall-run around the room to get to a high balcony.

Area 10: Upper Custodian Hold

Activate a second Maker Custodian up here. Roll north and park the Custodian on the orb slot near the east wall. This activates the elevator, raising the first Custodian up to the balcony.

Mount the elevator Custodian and roll it up the south stairs. Turn left and park on another orb slot, which lowers the nearby south gate. Dismount and take control of the previous Custodian. Then, roll south and explore the passage that the gate had formerly blocked.

Ignore the Book of the Dead page that's kept behind a gate in the south passage, and keep rolling until you reach another orb slot. Station the Custodian here and fire its chain to destroy the far Corruption crystals, exposing a target. Link the chain to this target, and then tiptoe across.

Notice the chest on the ledge below the chain as you cross. Carefully jump down to the chest ledge and claim your plunder, and then climb the nearby growth to return to higher ground.

You are now back near the other Custodian. Hop aboard and roll west, parking on yet another orb slot that lies near the pit you've just emerged from. Activating this orb slot unbars the far west door; dismount and hop across a beam to reach the other Custodian's chain.

You didn't forget that Book of the Dead page, did you? Tiptoe back across the chain to return to the south passage, and you'll find that the page can now be claimed. That wraps up this area! Cross the chain again and hop across the beam to reach the west door and proceed through it.

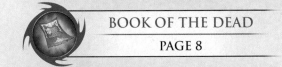

BOOK OF THE DEAD
PAGE 8

Area 11: Outer Wall

Cut down a few Constructs that ambush you in this outdoor area, and then wall-run north toward a hand hold.

Jump from the hand hold to reach the beams that follow, hop across them, and leap from the final beam to land on a ledge.

Scale a wall to grab another hand hold, and then wall-run to the left. Vault off of the pegs as you round the corner, heading for a wide balcony.

Balcony Beatdown

Once you slay the pack of Savage Prowlers that ambush you on the balcony, a formidable pair of Savage Stalkers will join the fight. Remain elusive as you combat this deadly duo. Focus on eliminating one Stalker first, and then take on the other. The north door becomes unbarred once all enemies have been slain.

Area 12: Orb Junction

Dispatch the lesser Constructs and Stingers in this chamber so that you can concentrate on the puzzle solving required to open the room's west door.

Scale the north wall by navigating a short series of pegs and hand holds.

When you arrive at the upper ledge, turn and shoot the Shadowbomb pod near the south wall's Corruption crystals. The blast dislodges the nearby orb.

INTRODUCTION

EXPLORATION AND COMBAT

SKILLS AND COMBOS

WALKTHROUGH

SIDE QUESTS AND AREAS

APPENDIX

BEHIND THE SCENES

Before dropping down to the ground, blast the Stonebite on the high east wall, then hop across the broken beams to reach an alcove that houses a missing page from the Book of the Dead.

BOOK OF THE DEAD
PAGE 9

STONE OF POWER
3

Once you have the page, drop down to the ground and roll the orb onto the orb slot to unseal the west door.

Area 13: Chamber of Champions

Beware: A pair of powerful Tainted Construct Champions storm toward you as you enter this room. Use evasive tactics to avoid being surrounded, and dodge around the thick pillars to keep the Champions from surrounding and double-teaming you. A small army of Tainted Construct Warriors will join the fight after the first Champion falls, so try to weaken both Champions before cutting down one of them—this lets you quickly dispatch the second as the lesser minions begin to swarm.

ENEMY: TAINTED CONSTRUCT CHAMPION

Class: Brute

Tainted Construct Champions are immensely powerful and they attack with relentless fury and aggression. It is vital that Death outmaneuver these formidable foes by Evading laterally around their linear charge attacks. Call upon the Rider's most powerful skills as you whittle away at the Tainted Construct Champion's health, and don't hesitate to consume potions and keep the Reaper's health in good standing since the lingering effects of their attacks can quickly bring about Death's demise.

Smash the plentiful array of debris in this room to find more healing potions. A Boatman Coin is hidden amongst the junk to the south—be sure to grab it before advancing through the west door.

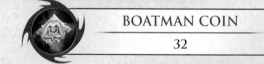

BOATMAN COIN
32

⌖ CAUTION
The final showdown lies ahead. If you're low on potions, consider fast-traveling to Tri-Stone to restock your supply.

Area 14: Circle of Worship

At last, you've advanced to the temple's final area. A formidable adversary awaits you here, and it must be defeated before the Reaper can awaken the Makers' great Construct Warden.

BOSS BATTLE: CONSTRUCT HULK

The Construct Hulk pounds the earth with unbridled fury. Keep your distance from the monster and note that each time it slams the ground, a number of Shadowbombs fall from the high pods around the arena. Grounded Shadowbombs will erupt after a short time, so you'll have to be quick when rushing over to the nearest bomb to use it.

◈ CAUTION

Beware the Construct Hulk's charge attack, when it slams the ground multiple times as it rampages toward Death. The wide radius of the boss's single ground-pound is also worthy of concern—jump to avoid being caught by the shockwave.

Once you've obtained a Shadowbomb, immediately focus on the Construct Hulk and toss the bomb at it. The bomb will soon detonate, causing the boss to momentarily collapse.

Now's your chance! Rush toward the Construct Hulk and strike at its exposed core with your most devastating combos. Call upon Death's skills to pile on as much damage as possible in your brief window of opportunity.

Damaging the Construct Hulk only fuels its fury. When you do, the monster calls lesser Construct Warriors and Adjuncts to its aid. Avoid the boss and cut down its minions to simplify matters before focusing your attention on stunning the Construct Hulk again.

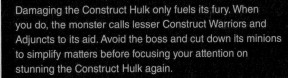

cont. ➤

Continue to stun the Construct Hulk and punish its core until the monster can take no more. With this final adversary lying in ruin, there's nothing left to stop Death from completing his mission.

Rousing the Warden

Collect any loot that may lie strewn about the battle area, and then scale the west stairs and empty a quartet of chests to claim even more spoils. After pocketing your plunder, approach the giant stone Construct to the west and activate it with the Makers' Key.

The Makers' Key does its work, and the great Construct Warden awakens from its long slumber. As luck would have it, Corruption has not yet spread to this great Construct. The Warden agrees to assist the Rider in his quest to awaken the Guardian—the only being capable of destroying the Corruption that surrounds the Tree of Life.

Quest Advancement

The Construct Warden carries the Reaper to the foot of Tri-Stone. Enter the Makers' city and find Eideard standing near the south door. Speak with Eideard to advance your quest.

Next, chat with Muria to complete her side quest. The special item she gives you in reward can be used to .

> **NOTE**
>
> The Grim Tailisman causes Death to gain Reaper Energy with each successful attack. Equip this item after unleashing Reaper Form, and Death's Reaper Gauge will refill more quickly.

GRIM TALISMAN

SIDE QUEST COMPLETE: "SHAMAN'S CRAFT"

> **TIP**
>
> Return to the Lost Temple and search the area behind where the Warden had been standing to discover a secret chest!

Finding the Foundry

Trade with Alya if you like, and then proceed through the Forge's south door. Speak with the towering Construct Warden who awaits you just outside. Then, watch in awe as the Warden uses its ancient power to restore the bridge leading to the Foundry. Time is short, Rider—hurry across the bridge without delay!

Before entering the Foundry's front door, crack open the chest that's stashed off to the left. Once you've done that, head west and search behind a giant statue to the right of the door to discover a Boatman Coin in the shadows. All right, *now* you're ready to enter the Foundry and begin your quest to awaken the Guardian.

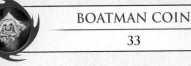

BOATMAN COIN
33

Heart of the Mountain

HAVING AWAKENED THE CONSTRUCT WARDEN AND RESTORED TRI-STONE'S SOUTHERN BRIDGE, DEATH MUST NOW EMBARK ON A PERILOUS JOURNEY THROUGH THE FOUNDRY— A GIANT, SWELTERING DUNGEON FILLED WITH ALL MANNER OF TRAPS AND HAZARDS. THE HORSEMAN MUST LOCATE THREE HEART STONES WITHIN THE FOUNDRY, FOR THESE ANCIENT OBJECTS SERVE AS THE ONLY MEANS OF AWAKENING THE GUARDIAN, THE GREATEST CONSTRUCT EVER CONCEIVED OF BY THE MAKERS. ONLY THE POWER OF THE GUARDIAN WILL BE ENOUGH TO ERADICATE THE NEST OF CORRUPTION SURROUNDING THE TREE OF LIFE.

THE FOUNDRY

The Foundry is a frightful site, so it's fortunate that Death is aided by the young Maker, Karn, during this quest. Karn will help the Pale Rider traverse this inhospitable place, and will also lend Death a hand—and the weight of his massive hammer—in battle.

1ST FLOOR

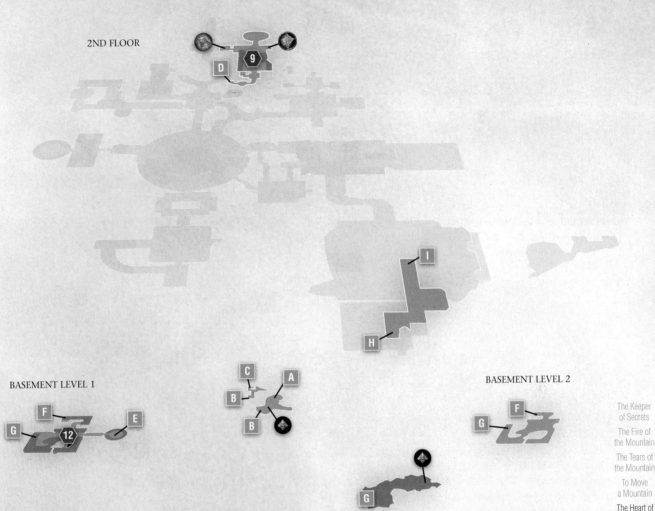

2ND FLOOR

D | 9

I

H

BASEMENT LEVEL 1

C
B | A
B

F
G | 12 | E

BASEMENT LEVEL 2

C
A
B
B

F
G

G

Area 1: Foundry Entrance

Pause as you pass through the Foundry's entry door and watch as hanging cauldrons slowly pass by overhead. Blast the Stonebite that's affixed to the top of fourth cauldron, then loot the chest that lies in shallow water to the east before advancing.

⚑ TIP

If you miss the cauldron with the Stonebite, simply remain near the north entry door and wait for the cauldrons to cycle past again.

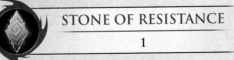

STONE OF RESISTANCE

1

Area 2: Foundry Forge

Massive chains support a giant stone hammer in the center of the Foundry's circular entry chamber. Not exactly a welcoming sight! Circle around the central forge, passing a clutter-filled corridor to the east and a giant sealed door to the south.

When you reach an apparent dead-end, Karn offers to help Death progress. Approach the young Maker and press the Action button, and he'll hurl the Rider up to an otherwise unreachable ledge.

Area 3: Cauldron Corridor

After being tossed by Karn, run up the wall and vault from the peg to reach a high hand hold.

Shimmy around the corner and perform a 180 leap to grab a passing cauldron and hitch a ride southward.

Circle around the cauldron as you're ferried along and jump to the west when you pass a ledge.

Wall-run south along the smooth west wall to clear a fiery gap.

Construct Clash

Several Tainted Construct Warriors attack once you complete your wall-run. Secure the area, and then approach the nearby lever.

Before pulling the lever, peer north to spy a chest on a ledge. Wall-run over to the chest, claim your treasure, wall-run back to the lever, and then pull it to unbar the nearby door.

Area 4: Crossroad Chamber

Karn calls out from beyond a massive door when Death enters this large chamber. Better find a way to open that thing!

Ignore the northeast passage; it leads back to the Foundry Forge. Instead, find a long lever sticking out from the east wall and perform a vertical wall-run to climb onto it. Wait there for a moment until Death's weight causes the lever to lower.

Lowering the lever raises the huge north and south doors, allowing Karn to join you. Remain on the lever while the Maker crosses the room and positions himself under the south door.

Step down from the lever once Karn is in position. The doors slam down again, but the Maker's great strength allows him to hold the south door open. Hurry and sprint through!

Area 5: Guardian Assembly

Fresh air greets Death as he enters this sizeable outdoor area. The center of the site is dominated by a towering, lifeless construct of immense size. Karn informs the Rider that this is the Guardian, which only the power of the Heart Stones can wake.

Smash the outlying debris to claim some loot, and then enter the northeast passage, which is filled with yellow Corruption crystals and Tainted Construct Warriors. Dispose of the fiends with Karn's help to secure the passage, and then follow it to the next area.

NOTE
Don't worry about Karn; he can't be slain.

Area 6: Lift Chamber

All is quiet in this spacious chamber. Smash the surrounding clutter in search of minor items before allowing Karn to heave the Horseman up and onto the east wall. Explore the small network of passages and underwater tunnels that surround Area 5 while Karn waits patiently behind.

Waterway Romp

First, circle around the high ledge and smash the clutter to expose a chest.

Drop to the lower level after looting the chest, shatter some more debris, and then leap into the central pool.

Swim north and claim an underwater Boatman Coin. Surface and scamper up the smooth north wall to reach a room with an orb.

Swim east and surface. Scale another smooth wall to return to the room with the orb.

Cross the room and ignore the orb—you'll soon return for it. Plunge into the west pool and swim toward the ray of sunlight.

Stand on the pressure plate to lower the bars ahead and raise the far door. Let Karn move into position before stepping off the pressure plate.

Turn left when you reach the sunlight, and then swim north. Surface and scale another smooth wall.

Raising the Lift

With Karn supporting the door, grab the nearby orb and roll it into the Lift Chamber. When you reach the south slope and can roll it no farther, press the Special Item trigger to shove the orb up the slope and into the slot on the south wall. The orb glows with power, and energy is quickly sent to the room's center, causing the central lift to rise and delivering a Maker Custodian into the room.

Open the chest you find in a nook, and then step on the nearby pressure plate to lower the bars ahead. Sprint forward and drop back into the water.

> **NOTE**
> If the orb does not lock into place, roll it up the slope and try shoving it again. Use the symbols on the floor to help you line up.

Custodian Crusher

A small army of Constructs storms into the chamber after you activate the orb and raise the lift. Immediately activate the Maker Custodian and lay waste to the swarming foes.

Take aim and fire the Custodian's chain at the distant target on the far wall, and then tiptoe across the lava pit.

TIP

After the battle, take aim and fire the Custodian's chain at the yellow Corruption crystals on the west ledge. Dismount and scale the wall to inspect the ledge and discover a hidden chest.

As you near the end of the chain, jump to the growth on the left wall and climb up.

Roll up the south passage, heading back toward the Guardian Assembly site.

Smash more crystals in the passage to expose another chest in a nook. Roll onward and turn right before you reach the Guardian Assembly area. Use the Custodian's heavy attacks to destroy the crystals blocking a passage back to the Crossroad Chamber.

Perform a 180 leap from the top of the growth to grab the wooden post that hangs from the ceiling.

Chain Game

Back at the Crossroad Chamber, roll the Custodian directly down the west passage and park it atop the orb slot at the far end.

Perform two more 180 leaps to reach a horizontal beam, and then enter the door that follows to reach the next area.

Area 7: Lava Passage

Wall-run along the right wall and jump as you near the corner to continue your run.

Beware: a monstrous Corrupted Construct Champion appears after you've slain the Warriors. Though stalwart, this lone brute should pose little threat to a Horseman of your experience.

When you reach a hand hold, wait for the lava waterfalls to stop flowing, then quickly wall-run over to the west ledge and proceed through the door.

Area 8: Corrupted Construct Ambush

Death becomes trapped in this small chamber and is forced to battle a trio of Corrupted Construct Warriors. Unleash anti-group attacks and Evade often to present an elusive target for these aggressive minions.

ENEMY: CORRUPTED CONSTRUCT WARRIOR

Class: Minion

These ultimate versions of the Construct Warrior have been fully consumed by Corruption, gaining incredible strength and resilience. Their relentless attack patterns remain largely similar to those of the other Construct Warriors you've faced, but their blows land with significantly greater impact, and they can suffer far more punishment before falling to the Rider's fury.

ENEMY: CORRUPTED CONSTRUCT CHAMPION

Class: Brute

Corrupted Construct Champions pack a mighty punch and can withstand tremendous amounts of damage. Evade around their drilling blows and strike from flanking positions to reduce the odds of being ground to bits. Employ skills such as Teleport Slash and Unstoppable to pile on the punishment and hasten battles against these durable brutes.

Prima Official Game Guide   www.primagames.com

Proceed through the south door after defeating the Champion. Open the ornate chest you discover to claim a Skeleton Key.

Cut down the Corrupted Constructs that attack after you land. One of these is an Adjunct, so deal with it first. Drop down from the ledge's east side after clearing the room of enemies, and locate an ornate chest containing the Dungeon Map.

SKELETON KEY

DUNGEON MAP

Gaze across the pit beyond the ornate chest to spy the Maker Custodian, whose chain remains extended. Carefully jump down to the chain and run across. Leave the Custodian as it stands and travel back to the Crossroad Chamber on foot.

NOTE

Did you get a glimpse of the chest in the north nook as you crossed the chain? You need a special item to reach it, which you'll soon possess.

Open the Crossroad Chamber's locked door with the Skeleton Key and go through. Karn will join you in climbing the winding stairs beyond.

Area 9: Chasm Cavern

The stairs lead up to a spacious cavern. Allow Karn to toss you over the first expanse.

ENEMY: CORRUPTED CONSTRUCT ADJUNCT

Class: Minion

The combination of powerful ranged attacks and resilient durability make these Adjuncts quite troublesome. Still, Death's tactics for battling them remain the same: pressure Corrupted Construct Adjuncts to keep them off-balance, and prioritize the slaughtering of these adversaries whenever they're encountered alongside melee-oriented cohorts like Construct Warriors.

Return to the upper ledge after claiming the Dungeon Map and proceed through the north door. Attack the curious object in this small room to receive an awesome new ability: the Deathgrip!

DEATHGRIP

Get a Grip

Exit the room with your newfound power and notice the small hoop on the ceiling. Now that you've found the Deathgrip, hoops such as these will glow with purple light. Jump and press the Special Item trigger to grasp the hoop with the Deathgrip and flip over to Karn's ledge.

Claim a missing page from the Book of the Dead, and then drop down to a lower ledge. Flip back over to Karn by using the Deathgrip as you did before, and then take your leave of this place.

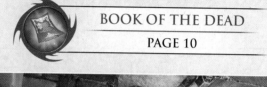
BOOK OF THE DEAD
PAGE 10

Before you leave this area, turn around and gaze down the pit. Look for another hoop far below the previous ledge. Swing back across the overhead hoop, then carefully hang and drop from the ledge. Fire the Deathgrip as you plummet and you'll zip over to the lower hoop. Death will then automatically wall-run up to a hand hold.

As you exit the area, pause near the yellow Corruption crystals at the top of the winding stairwell. Find the Shadowbomb pod on the ceiling in the nook beyond the crystals, enter aiming mode, and use the Deathgrip to snatch a bomb from range. Toss the bomb at the crystals to destroy them, and then enter the nook to discover a hidden chest. Sneaky!

Enter the passage above the hand hold and slay the constructs that prowl this secret corridor. Look up when you reach an apparent dead-end and you will find an overhead hoop. Wall-run up toward the hoop, then Deathgrip it to extend your run up to a high ledge.

THE FIRST HEART STONE

Armed with the Deathgrip, you're ready to begin your search for the first of three Heart Stones needed to awaken the Guardian. But first, backtrack to the Maker Custodian you left near the lava pit and cross its chain once more. Turn to the right as you near the end, and then jump and Deathgrip a low-hanging hoop to flip over to a chest.

Return to the Crossroad Chamber and take the west passage back to the Guardian Assembly area. (Leave the Custodian behind; he can't follow.) Cut down the hostile constructs in the area's lava-filled west passage, and then use the Deathgrip to collect an out-of-reach Shadowbomb from the passage's right wall. Toss the bomb at the far switch to activate it and extend a bridge. Cross over to the far door.

Area 10: Drawbridge

Turn left as you enter this area and hop across a row of beams.

Leap from the last beam to reach a ledge with a lever. Pull it to extend one half of the central drawbridge.

Run up the south wall to reach the beam above. Jump from the beam's end, Deathgrip the overhead hoop, and swing over to some ceiling growth.

Climb north along the growth, heading toward the north lever. When you reach the end, drop down and immediately Deathgrip the hoop ahead.

Drop from the beam you land on and pull the lever below. The central bridge is now fully extended.

Scamper back up to the overhead beam, and then climb to a higher hand hold. Shimmy to the right and jump to another hand hold on the east wall.

Perform a wall-run from the end of the east hand hold to reunite with Karn on the entry ledge. Cross the bridge and proceed through the west door.

Area 11: Elevator

Pull the lever in this circular chamber to make the floor slowly lower. Enjoy the ride as you wait for the floor to stop, and then advance through the west door.

Area 12: Heart Stone Chamber

The first Heart Stone tempts you from the center of this room, but even with the Deathgrip it's too high to reach.

Let Karn toss you over to a distant ledge, and then skip across the beams that follow to reach a hand hold on the south wall.

Wall-run to the right and fire the Deathgrip at a distant hoop to extend Death's run to the far hand hold.

Use the Deathgrip again to swing from an overhead hoop and reach a distant hand hold.

Shimmy around the corner and wall-run to another hand hold. Round another corner, and then drop down to a ledge.

Wall-run to the left and vault a peg. Jump the corner to continue running along the adjacent wall.

Hidden Chest

Before messing with the ledge's pressure plate, turn around and jump toward the hoop on the south wall, which you exploited during your recent wall-run. Deathgrip the hoop in midair to zip up to a high nook with a chest. Wall-run back around to the pressure plate ledge afterward.

Pause at the next hand hold after rounding the corner. Perform a vertical wall-run to reach another chest in a small nook.

Under Pressure

Stand on the pressure plate to lower the gate ahead. Remain on the plate and Deathgrip Karn, who quickly heaves you over to a remote ledge.

Drop down to the hand hold again and wall-run to the left to reach a wooden wall post. Perform a 180 leap to reach the hanging post behind you.

Execute another 180 leap to reach another hanging post. Perform one last 180 leap to reach solid ground below.

Custodian Comrade

Drop down to a lower ledge, then wall-run over to the Maker Custodian that rests amongst boiling lava. Power it up and climb aboard.

Roll the Custodian south, over the shallow lava, and veer left to locate a patch of solid ground. Carefully dismount the Custodian and crack open the chest you find here.

Backtrack a bit so you that can veer right and ride the Custodian farther south. Destroy the Corruption crystals that get in your way, and then continue toward an orb slot. Park there and launch a chain at the north wall's high target, and then tiptoe across.

Leap from the end of the chain and scale the west wall's hand holds. Shimmy around the corner and climb up.

Have a Heart Stone

At last, you've reached the Foundry's first Heart Stone. Simply use the Deathgrip to latch onto the precious object and cut it down.

Returning the First Heart Stone

Karn quickly collects the massive Heart Stone from the ground. Go east to return to the elevator and pull the lever to begin your ascent. Beware: an army of Corrupted Constructs will assault you on your way up!

> ### TIP
> Remain close to Karn during the elevator ride, and his heavy Heart Stone attacks will crush the daylights out of your swarming foes.

Return to the Guardian Assembly area, and the Heart Stone will magically find its way onto the hulking creature. Two more to go!

THE SECOND HEART STONE

Some nearby scaffolding collapses after you place the first Heart Stone, exposing a hoop. Jump and Deathgrip the hoop to swing past the bubbling lava which now fills the Guardian Assembly area. Proceed into the dark tunnel beyond.

Area 13: Foundry Drainage

An out-of-reach Boatman Coin taunts you from across this pipe-filled chamber. Ignore it for now and pass through another nearby tunnel to reach a wide passage to the north. Stand on the pressure plate here to raise the east and west doors, then wait for Karn to position himself beneath the east door. Sprint through to the next area while Karn holds the door for you.

Area 14: Waterway

Let Karn heave you over to the this chamber's central ledge, and then Deathgrip the hoop that hangs from the ceiling to reach the east ledge. Proceed into the roofless room beyond.

Area 15: Custodian Storage

Slay a few Savage Prowlers in this crumbling room, and smash the clutter in the northeast corner to discover a hidden Boatman Coin.

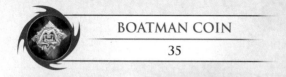

BOATMAN COIN
35

Activate the Maker Custodian here and park it on the nearby orb slot. Once in position, fire a chain to the nearby target and mount the chain. Drop down to the floor and climb atop the nearby platform to reach a lever.

Grab and rotate the lever to raise the Maker Custodian, along with the chain target platform.

Release the lever, and then quickly jump at the chain target platform to perform a vertical wall-run up to its hand holds.

Climb onto the chain and leap over to the growth on the far wall.

Wall-run from the end of the growth to reach the hand hold on the right. Wall-run again and jump the corner to reach more growth.

Climb down the growth and drop down to the ledge below. Go west and pull a lever to raise a series of bridges back in the Waterway area.

Turn around and scale the wall behind you before boarding the Maker Custodian and rolling back to the Waterway area. Cross the south bridge and use the Custodian's heavy blows to smash through the Corruption crystals that block the south passage. Proceed to the next area.

Next, swim northeast and climb the east wall's growth to reach a high hand hold. Shimmy to the right until you can shimmy no farther, scamper up the wall, and Deathgrip a hoop to reach more growth above. Make your way up to the top of the wall.

Area 16: Foundry Plaza

The second Heart Stone catches Death's eye here, but it will take some effort to obtain.

Roll all around this wide open area and use the Maker Custodian to annihilate the Savage Prowlers that foolishly attack you here.

Dismount the Maker Custodian after the battle. Ignore the lever near the northwest machinery for the moment, and instead plunge into the surrounding water. Swim west and claim the underwater Boatman Coin near a broken drainage grate in the west wall.

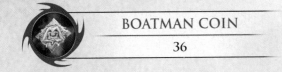

BOATMAN COIN
36

Area 17: Eastern Ruins

A series of crumbling ruins must be navigated in order to reach a high lever in this area. First, run north along the top of the wall, exploring the east grassy ledge to locate a chest. Then, drop down into the water below and swim east to discover an underwater Boatman Coin.

BOATMAN COIN
37

Surface and search for a smooth nearby wall sporting a hoop. Deathgrip the hoop to reach a high hand hold, and then shimmy and wall-run to the right to reach a ledge.

Climb the west wall to reach a balcony. Slay the Savage Prowlers that ambush you here in order to secure the balcony's chest. Then, shatter all of the balcony's clutter to cause a second, larger chest to materialize as well.

Backtrack away from the balcony, dropping down to the lower ledge and returning to the east wall's hand holds. This time, wall-run to the left and shimmy around a corner. Keep going until the viewpoint expands to reveal a hoop on a far wall. Perform a 180 leap and Deathgrip the hoop in midair to reach a balcony where more Prowlers lurk.

Clear the balcony of hostiles, then pull the nearby lever. This releases a torrent of water into the Foundry Plaza, activating the machinery back in the previous area.

There's nothing else to accomplish here. Drop down into the water and swim west, and then use the west wall's hoop to help you climb to the top again.

Make the long drop down to the Plaza area's water, surface, and look for a peg on the smooth wall opposite the growth you climbed to enter the Eastern Ruins. Vault from the peg to scale the wall and rejoin Karn on the Plaza's main level.

Sprint south and stand before the large Corruption crystals that are blocking a high ledge. Use the Deathgrip to snatch a Shadowbomb from one of the cauldrons that pass by, and then toss the bomb at the crystals to destroy them.

> **NOTE**
> If no cauldrons are passing by, return to the Eastern Ruins and make sure you pulled the lever there.

With the crystals gone, Karn now offers to toss Death over to the ledge that the Corruption was previously covering. Open the ornate chest you discover there to claim a Skeleton Key. Drop down and unlock the nearby door to the south.

> **NOTE**
> The Maker Custodian can't fit through the doorway, so don't bother bringing it along.

SKELETON KEY

Area 18: Earth Crag Lair

Beware: a monstrous Earth Crag resides in this clutter-filled chamber. Stay mobile, use Death's abilities, and allow Karn to assist in bringing down this vicious brute.

Smash the surrounding debris for items after the battle, and take notice of the orb slot on the ground. Backtrack to the Maker Custodian and roll it toward the Plaza's northwest lever. Hop off and pull the lever to crush the rocks on the nearby mechanism, and then park the Custodian where the rocks formerly sat. Pull the lever again to smash the Custodian to bits, freeing the orb it uses to move. The orb is then sucked into the ground and pops out near the moving cauldrons to the south.

Grab the orb and roll it back to the Earth Crag Lair, placing it into the slot you noticed before. This lowers a nearby gate; jump up the parallel walls beyond, leaping between them to climb to the top.

Shimmy around a hand hold and drop down to a ledge. Run north until you finally arrive within reach of the second Heart Stone. Deathgrip the stone to knock it down so that Karn may collect it.

Returning the Second Heart Stone

You're back in the Plaza. Backtrack up the north passage to return to the Waterway area. Beware: dangerous Nightmare Prowlers now lurk in the north passage. Consider falling back to the Plaza where you have more room to battle these challenging new foes.

ENEMY: NIGHTMARE PROWLER

Class: Minion

These nimble minions are even more vicious than Savage Prowlers, attacking more often and with greater fervor. Nightmare Prowlers can also absorb far more punishment than their predecessors, making them the ultimate incarnation of these agile adversaries. Evade and avoid becoming surrounded when you encounter these creatures in packs, or else they'll quickly overwhelm the Horseman with their numbers.

Back at the Waterway, dive into the water and scale the west wall. Shimmy to the nearby balcony and drop down, and then enter the tunnel to return to the Foundry Drainage area. Beware the Noxious Stingers that now swarm this place.

Claim a Boatman Coin from within the drainage pipe on the left. This is the one you noticed a while ago.

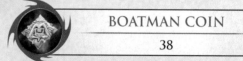

ENEMY: NOXIOUS STINGER

Class:
Fodder

Though slightly more dangerous than the common Stinger, these pint-sized pests pose little threat to the Reaper. Evade to avoid becoming surrounded as you pick them off with Redemption, or allow the Noxious Stingers to swarm you before culling them all with one clean anti-group skill, such as Harvest.

Now, either swim across the water-filled channel, or wall-run between the south wall's posts to reach the Drainage area's west side. Enter the north tunnel to return to the pressure plate passage, then stand on the plate and allow Karn to pass through to the Guardian Assembly area. Backtrack to the Drainage area afterward and use the west tunnel to join up with Karn.

The Guardian Assembly area's lava has now cooled, so you can safely cross it. Sprint over to Karn and watch as the second Heart Stone drifts into place.

THE THIRD HEART STONE

Your business at the Foundry is almost finished—the third Heart Stone isn't far. With the second Heart Stone in place, sprint south to locate a Maker Custodian that sits near a gate. Before activating the Custodian, allow Karn to toss you over the gate and into the passage beyond. Pull the nearby lever to lower the gate, and then return for the Custodian. Smash away the passage's Corruption crystals as you head for the Foundry's final area.

Area 19: Chamber of Corruption

Roll the Custodian down to a small, crystal-filled chamber, where the third and final Heart Stone is housed. Park the Custodian on the nearby orb slot to lower a high gate on the west wall. Dismount and climb the west wall to reach the ledge above.

Deathgrip the hoop in the fiery passage that follows to swing to a hanging post.

Slide down the post and 180 leap to the smaller post at the corner of the nearby wall.

Perform two more 180 leaps to cross the next two posts, and then wall-run toward a hoop.

Deathgrip the hoop, along with the next one ahead, to extend your run to the far ledge.

Hearty Congratulations

The final Heart Stone is now within your grasp! Use your Deathgrip to knock it free.

BOSS BATTLE: CORRUPTED CUSTODIAN

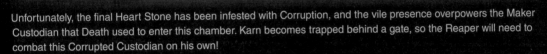

Unfortunately, the final Heart Stone has been infested with Corruption, and the vile presence overpowers the Maker Custodian that Death used to enter this chamber. Karn becomes trapped behind a gate, so the Reaper will need to combat this Corrupted Custodian on his own!

You've piloted enough Custodians to know that their blows are devastating—it takes only a few hits to spell Death's end. Evade each blow, and then be quick to counter with combos of your own.

Don't mess around with the Corrupted Custodian. Call upon your Reaper Form to pile on the damage, and then use Wrath-based skills to facilitate its destruction. Above all, ensure that you avoid this powerful construct's crushing blows.

TIP
Deathgrip the Custodian to quickly zip into striking range after each dodge.

CAUTION
Beware the Custodian's powerful spinning whirlwind attack. The damage is immense, so evade out of harm's way!

The Guardian Awakens

With the Corrupted Custodian reduced to rubble, Death and Karn are at last able to slot the final Heart Stone onto the Guardian. The young Maker has misgivings about placing the Corruption-laden stone onto the titan, but the Horseman wagers that the purity of the other two Heart Stones will be enough to cleanse the third.

Unfortunately, the Reaper couldn't have been more wrong. With a terrible roar, the towering Guardian rips free of its bonds and storms off, causing immense damage to the Foundry along the way. Something must be done to stop this monstrosity!

Trek to Tri-Stone

Make your way back to Tri-Stone, taking the north passage back to the Crossroad Chamber, whose north door has been shattered. As you pass through the Foundry Forge area, notice that the massive central hammer is now missing. The Guardian seems to have armed itself!

Tri-Stone has paid a terrible price for Death's lapse in judgment. The Makers' once great city now lies in ruins, and Eideard is nowhere to be found. Question the other Makers to learn that the old one has pursued the Guardian to Stonefather's Vale. It is there that the Maker's greatest construct must be confronted...

The Tree of Life

DEATH HAS SUCCEEDED IN ROUSING THE GUARDIAN FROM THE FOUNDRY, BUT THE RIDER NOW FINDS HIMSELF IN A DESPERATE SITUATION. THE MAKER'S GREAT TITAN HAS FALLEN UNDER CORRUPTION'S SWAY, AND NOW THE TOTAL DESTRUCTION OF THE FORGE LANDS IS AT HAND. EVEN EIDEARD'S ANCIENT MAGIC PROVES NO MATCH AGAINST THE GUARDIAN'S UNBRIDLED IRE. THE TASK OF DEFEATING CORRUPTION'S NEWFOUND COLOSSUS FALLS TO THE REAPER.

BOSS BATTLE: THE GUARDIAN

No amount of Eideard's wizardry can tame this monstrous construct. The Pale Rider is forced to confront the Guardian in the vastness of the Stonefather's Vale.

cont. ➤

Focus on the Guardian as you ride toward it on Despair. Circle to the left around the colossus, and the great monster will soon attack with its massive hammer. Press the Evade trigger to charge to the left when you see the Guardian raise its hammer, riding hard to avoid the devastating blow.

Whether or not you managed to slip past the Guardian's attack, immediately enter aiming mode and blast the yellow Shadowbombs lining the outside of the titan's right arm. Shoot these with Redemption to cause a massive explosion that temporarily severs the arm.

Now's your chance! Ride close to the Guardian's lowered shoulder before banishing Despair. Switch to the Deathgrip and grasp the Heart Stone affixed to the Guardian's shoulder. Attack the Heart Stone with Death's scythes once you've zipped into range. Repeat this sequence until you manage to destroy the Heart Stone and permanently disable the Guardian's right arm.

Phase II

Having lost the use of its enormous hammer, the Guardian changes tactics and begins to fire massive, spike-covered orbs at Death from its remaining arm. Summon Despair once more, and then focus on one of the orbs and blast it with Redemption. Ride in circles to avoid the orb as you pepper it with shots.

Once the orb is nearly destroyed, it begins to glow and rise. Immediately ride toward the Guardian and slip between its massive feet. The damaged orb will race after you, but ultimately smash into the Guardian's feet instead! The impact knocks the titan to its knees, leaving it vulnerable.

There isn't much time! Ride to the Guardian's lowered arm, banish Despair, and wall-run up the arm. Vault off of two pegs to reach a wooden beam, and then move to the beam's end and look for the nearby Heart Stone. Jump toward the Heart Stone, Deathgrip it, and attack without mercy. Repeat this sequence until the second Heart Stone is destroyed.

Corruption Cleared

The Guardian can suffer no more. With a tremendous shudder, the monstrous Construct collapses into a vast pile of rubble. The Forge Lands have been spared!

Death has stopped the Guardian's rampage, but Corruption still surrounds the Tree of Life. Eideard uses the last of his life force to raise the Guardian once more, restoring the great construct to its natural purity.

The Guardian wastes little time in eradicating the nearby nest of Corruption, but the epic clash destroys the Guardian mere moments after it had been reformed.

Congratulations, you've banished Corruption from the Forge Lands! Many side ventures are still available in this realm, however, and completing these now will give you an advantage in the lands ahead. Here's a quick list of everything you can now accomplish in the Forge Lands—refer to the "Side Quests and Areas" chapter for further details.

The Crucible: Return to Tri-Stone and check the Tome—you've been sent a special item that lets you visit a special side area called the Crucible! This area now appears on the in-game map; simply fast-travel there and see what awaits you.

Death Tomb 1: If you've been following this walkthrough carefully, then you'll claim your 10th page of the Book of the Dead while exploring the Shattered Forge as part of Valus's side quest. This completes the Book's first chapter; trade the chapter for a special key from vulgrim, then fast-travel to the Lost Temple's entrance and use the key to open the colorful door you noticed before. This leads to a treasure-filled Death Tomb!

Baneswood Loot: Use the Deathgrip to perform a long wall-run at the east ruin and reach a chest on the ruin's south ledge. Drop from the south end of the chest ledge afterward to snag a Boatman Coin.

Fjord Loot: Now that you have the Deathgrip, you can reach a chest around the Fjord's harbor. It's found atop the mooring station (Deathgrip the hoop on station's exterior wall). Leap from the top of the mooring station to claim the high-hovering Boatman Coin.

The Weeping Crag: Now is a good time to revisit the Weeping Crag and defeat its resident boss enemy, Gorewood. See the "Side Quests and Areas" chapter for a complete walkthrough.

The Nook: Return to the Nook and use the Deathgrip to claim a Book of the Dead Page, a Boatman Coin. Slay Bheithir in the basement to complete a side quest for Thane as well.

A few tasks in the Forge Lands remain inaccessible. Here's a quick rundown of those to prevent you from wasting time:

✦ The Scar can be attempted at this point, but its many challenges are likely beyond Death's current skills. A future side quest will direct you to the Scar, so forgo visiting this side dungeon for now.

✦ All puzzles involving warp portals and multiple pressure plates cannot currently be solved. These include the puzzles in the Weeping Crag, the Nook (basement of the interior ruin), and the Fjord (east ruin, and also the harbor enclosure where Vulgrim is found). For this reason, we recommend that you wait to revisit these areas until later in the adventure. We'll inform you when the time is right!

Don't worry; we'll let you know when these lingering side adventures become available!

STONE OF MYSTICS
15

STONE OF POWER
4

GOREWOOD MAUL

BHEITHIR'S TALONS

HEARTSTONE TALISMAN

BOOK OF THE DEAD
PAGES 11-12

BOATMAN COINS
39-42

SIDE QUEST COMPLETE:
"FIND AND KILL GOREWOOD"

SIDE QUEST COMPLETE:
"FIND AND KILL BHEITHIR"

THE VERDANT HOLLOW

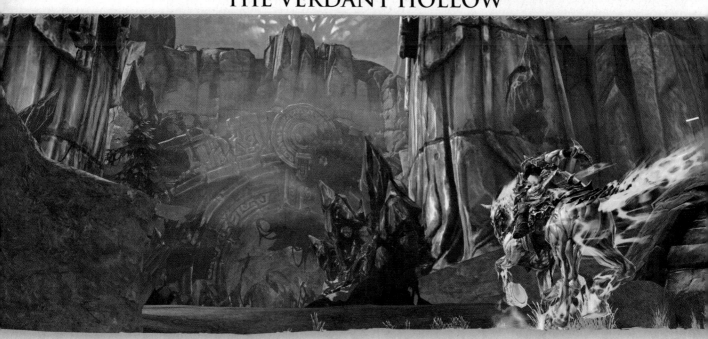

This lush trail leads to the Tree of Life, a gargantuan growth that serves as a mysterious portal between worlds.

Take the north trail out of Stonefather's Vale, which is now free of Corruption, and ride up to the towering Tree of Life. Approach the giant door carved into the Tree's trunk, and Death will be sucked in by a sickening tendril of Corruption. Where the Pale Rider might emerge is a mystery that will soon be revealed...

The Kingdom of the Dead

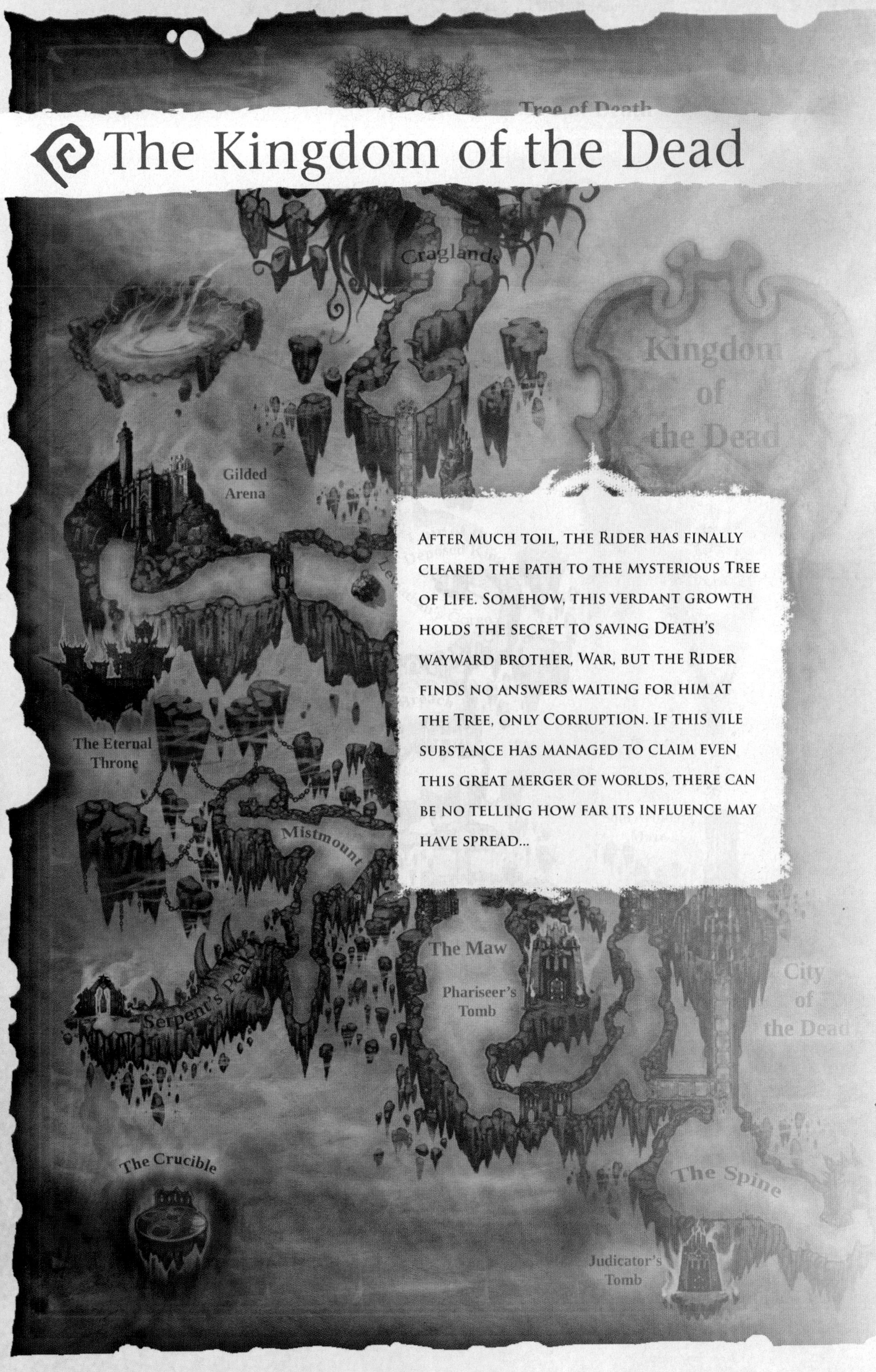

AFTER MUCH TOIL, THE RIDER HAS FINALLY CLEARED THE PATH TO THE MYSTERIOUS TREE OF LIFE. SOMEHOW, THIS VERDANT GROWTH HOLDS THE SECRET TO SAVING DEATH'S WAYWARD BROTHER, WAR, BUT THE RIDER FINDS NO ANSWERS WAITING FOR HIM AT THE TREE, ONLY CORRUPTION. IF THIS VILE SUBSTANCE HAS MANAGED TO CLAIM EVEN THIS GREAT MERGER OF WORLDS, THERE CAN BE NO TELLING HOW FAR ITS INFLUENCE MAY HAVE SPREAD...

Tree of Death

Craglands

Kingdom of the Dead

Gilded Arena

The Eternal Throne

Mistmount

Serpent's Peak

The Maw

Phariseer's Tomb

City of the Dead

The Crucible

The Spine

Judicator's Tomb

INTRODUCTION

EXPLORATION AND COMBAT

SKILLS AND COMBOS

WALKTHROUGH

SIDE QUESTS AND AREAS

APPENDIX

BEHIND THE SCENES

THE TREE OF DEATH

There are two sides to everything in existence. Even as the vibrant Tree of Life exists in many worlds, so too does its shadowy reflection.

Mysterious Merchant

Emerging from the grip of Corruption, Death finds himself in eerily familiar surroundings. This is not the Verdant Hollow, however. No—the Horseman has somehow been thrust into a twisted realm of gloom and despair.

An unusual fellow greets the Reaper at the foot of the great Tree, and casts welcome light on Death's current dilemma. Question the creature, whose name is Ostegoth, to learn more about the twisted realm in which the Horseman now finds himself. Ostegoth also offers a selection of fine wares, and bestows a special side quest upon the Rider, which involves the collection of scattered Relics.

SIDE QUEST ACQUIRED:
"LOST RELICS"

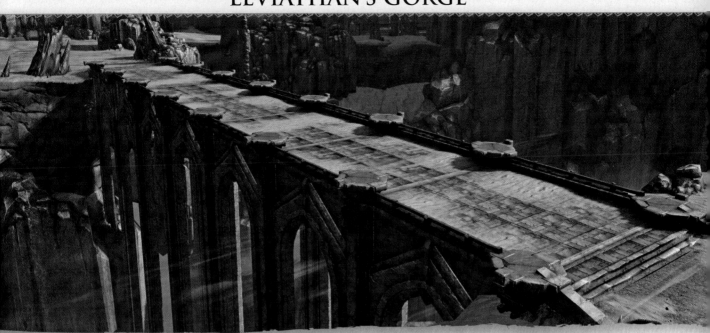

LEVIATHAN'S GORGE

This vast chasm lies south of the Tree of Death. A massive stone bridge spans the yawning abyss.

The Walking Dead

When you've finished bartering with Ostegoth, call upon Despair and ride south through the eventless Craglands and into Leviathan's Gorge. Beware the Skeletons that guard the Gorge's bridge—though easily slain, their vicious sword attacks are surprisingly strong.

ENEMY: SKELETON

Class: Minion

Skeletons are the most common form of minion encountered in the Kingdom of the Dead. Though their lack of armor makes them easy prey for the Reaper, they can inflict fast damage with their massive swords. Lone Skeletons are no match for Death, but these deceased warriors become quite dangerous when they manage to overwhelm the Horseman with their numbers. Ensure this doesn't happen by Evading and striking from advantageous angles.

Before crossing the Gorge's great stone bridge, search near the edge of the east cliff to discover the first of many lost Relics that Ostegoth has asked Death to acquire. This one happens to be of the most common variety: a Relic of Etu-Goth.

RELIC OF ETU-GOTH
1

Southern Wastelands

Cross the bridge after pocketing the Relic to reach the south end of Leviathan's Gorge. Here lies the entrance to the Lair of the Deposed King; an underground tomb that you can opt to explore now or later. See the "Side Quests and Areas" chapter for further details on this optional area.

BOATMAN COINS	43 - 44
RELIC OF ETU-GOTH	2
SOUL ARBITER'S SACRED SCROLLS 1 - 2	
STONE OF POWER	5

SIDE QUEST COMPLETED:
"FIND AND KILL ARGUL"

Underbelly Treasure

A massive door stands to the west, and can be opened if you wish. This would take you off the beaten path, however, and you'll naturally explore the lands beyond later, so ignore the door for now. Instead, scamper up the nearby wall and grab a hand hold, and then wall-run to the right to reach a wooden post. Slide down and navigate the series of hand holds and posts that follow until you reach solid ground.

Sprint east, and then north, heading toward a ledge. Before Deathgripping across the overhead hoops, look for a distant Shadowbomb pod near some Corruption crystals. Shoot the pod to obliterate the crystals and expose another pod.

Deathgrip across the hoops to reach a hanging post. Perform a 180 leap to reach the ledge with the Shadowbomb pod you just exposed. Collect a bomb, and then toss it at the hanging crystals ahead to banish these obstacles.

Return to the post and Deathgrip across the remaining hoops. Leap from the final post to reach a ledge with two pressure plates and a chest. You can't solve this pressure plate puzzle at present, so simply plunder the chest before backtracking out of this area.

Reaching the Breach

When you're ready to move on, climb the Gorge's south steps and open the giant door to enter an ancient stronghold known as the Breach.

BREACH

This derelict fortress connects Leviathan's Gorge with the lands to the south.

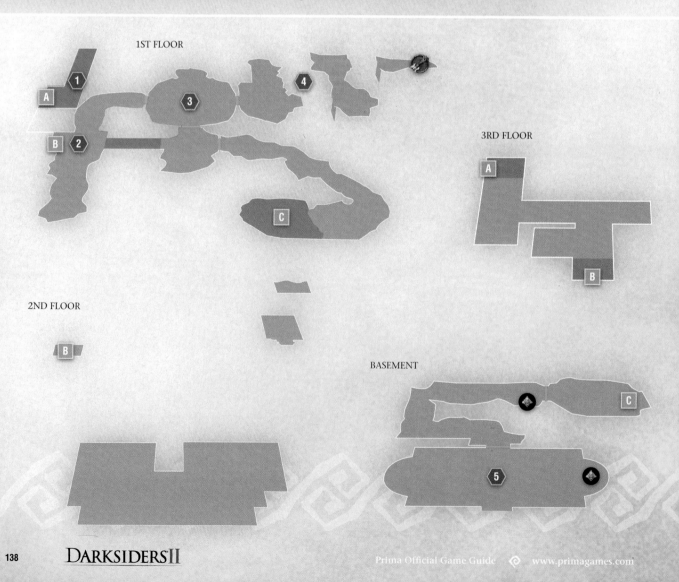

Area 1: Ruined Entry

Wall-run along the Breach's entry corridor, Deathgripping a hoop and jumping at the corner to reach some growth.

Don't scale the wall growth, but instead, perform a 180 leap and Deathgrip the hoop behind you.

Scale the hoop, and the next one above, then jump off of the wall to reach a high passage with a chest. Stand on the pressure plate after looting the chest, then sprint past the nearby gate before it rises.

A special power is needed to acquire the chests in the passage beyond. Ignore them and descend through the nearby hole to reach a lower ledge. Drop again to reach a passage with more pressure plates.

Area 2: Pressure Plate Passages

The passage below the post features a pair of pressure plates. One lies before a chest; the other, before a corridor with no floor. You can't reach the chest without possessing a new special ability, so stand on the plate near the east corridor which leads to a locked door. Allow the corridor's many gates to retract, and then quickly wall-run toward the locked door, jumping between the walls to extend your run.

Area 3: Arena Ambush

A Skeleton Key is needed to open the locked door. Proceed through the unlocked north door instead to enter a circular arena, where a horde of Skeletons stage a deadly ambush. Among their numbers are formidable Skeletal Warriors. Stay mobile and Evade often to prevent the dead from mounting a proper offense. Proceed through the east door when the mayhem finally subsides.

ENEMY: SKELETAL WARRIOR

Class: Minion

Like Skeletons, these soldiers of bone are skilled with their massive swords. However, Skeletal Warriors also enjoy the added benefit of protective armor, allowing them to absorb much more damage than their unarmored peers. Dodge their leaping sword strikes, and then counter with lengthy attack combos to chop away most (if not all) of a Skeletal Warrior's health.

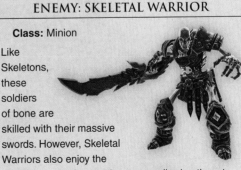

ENEMY: SCARAB

Class: Fodder

Scarabs are comparable to Stingers: they fly about, attack in swarms, and are easily squashed. Blast these overgrown bugs with Redemption, or wipe out whole swarms with the well-timed use of skills such as Harvest.

This quiet cavern features two bridges, but only one of them is extended. Before crossing the bridge, Deathgrip a Shadowbomb from the northeast pod. Toss the bomb at the wall, sticking it near the switch. Deathgrip two more bombs and stick them to form a line between the Shadowbomb pod and the switch. Leave the bombs

be and cross the bridge.

Stand near the foot of the second bridge, which is not extended and cannot be crossed. Enter aiming mode and target the Shadowbomb pod back near the switch. Blast the pod with Redemption to detonate it, along with the bomb you stuck to the nearby wall. If you did it right, the chain reaction will trigger the switch, causing the first bridge to lower and the nearby bridge to rise. Cross over and open the ornate chest to claim the Skeleton Key you seek.

SKELETON KEY

Scarab Scare

After retrieving the key, a swarm of Scarabs descends upon the Rider. Unleash anti-group attacks to make short work of these pests before they make a meal out of you.

Escape Plan

You've found the key you needed, but you've no way of manipulating the bridges again. No matter; go south and scale a wooden post, then perform a 180 leap to reach the nearby wall's hand hold.

Before shimmying around the corner, perform a vertical wall-run and Deathgrip a high hoop to reach the top of the wall. Plunder the pair of chests up here, and then return to the hand hold and make your way back to the area's entry by performing a 180 leap from the wall's corner post.

> ◈ NOTE
> It will be some time before you gain the ability to travel through the portal found near the chests. Rest assured that we'll remind you when the time comes!

Area 5: Breach Basement

Backtrack through the arena and open the locked door you noticed earlier to enter a passage. Wall-run to a post, then drop down to a small basement chamber where a handful of Skeletons lurk.

Proceed through the east door after dispatching the Skeletons, and then turn around and collect the Boatman Coin that hovers near the door's other side.

BOATMAN COIN
45

Slaughter a few more Skeletons in the chamber that follows before searching behind one of the room's two statues to discover another Boatman Coin. Find a Shadowbomb pod behind the opposite statue, and use a bomb to obliterate the Corruption crystals on the ledge above.

BOATMAN COIN
46

Rooftop Loot

Scale the south wall after clearing the Corruption, and then work your way up to the ledge that the crystals were covering. Grab the north wall's hand hold, shimmy around the corner, and perform a vertical wall-run to reach two chests cleverly hidden on the Breach's roof.

> ### NOTE
> You can raid only one of the roof's chests at present. The other is kept beyond a gate, and the requirements for reaching it won't be made clear for some time.

Last Chest

Drop back into the Breach's interior and navigate the north wall's hand holds. When you reach the last hand hold, wall-run toward a distant hoop, jump off the wall, and quickly Deathgrip the hoop to flip to the far ledge. Crack open the chest, and then drop down to the ground and slay the Skeletons that emerge from the floor. Exit the Breach afterward through the south door.

South of the Breach, another bridge spans a dizzying chasm. This one is made of wood and serves as a vital junction between the Breach and the Maw.

Make for The Maw

The Breach's southern grounds offer few distractions. Cut down the odd Skeleton on your way to the bridge. Your destination lies to the west, beyond Mistmount, but take a moment to inspect the bridge's ruined east wing and claim a Boatman Coin.

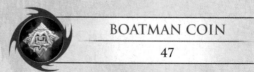

BOATMAN COIN

47

THE MAW: WEST VALLEY

This barren wasteland lies west of the Breach, and is home to more roaming dead.

Northwest Ruin

Before proceeding south toward Serpent's Peak, take a moment to explore the valley's northwest ruin. Drop down two ledges to reach the ruin's entrance, and then slay a number of Skeletal Warriors lurking within the ruin. Smash the clutter in the nearby alcove to discover a Boatman Coin. You can't reach the ruin's chest without the aid of a future ability, so blast the Stonebite on the high west wall before taking your leave of this place.

BOATMAN COIN
48

STONE OF POWER
6

Ride south, toward Serpent's Peak. As you near a tall arch, check behind the warped tree to the south to discover another Boatman Coin.

BOATMAN COIN
49

Scale the sand-covered stairs beyond the arch, cutting through Skeletons as you go. Before venturing up the west stairs that lead to Serpent's Peak, take a moment to explore another ruin to the south.

South Ruin

Crack open the chest on the ruin's balcony, and then push the switch to cause two sections of the nearby wall to rotate, revealing a hoop and peg. The wall sections will quickly flip back around, so make haste in scaling the wall.

Collect the Relic you discover atop the wall. This one's an extremely rare Relic of Khagoth—Ostegoth will pay handsomely for this prize. Take your leave of the ruin afterward, and scale the west stairs to reach Serpent's Peak.

RELIC OF KHAGOTH
1

SERPENT'S PEAK

This western stretch of wasteland winds ever upward. Death's objective isn't far now.

Visit with Vulgrim

Cut down more roaming dead as you navigate this desolate passage. Shoot a Stonebite on the ceiling of the cave near a side trail that leads to Vulgrim, who offers his familiar array of goods. Continue toward the summit after trading with the demonic merchant and raiding the chest that lies in a nook to your right.

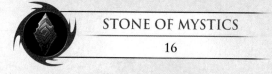

STONE OF MYSTICS
16

Wild Ride

Arriving at the summit, Death finds no sign of the Eternal Throne he seeks—only an ornate bell. In venting his rage on the ancient instrument, the Reaper creates a din that summons an ancient vessel. So *this* is the *Eternal Throne*: a monstrous airship driven by a pair of flying leviathans. Void of fear, the Reaper leaps onto the craft and begins his daring effort to reach the main deck.

Boarding the *Eternal Throne*

Locate a hand hold on a nearby wall. Climb up and Deathgrip the hoop above to reach a higher hand hold.

Perform a 180 leap from the second hand hold and Death will scamper up the pillar behind him. Quickly jump from the pillar to bound up to the deck above.

Loop around the deck and raid a chest. Cross the nearby walkway afterward and climb up to some growth.

Scale the growth to reach a higher platform. Wait for the massive anchor to swing to the right, then jump and Deathgrip an overhead hoop to flip onto the anchor.

Allow the anchor to swing to the left, leap to a stable wooden platform, and then jump onto the next anchor when it drifts close.

Jump from the second anchor to a third when it swings near. Deathgrip an overhead hoop to flip to another stable platform.

Round another corner and drop down onto a wooden beam. Deathgrip across a pair of hanging hoops to land on a distant beam.

Raid the chest on the platform, and then loop around and Deathgrip another hanging hoop to reach some growth on a pillar.

Scale the nearby hand holds and round the corner. Perform a vertical wall-run and jump to reach the high hand hold behind you.

Circle around the growth and climb up to a hand hold. Perform a vertical wall-run and jump off of the pillar to grab the hanging post behind you.

Cross the hand holds that follow and drop down onto another beam. Deathgrip across the hanging hoops and beams that follow.

Circle around the post and perform a 180 leap to reach some nearby hand holds. Round the corner, climb up, and 180 leap to the neighboring hand hold.

At last, you've come to the ship's interior. Follow the passage and scale a tall wall to reach a high hand hold, and then 180 leap to a higher passage. Drop down through the hole that follows and you will land near a door leading to the *Eternal Throne*'s main deck.

This haunted vessel is home to the Lord of Bones, high ruler of the Kingdom of the Dead.

1ST FLOOR

BASEMENT

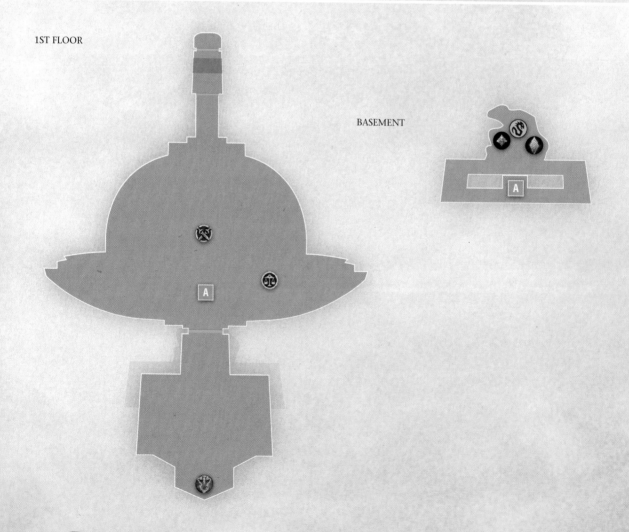

The Dead Crew

A host of ghastly soldiers stand at attention near the deck's center, but only one of them will speak with Death: a heavily-armed shade named Draven. Converse with this spectral warrior to gain some insight into the intrigue surrounding the Dead Court. Draven also offers to teach the Reaper an array of powerful new moves—for a price.

🖈 TIP

If you have coin to spare, consider paying to train with Draven; the techniques he teaches are quite powerful. See the "Skills and Combos" chapter for tips on how to best incorporate Draven's moves.

Scale the north stairs to reach the door to the throne room. The guards deny Death entry, and a robed specter appears. The shade introduces himself as the Chancellor, and informs the Reaper that no one sees the Lord of Bones without first proving their worth in the Gilded Arena. The Horseman must defeat the arena's champion before the Dead King will grant him an audience.

As luck would have it, the Gilded Arena isn't far—the *Eternal Throne* makes fast at the foot of the forsaken place. Before taking your leave of the Dead King's vessel, go below deck and smash the debris to discover minor items and a Boatman Coin. A Tome is also located down here. Shoot the Stonebite on the support post near the Tomb as well.

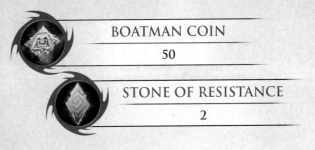

BOATMAN COIN
50

STONE OF RESISTANCE
2

To the Gilded Arena

When you're ready to brave the Gilded Arena, exit the main deck through the south door and climb the growth on the right wall to reach another door. Pass through the door to step out onto a stone jetty where the *Eternal Throne*'s terrifying leviathans have perched. Steel yourself, Rider—the Gilded Arena lies ahead!

The Toll of Kings

THE REAPER HAS SENT MANY SOULS TO THE KINGDOM OF THE DEAD, BUT THE DARK REALM'S CUSTOMS ARE NOT WELL KNOWN TO HIM. HAVING ARRIVED AT THE DEAD KING'S DOORSTEP, THE HORSEMAN IS SURPRISED TO LEARN THAT RULER OF THE REALM WILL NOT GRANT HIM AN AUDIENCE UNTIL A SPECIAL CHALLENGE HAS BEEN MET. WITH NO OTHER ALTERNATIVE, THE PALE RIDER MAKES READY TO DECIDE HIS FATE WITHIN THE GILDED ARENA...

Gilded Arena

GILDED ARENA

This ancient battleground must be braved, and its champion slain, before one can be granted an audience with the Lord of Bones.

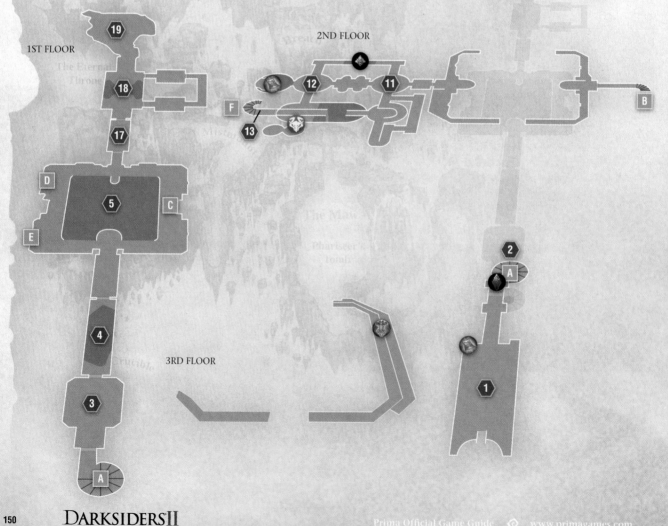

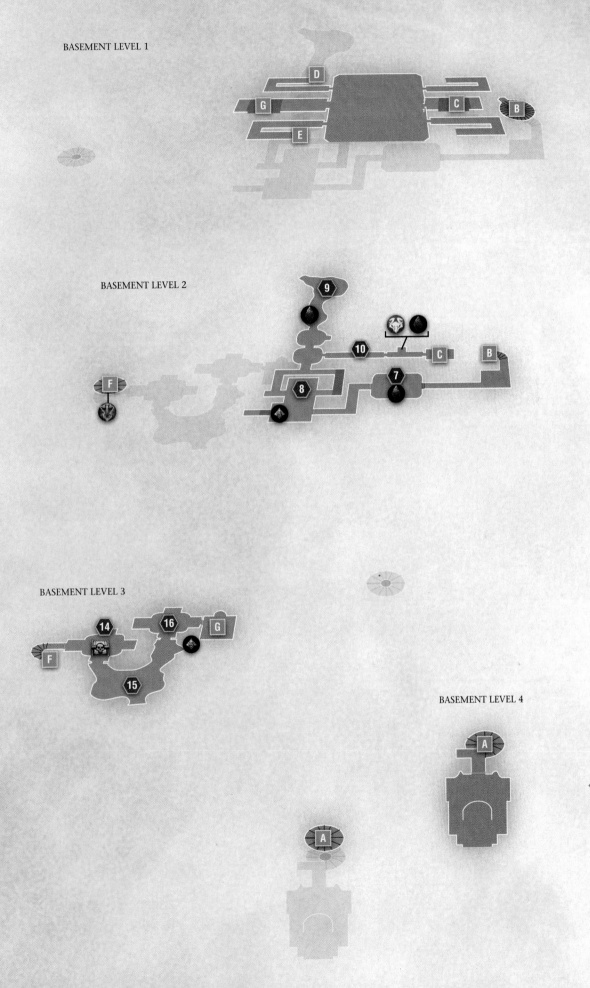

BASEMENT LEVEL 1

BASEMENT LEVEL 2

BASEMENT LEVEL 3

BASEMENT LEVEL 4

Area 1: Exterior Pier

Cross the pier to find the merchant Ostegoth waiting at the opposite end. Trade with Ostegoth if you wish, and collect the nearby page of the Book of the Dead. Enter the door to the north to begin your exploration of the Gilded Arena.

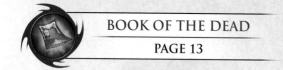

BOOK OF THE DEAD
PAGE 13

Area 2: Stairwell

Shoot the Stonebite on the statue that stands just beyond the Gilded Arena's entry door before descending the spiral stairwell that follows. Enter the first door you encounter—there's nothing of interest farther downstairs.

> **NOTE**
>
> The door at the bottom of the stairwell leads out to the Leviathan's Gorge, but there's no need to return there at present.

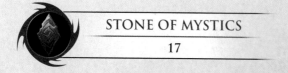

STONE OF MYSTICS
17

Area 3: Arena Entry

This small chamber houses an unusual statue. Grab one of handles on its side and rotate the fixture so that the beam of light from the statue strikes the crystal above the barred north door. The door then unbars, allowing you to advance.

Area 4: Broken Corridor

This hallway has fallen to ruin. Drop into the central pit, raid a pair of chests, and scale the wall growth to climb back out. Then, wall-run along the left wall and Deathgrip the hoop to clear the pit. Proceed through the door that follows to enter the arena proper.

Area 5: Arena

Voices call out to Death as he enters this spacious arena. The mysterious speakers inform the Rider that their champion awaits battle—but before the great fiend can be summoned, Death must seek out three special objects within the Gilded Arena known as Animus Stones. Only the power of these ancient artifacts can bring forth the champion.

Drop down two levels to return to the lowest balcony. Continue circling around the arena, optionally entering the side passages on your right to destroy the downstairs clutter (mainly coffins). Work your way around and climb the rubble in the southwest corner to reach the second balcony. Climb the outside wall to reach the highest balcony and open another chest.

Balcony Spoils

Run around the balcony, ignoring the side passages on the right for now. Look for the hand hold on the outside wall and use it to reach the second level. Go right and climb another hand hold, and then go left and scale a third to reach the highest balcony. Deathgrip the north hoop and wall-run to a hidden Relic.

Drop down to the second (middle) balcony and run north. Keep going to locate the Arena area's third and final chest.

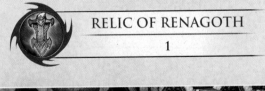

RELIC OF RENAGOTH

1

Drop down to the lowest balcony and circle back around the arena. Climb the east wall again to reach the second (middle) balcony. You've plundered the Arena, so pass through the east door here to begin your search for the first Animus Stone.

Drop down two levels from the Relic ledge, and then go north and use another hand hold to scale the northeast wall, reaching a chest.

THE FIRST ANIMUS STONE

Area 6: Broken Stairwell I

Beyond the door, a spiral staircase winds ever downward—but this, too, has fallen to ruin. Run along the outside wall to pass the collapsed stairs, and be sure to loot the chest you land near after the first wall-run.

The stairs wind down into a small crypt. Smash the ample array of clutter down here for potions and other minor items.

Area 7: Room of Death

The walking dead have massed in this small chamber. Rip them asunder with vicious anti-group attacks and skills, evading between combos to present a difficult target. Beware: more powerful Skeletal Warriors enter the fray after the initial horde of Skeletons have been cut down.

When the melee at last resolves, aim high and shoot the Stonebite on the ceiling to add to your your collection.

> **TIP**
> Blast the hanging coffins with Redemption in search of potions!

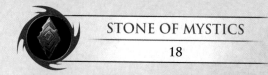

STONE OF MYSTICS

18

Area 8: Lantern Chamber

Claim a Boatman Coin from the southwest corner of this sizable chamber, where a puzzle must be solved in order to progress.

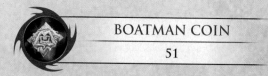

BOATMAN COIN

51

Stand on the room's central pressure plate to lower the east gate. Remain on the plate and Deathgrip a Shadowbomb from the pod beyond.

Wall-run through the pitfall passage that follows, jumping the corners to extend your run.

Toss the Shadowbomb at the south wall to obliterate some Corruption crystals and expose a chest.

Follow the passage to a switch that lowers a nearby gate. Press the switch, then Deathgrip the lantern you left on the pressure plate before.

Collect another Shadowbomb, and then hurl it at the crystals beyond the southwest pit to knock a massive lantern out of a statue's hand.

Backtrack a bit and go north to enter a small room. Press the Action button to place the lantern you're carrying on the statue here.

Deathgrip the lantern and return to the pressure plate. Place the lantern on the plate to keep it depressed, and then explore beyond the lowered east gate.

A beam of light now shines from statue. Rotate the statue 180 degrees to shine its light north and unbar the north door.

Area 9: Animus Stone Chamber I

This cavernous chamber is home to the first Animus Stone. Simply approach the far altar and claim your prize.

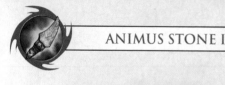

ANIMUS STONE I

A swarm of Scarabs stage an ambush after you swipe the first Animus Stone. Blast these minor threats with Redemption,

or cut them down with anti-group attacks and skills.

After the battle, blast the Stonebite that hangs on the nearby hanging cage to claim another Stonebite.

STONE OF MYSTICS
19

Back to the Arena

Backtrack out of the Animus Stone cavern and cut down the Skeletons that storm you in the outer room. The east passage near the

lantern statue is now open—hurry through.

Area 10: East Passage

Take aim and blast a glowing Stonebite held by a Skeleton hanging from the ceiling in a nook. Then, examine the writing on the nook's wallto gain a clue about a side dungeon known as the Soul Arbiter's Maze. See the "Side Quests and Areas" chapter to learn more.

STONE OF POWER
7

SOUL ARBITER'S SCROLL
1

Open the ornate chest at the passage's end to claim the Dungeon Map.

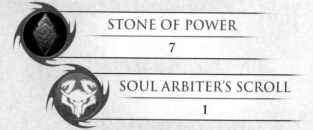

 ### DUNGEON MAP

Scale the east wall to reach a beam, and then jump onto a hanging post. 180 leap to the west balcony, and pull the lever there to open the nearby door. Pass through to return to the Arena.

Returning the First Stone

Back at the Arena, approach the altar to the north. Deathgrip the altar's hoop to zip up and insert the first Animus Stone.

THE SECOND ANIMUS STONE

A handful of Skeletons and a Skeletal Warrior ambush you in the Arena after the first stone has been placed. Show them no mercy, and then enter one of the western passages to return to the balcony. Climb the southwest rubble to reach the second level, smashing through the occasional Skeleton as you make for the west door, which is no longer barred.

Area 11: West Wing; East Statue

The Arena's west door leads to a network of small circular rooms connected by winding stairs and narrow corridors. Go south, following a statue's green beam of light to a stairwell. Go upstairs to find another statue that has no light-emitting lantern, and Deathgrip a Shadowbomb from the pod across the west pit.

Use the bomb to blast the Corruption crystals that block the nearby south passage. The passage is a dead-end, but at its end rests a large chest filled with plunder.

Collect another Shadowbomb and backtrack to the downstairs lantern statue. Use the bomb to destroy the Corruption crystals here, exposing another Shadowbomb pod in the north passage. Spin the statue to lower the west gate, and then collect a bomb and obliterate more crystals beyond the gate.

Enter the north passage and wall-run to clear its long pit. Jump from wall to wall to complete the run and claim a Boatman Coin in the process. You can also Deathgrip this collectible if you're having trouble grabbing it during the wall-run.

BOATMAN COIN

52

Rotate the statue you discover beyond the passage to direct its light west and raise a bridge. Sprint across and claim another lost page of the Book of the Dead.

BOOK OF THE DEAD
PAGE 14

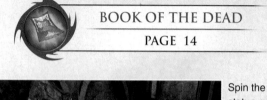

Spin the statue again, this time angling its beam south to open the south passage. Go through and loot a chest to your right. Continue south and claim a precious scroll from a nearby alcove.

SOUL ARBITER'S SCROLL
2

Search the south nook to discover a lantern. Beware: you're trapped in this confined space and ambushed by Skeletons as you try to leave. Set the lantern down so you may do battle unhindered.

Lantern Dash

Now that you've found a lantern, you must bring it all the way back to the lantern-less statue you noticed earlier above the south stairwell. Begin by setting the lantern down on the pressure plate near the previous light-emitting statue. This lowers the nearby gate.

Leave the lantern on the pressure plate and wall-run back through the north passage to return to the other light-emitting statue. Deathgrip the lantern you left on the pressure plate to obtain it once more, then set it down and rotate the nearby statue to open the south passage.

Carry the lantern up the south stairwell and give it to the statue atop the stairs. The lantern shines its light once placed, raising the west bridge. Cross and proceed through the far west door.

Area 13: Broken Stairwell II

Wall-run to descend this familiar stairwell. After landing from one run, backtrack up the stairs to discover a hidden Relic for Ostegoth. Continue to descend the stairwell afterward until you reach the door at the bottom.

RELIC OF ETU-GOTH
3

Area 14: Storage I

Destroy a large amount of clutter in this chamber to score plenty of potions and coin. Beware: Each of the large gravestones you destroy down here causes a crew of Skeletons to rise from the floor. However, smashing all three of these special gravestones also causes a secret chest appear, making it well worth the effort.

Area 15: Animus Stone Chamber II

At last, you arrive at the cavern that houses second Animus Stone. Tear through the Skeletal Archers, Warriors, and Scarabs that stand between you and your prize. Pry the stone from the altar after the dust settles, and then leave the cavern by way of the northeast passage.

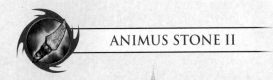

ANIMUS STONE II

ENEMY: SKELETAL ARCHER

Class: Soldier

Like Construct Adjuncts, Skeletal Archers use ranged attacks to assail the Rider from safe distances. Skeletal Archers can be difficult to catch, but become significantly easier prey when the Horseman utilizes his Deathgrip ability. Grasp these evasive minions from afar to pull them into range, and then strike without mercy.

With the second Animus Stone in your possession, proceed north and smash up the weapon racks in the circular room to obtain worthy gear. Pass through the nearby door and open the chest in the small room beyond.

Use the Deathgrip to scale the east wall and reach a higher passage. Before pulling the lever and proceeding through the east door, turn around and Deathgrip an overhead hoop to reach the west chest.

Returning the Second Stone

Before scaling the east wall, enter the south alcove and climb the side wall to reach a small balcony with some clutter. Wall-run to the neighboring balcony, and then smash a crate there to discover a hidden Boatman Coin.

Deathgrip the hoop to place the second Animus Stone onto the Arena's altar. No hostiles ambush you this time; simply proceed through the nearest passage to reach the balcony, and then pass through the north door, which is now open.

BOATMAN COIN
53

THE THIRD ANIMUS STONE

Area 17: Hall of the Dead

Beware: A formidable Skeletal Champion guards the hall beyond the north door, and calls a horde of Skeletons and Skeletal Warriors forth to its aid. Stay evasive and unleash violent anti-group combos and abilities to lay waste to this fearsome horde. The Champion is much stronger than other dead soldiers you've faced to this point, but it can still be Deathgripped and juggled with air combos like other minion-class foes.

ENEMY: SKELETAL CHAMPION

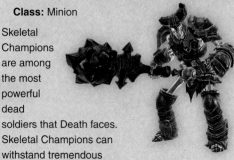

Class: Minion

Skeletal Champions are among the most powerful dead soldiers that Death faces. Skeletal Champions can withstand tremendous punishment, and their attacks cover great distance, landing with crushing force. Be patient and evade a Skeletal Champion's mighty blows, dodging twice to slip their two-strike combos. Quickly counter afterward, landing your best moves while the fiend is off-balance.

Area 18: North Drawbridge

The bridge beyond the Hall of the Dead is not extended, and there's no easy way across. Explore the east passage and take a roundabout route to the north, but beware: two more Skeletal Champions lurk in these narrow corridors.

Death faces a seemingly endless onslaught of Skeletons after the final Skeletal Champion falls. Stay agile and don't let down your guard until the torrent finally subsides.

A Game of Throne

You've bypassed the drawbridge and reached the north side of the bridge. Stand on the nearby pressure plate to raise the bridge, and then Deathgrip a Shadowbomb from the bridge's pod.

Bring the bomb over to the north throne, stand next to the throne, and toss the bomb at the nearby switch.

The resulting blast triggers the switch, causing the throne platform to rotate and delivering Death to a new area.

Area 19: Animus Stone Chamber III

Beware: a horrific Scarab Hulk attacks you in this final cavern. Evade this brute's attacks and counter with vicious combos. The Scarab Hulk's a worthy adversary, but try to preserve Death's Reaper Form ability for the coming battle against the arena's champion. Use timely counters and wear down this overgrown insect with wrath-based skills, instead.

ENEMY: SCARAB HULK

Class: Brute

Scarab Hulks are monstrous insects that move with frightening speed and possess lethal, far-reaching attacks. Dodging and countering effectively is vital when battling these grotesque foes. Start evading the moment you see a Scarab Hulk's wings begin to flap, for this signals a forthcoming attack. Scarab Hulks commonly strike by dashing forward and swiping with their long claws, or by taking to the sky and divebombing Death with heavy momentum. Evade to one side to avoid these assaults, then counter with your best single-target attacks and skills.

Approach the far altar after the Scarab Hulk falls to claim the third and final Animus Stone. Excellent work! Return to the Drawbridge area by pulling the switch back near the throne, and then quickly stepping aboard the throne platform before it spins.

ANIMUS STONE III

Returning the Third Stone

Make the short jaunt back to the Arena, and place the final Animus Stone onto the altar. At last, the Arena's champion has been called!

BOSS BATTLE: GNASHOR

Gnashor is a terrible fiend whose vile power has steadily grown over the ages with the slaying of each of its countless victims. Death must best this mighty adversary to prove his worth.

Focus on Gnashor and remain evasive as the fiend tunnels around beneath the Arena's floor. Gnashor will briefly emerge to strike several times before fully bursting out of the earth, exposing itself. Immediately Deathgrip Gnashor's skull to rip the beast to the ground, then punish its vulnerable skull with a furious combo.

Stagger Gnashor with a powerful combo, and then wait for it to let out a terrible scream. Immediately Deathgrip Gnashor's skull during this howl to bring the beast crashing down.

After suffering significant damage, Gnashor will call upon all of its power and summon its true form. Gnashor now attacks by whipping around its skull and spine with thunderous impact. Prioritize avoiding these deadly blows, and strike hard at Gnashor's feet at every opportunity.

Now's your chance! Assail Gnashor's skull while the monster is helpless. You can inflict great amounts of damage at this point without fear of counterattack. Continue staggering and stunning Gnashor in this fashion to pile on the damage and emerge victorious!

THE GOLDEN SKULL

The Dead King's Court

Take your leave of the Gilded Arena after slaying Gnashor and claiming its Golden Skull. Ascend the spiral stairwell and cross the pier to return to the Eternal Throne. If you wish, trade with Ostegoth, who now stands near the far stairs.

Scale the north stairs and speak with the Chancellor to at last gain an audience with the Lord of Bones. Sadly, the Dead King has no interest in aiding the Reaper—or at least not until the Horseman succeeds in bringing his three Dead Lords back to court to serve their master. Death has little choice in the matter, and accepts a new ability that will aid him in his efforts.

INTERDICTION

After speaking with the Dead King, search behind his throne to discover a lost Relic for Ostegoth.

RELIC OF ETU-GOTH

4

Court of Bones I: The Phariseer

HAVING BESTED A POWERFUL CHAMPION WITHIN THE GILDED ARENA, THE PALE RIDER EARNS HIS AUDIENCE WITH THE LORD OF BONES. THE MEETING DOES NOT UNFOLD AS THE HORSEMAN MIGHT HAVE HOPED, HOWEVER. THOUGH THE DEAD KING PROMISES TO AID THE REAPER, DEATH MUST FIRST SUCCEED IN RETURNING THREE WAYWARD DEAD LORDS TO THE *ETERNAL THRONE*. THE FIRST OF THESE IS A BEING KNOWN AS PHARISEER, WHO RESIDES WITHIN A GREAT TOMB IN THE KINGDOM OF THE DEAD'S SOUTHERN BARRENS...

GILDED ARENA (EXTERIOR)

The west end of Leviathan's Gorge is, like many places in the Kingdom of the Dead, a desolate wasteland.

Gilded Arena

To the Tomb

Take your leave of the *Eternal Throne* and return to the Gilded Arena's tall entry stairwell. Descend all the way to the bottom this time, ignoring the first door you encounter, which leads into the Gilded Arena proper. Pass through the basement door to reach a large, still chamber. Pull the lever to open the far door and enter the western half of Leviathan's Gorge.

The Gorge's west valley is spacious, but holds only one item of note. Stick to the edge of the west cliff as you explore the area to discover a lost Relic hidden behind a large, gnarled vine.

RELIC OF RENAGOTH
2

Proceed through the giant door at the valley's east end to reach the Gorge's south section, where the entrance to the Breach is found. There's nothing new for you to discover within the Breach, however, so hasten your journey by fast traveling to the stronghold's southern grounds.

THE MAW

Much more of the Dead King's desolate realm lies beyond the bridge south of the Breach.

Run directly south across the bridge that spans the chasm and enter the southern barrens known as the Maw. Two ruins stand just beyond the bridge; enter the northwest ruin (on the right) and slay a Skeleton as you follow the interior passage to claim a hidden Boatman Coin.

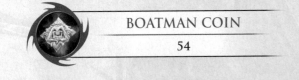

BOATMAN COIN
54

Backtrack a bit and scale a wall by vaulting from a peg to reach the hand hold high above it. Work your way up and around some wall growth to reach an exterior balcony. Claim the valuable scroll from within the far rooftop alcove.

SOUL ARBITER'S SACRED
SCROLL 3

Statue Tag

You can't claim the two chests here until you rotate the lantern statue that stands atop the Breach's southern entrance. But before you can do that, you must first spin the statue found within these ruins. Scale the wall near the scroll alcove and climb up to the roof above to find a lantern statue. Spin the statue 180 degrees so that its light shines north, toward the distant Breach stronghold.

If you like, you may now exit these ruins and backtrack over the bridge to reenter the Breach and rotate its statue 180 degrees as well. This will aim its beam of light back down south at these ruins, lowering the gate that blocks a switch here. Activating this switch will open another gate, exposing a large chest. You're also able to plunder another chest during this process, which is found atop the Breach's roof near its statue. Shoot the Stonebite on the wall near the Breach's final chest as well.

> **TIP**
>
> To return to the Breach's roof, simply enter its south door and climb around the very first room, springing up through the small hole in one corner of the ceiling.

STONE OF RESISTANCE
3

Sentinel's Gaze

Find a Boatman Coin hovering near the entry to this underground tomb. Head inside and run along the stairwell's outer wall to reach a post. Slide all the way down to the bottom, then wall-run to the left to discover a chest.

BOATMAN COIN
55

Return to the wall post and climb it, then wall-run to the right and descend a stairwell to visit an underground barrack. Smash through the skeletal minions down here, and then pocket another Boatman Coin found in the grounds' northeast corner.

Maw Blockage

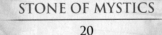

BOATMAN COIN
56

Climb the nearby wall to reach the northeast lookout. Claim the Relic that's hidden behind the torch up here, then collect a Shadowbomb from the nearby pod. Drop down and use the bomb to destroy the Corruption crystals in the alcove directly below. Claim valuables from the chest you discover within the alcove afterward, and destroy the weapon racks to obtain worthy gear.

> **NOTE**
>
> You can wall-run around the central tower to reach another crystal cluster inside the high walls, but you will not be able to solve the mystery of how to destroy these crystals for quite some time.

RELIC OF ETU-GOTH
5

You're unable to pass through the Maw's south gate and explore the lands beyond, but it doesn't matter—the entrance to Phariseer's Tomb is found along the valley's east wall. Still, swing by the Maw's south gate and shoot the Stonebite in the high left window to add to your collection.

STONE OF MYSTICS
20

PHARISEER'S TOMB

The Maw

Phariseer's Tomb

The first Dead Lord that Death must summon resides within this frightful tomb. The Rider's skills will be put to the test in this unholy place.

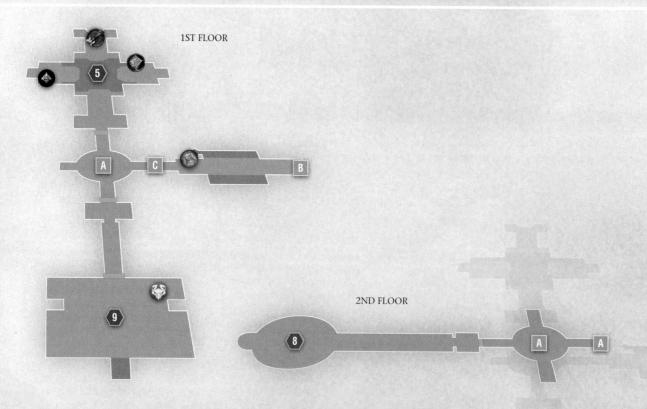

1ST FLOOR

2ND FLOOR

3RD FLOOR

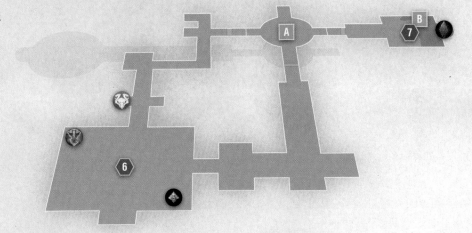

4TH FLOOR

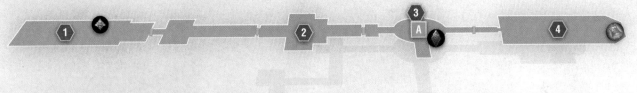

Area 1: Entry Elevator

Approach the dark crystal in the center of the tomb's quiet entry chamber. Strike the crystal to activate a lift that lowers you into the crypt's unknown depths.

When at last you come to a stop, advance and slay the roaming Mummies in the passage that follows. These shambling fiends pose little threat to Death. Swipe a nearby Boatman Coin before proceeding through the east door, where more dead minions must be battled in a spacious hall.

BOATMAN COIN
57

ENEMY: MUMMY

Class: Soldier

These lumbering minions wander mindlessly until a threat is detected, and then attack with shocking hostility. Still, the Reaper has little difficulty in cutting down these unarmored adversaries.

A massive gate bars your progress in this chamber. Standing atop the central pressure plate raises the gate, but it quickly collapses again when you step off the plate. A bit of ingenuity is needed to gain entry to the tomb's deeper reaches.

Drop down to the ground, and then wall-run up to the chest ledge. Claim your plunder from the chest.

Scale the south wall to reach a ledge with a Shadowbomb pod.

Return to the ground again and Deathgrip the tall pillar that the crystals had been covering to pull it down into the center of the room.

Grab and shove the pillar right up next to the large gate. Return to the pressure plate and Deathgrip a Shadowbomb from the nearby wall pod.

Hurl Shadowbombs at the Corruption crystals on the north ledges to blast them away, exposing a chest, a tall pillar, and a second Shadowbomb pod.

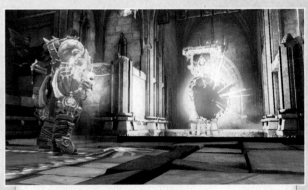

While standing on the pressure plate, toss a Shadowbomb onto the pillar. The ensuing blast knocks the pillar directly beneath the gate. The pillar will now catch the gate when you step off the plate, supporting it.

Area 3: Elevator Chamber

Another elevator lies beyond the gate. This one serves as your main means of transportation between the tomb's four primary floors. Notice that the surrounding walls are marked with the number IV—this denotes your current floor. Shoot the Stonebite on the southeast wall before proceeding through the east door.

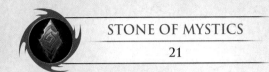

STONE OF MYSTICS

21

Area 4: Hall of Worship

A wide hall filled with bones and coffins lies beyond the east door. Slaughter the Mummies that roam this place, and then crack open the chest that sits before the east statue. Search behind the statue to discover a lost page of the Book of the Dead.

BOOK OF THE DEAD

PAGE 15

Going Down

Backtrack out to the elevator and strike the crystal with the number "III" etched into the floor before it. The elevator then descends to the third floor, where a locked door blocks your progress.

Next, strike the crystal with the number "II" etched before it. Instead of stopping on the second floor, the elevator is sabotaged by the Phariseer, who appears with a warning before sending you crashing down to the first floor. The elevator won't stop at the second floor, so your only option is to explore the first floor. Proceed through the north door.

Area 5: Pit of Bone

Countless bones fill a giant pit in this spacious chamber. A puzzle that demands precise timing must be solved in order to progress.

The East Chest

Ignore the hoop that hangs from the cage near the ceiling and turn left. Run up the west wall to reach a hand hold, and then shimmy around the corner.

Jump and Deathgrip the new hoop to swing over to the east ledge. Open an ornate chest here to claim the Dungeon Map.

DUNGEON MAP

When you near the end of the hand hold, perform a 180 leap to grab a high-hovering Boatman Coin.

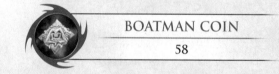

BOATMAN COIN

58

The North Chest

Next, Deathgrip a Shadowbomb from the pod above the hoop you've just used.

You land near a switch. Push it to lower a second hoop from the ceiling. The initial hoop then retracts after a brief time.

Throw the bomb at the west ledge's switch. The bomb remains inert until you shoot it, but don't do so just yet.

Prima Official Game Guide · www.primagames.com

Traverse the south wall's hand holds to round the corner and return to the entry ledge. Now, aim and blast the Shadowbomb to trigger the west switch.

Wait for the original hoop to lower from the ceiling, Then, hurry and Deathgrip across the two hoops before the second one retracts. If you time it right, you'll land near the north chest.

Key Acquired

Swinging across the hoops lands you near the ornate north chest. Crack into it to acquire a Skeleton Key.

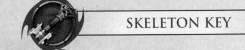

SKELETON KEY

With the Skeleton Key in your possession, drop into the bone-filled pit and cut down the lowly dead that lurk down here. Vault off of the south wall's peg afterward to climb out of the pit

Wraith Ambush

A gate rises behind Death as he exits the pit, and a new enemy known as a Wraith appears to challenge him. Keep your distance at first and gauge the Wraith's attack patterns, timing your dodges and counters well. Take your time in slaying the first Wraith since two more appear afterward, presenting a far greater challenge. Dodge often as you work at cutting down these agile foes.

ENEMY: WRAITH

Class: Minion

There's a certain degree of elegance to the Wraith's violence. These wispy vixens hover about with fluid grace, and then suddenly unleash lethal strikes with their twin swords. While a lone Wraith won't present much challenge for the Reaper, these fiends become exponentially more dangerous when encountered in groups. Remain focused on one Wraith at a time, cutting down each one in turn. Evade regularly to avoid the far-reaching attacks of other Wraiths that attempt to surround you.

With the Wraiths slain, your path to the elevator is clear. Attack the crystal with the number "III" etched before it to ride up to the third floor. Then, use your newfound key to open the locked south door and advance.

Cut down the odd Mummy as you navigate the wide corridor that leads to this square chamber, where many more Wraiths await. Stay mobile and evade around the room's many pillars to present a challenging target for these vicious fiends to focus on.

After all of the Wraiths have fallen, a massive brute in heavy armor storms into the fray. This Undead General is one of the most dangerous Brute-class enemies you've faced thus far, so steel yourself for a difficult battle. The General will block most of your attacks with his massive shield, but heavy secondary weapons, such as axes, hammers, and maces, will reach around and strike the General. Try to land a few hits with one of those weapons, and then quickly evade to one side to dodge the General's charge.

North Corridor Loot

After the General at last collapses, destroy the crate near the room's northwest pillar to discover a lost Relic. Smash another crate in the southeast corner to score a Boatman Coin. Proceed north afterward, slaying the odd minion as you navigate a long hall. Claim a Soul Arbiter's Sacred Scroll from the west nook as you go.

	RELIC OF ETU-GOTH
	6
	BOATMAN COIN
	59
	SOUL ARBITER'S SACRED SCROLLS 4

Elevator Action

You emerge in the Elevator Chamber, but the elevator platform is far below. Don't drop from the entry ledge; instead, turn left and grab the hand hold on the wall, and then work your way around to the east door by wall-running and 180 leaping between the hand holds that follow. Find your way to a wall post, then slide down and drop to reach the east ledge. Enter the door here to advance to the next area.

ENEMY: UNDEAD GENERAL

Class: Brute

Undead Generals are dangerous brutes that pressure Death with relentless aggression. Their massive shields nullify most of the Horseman's frontal attacks, and their heavy armor can absorb plenty of punishment. Utilizing skills is vital against these formidable foes; use Unstoppable to increase Death's attack damage, or summon ghouls with Exhume to distract a General so you may strike him freely from behind. The Undead General's attacks are devastating, but most can be avoided simply by evading to one side. When flanking efforts are proving fruitless, stand before the General and batter him with heavy secondary weapons. Charged attacks from glaives, and other attacks that deal Piercing damage, are very effective at bypassing the brute's armored defenses.

Area 7: Pillar Pit

Shoot the Stonebite atop the tall statue on the opposite side of this room, and then shoot the Shadowbomb on the nearby wall to obliterate a crop of Corruption crystals. This exposes a wall post; wall-run and grab the post, and then slide down to begin your exploration of this dizzying chamber.

Wall-run back to the previous wall post, and then wall-run to a third post on the right. Perform a 180 leap from this post to reach the broken post behind you.

STONE OF POWER
8

When you reach the bottom of the post, wall-run to the left to grab a second wall post.

Circle around the broken post and perform another 180 leap to reach the corner post to the right. Wall-run to the right to reach some growth that leads up to a ledge with a lever.

Pillar Shifter

When at last you reach the room's east ledge, pull the lever to raise a bridge below you. Drop down and slay the Mummies that roam the bridge, and then Deathgrip the tall east pillar to pull it down onto the bridge.

Slide down a bit and wall-run to the left again to reach a hand hold that leads to a tiny ledge with a chest.

Push the pillar to the west until you reach a step. Leave the pillar be, and then locate a hoop on the nearby wall. Deathgrip up to a small ledge, where a missing page of the Book of the Dead is found.

Area 8: Phariseer's Lair

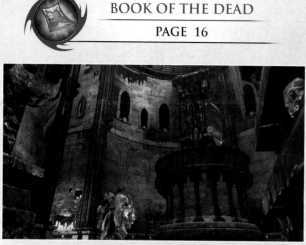

Descend the stairs that lead down into this large, circular chamber to awaken and face the Phariseer.

Now push the pillar off the step an into the west room, which turns out to be the Elevator Chamber. (The elevator platform is still resting on the third floor.) Move the pillar onto the Elevator Chamber's central pressure plate. This places the pillar in position to catch the elevator platform the next time you try to visit the tomb's second floor.

Back to the Elevator

With the pillar in position, backtrack out of the Elevator Chamber. Smash through the hoard of Skeletons that ambush you on the bridge, and then scale the east wall growth. Wall-run back to the corner post and work your way back up to the top of the room.

You've done well thus far, Horseman. Return to the Elevator Chamber and drop down to the elevator platform. Strike the crystal with the number "II" etched before it to descend to the second floor. This time, the pillar you recently shifted catches the elevator platform, allowing you to at last explore this floor of the tomb. Proceed through the west door to at last face off against your quarry: the first Dead Lord, Phariseer.

> **◊ NOTE**
>
> You can still return to the tomb's first floor by dropping off the elevator platform's east side. There's no reason to do so at present, however.

BOSS BATTLE: PHARISEER

Phariseer is not pleased to have his slumber disturbed by a meddling Horseman, and battle quickly commences. Immediately call upon your best abilities and have at the Dead Lord. Unstoppable and Aegis Guard are excellent here, helping you inflict more damage and mitigate Phariseer's swift and far-reaching attacks.

TIP

Don't forget to unleash your Reaper Form against Phariseer—it helps even the odds!

The Dead Lord doesn't give much warning before he strikes, and he often attacks in fluid combos. Evade often to avoid this nimble boss's crushing blows, especially when you see him swinging away with abandon. Immediately counter with combos of your own each time Phariseer misses or leaves himself open.

Defeating Phariseer is no easy feat, so expect to burn through several potions during the struggle. When the Dead Lord finally falls, he becomes yours to command. Excellent work, Rider—you've just gained an ally of immense power!

After suffering significant damage, Phariseer will begin to glow and rise, calling forth skeletal minions to aid him. These Skeletons and Skeletal Warriors add unwanted chaos to this already frantic battle—use skills such as Exhume and Harvest to keep them off your back while you focus on combating their master.

The Horseman's Slave

The time has come to leave this unholy place. Ready the Interdiction ability, and then stand on the chamber's central Summoning Circle and use Interdiction to summon Phariseer. The Dead Lord will obediently await your command; enter aiming mode and target the pressure plate beyond the east gate, and then use Interdiction again to send Phariseer off to activate the plate. The Dead Lord passes through the gate unhindered, then depresses the plate to banish the obstacle.

Before taking your leave of Phariseer's Tomb, drop down from the east end of the elevator platform to return to the first floor one last time. Now that Phariseer is under your command, you can raid the first floor's south chamber, which houses valuable treasure. Pass through the first floor's south door and summon Phariseer at the circle beyond. Enter aiming mode and order the Dead Lord to trigger the pressure plate past the nearby gate. This lowers the gate, which had previously blocked your progress.

Area 9: Phariseer's Hoard

Slaughter a few lowly Mummies in this chamber and smash the surrounding weapon racks to obtain valuable gear. Grab a Shadowbomb from the west pod and use it to obliterate the south Corruption crystals so that you may descend into the pit beyond to reach a lower chamber.

Use the lower room's Summoning Circle to call forth Phariseer, and then command the Dead Lord to stand upon the central pressure plate. This lowers the surrounding gates that block three alcoves, each of which features a chest. Beware: you're ambushed by enemies each time you open a chest. First you face a mob of Mummies, second you face an Undead General, and finally, a pair of deadly Wraiths. Raise Phariseer at the Summoning Circle to gain his aid during each fight. Phariseer can be slain by enemies, but you can simply summon him again whenever this occurs.

Make sure to inspect the scrawl on the wall in the room's dark northeast corner before taking your leave of his place; it provides you with a Soul Arbiter's Sacred Scroll.

SOUL ARBITER'S SACRED SCROLL 5

Fast Travel Time

Phariseer's Tomb holds no further secrets. Call up the World Map and fast travel out of the dungeon, returning to the *Eternal Throne* to barter with Ostegoth. Then, fast-travel back to Phariseer's Tomb and venture toward the Maw's south gate. You couldn't open this gate before, but with the aid of Phariseer, no roads are blocked to you...

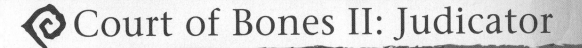

Court of Bones II: Judicator

ONE DEAD LORD HAS BEEN BENT TO THE PALE RIDER'S WILL, BUT TWO OF THE DEAD COURT'S WAYWARD SERVANTS STILL REMAIN UNSUMMONED. THE NEXT LORD ON DEATH'S LIST IS KNOWN AS THE JUDICATOR AND RESIDES WITHIN A FRIGHTFUL TOMB AT THE SOUTHEAST REACHES OF THE KINGDOM OF THE DEAD...

THE SPINE

Only with the aid of the Dead Lord, Phariseer, is Death able to venture into the dreary wastes where the Judicator's Tomb is found.

South Gate

Summon Phariseer at the circle near gate that separates the Maw from the Spine. Order the Dead Lord to pull the lever to the north so that you may explore beyond this checkpoint unimpeded.

Grab the hand hold at the passage's end and shimmy around a corner to reach a ledge with a chest. Drop from the ledge after claiming your plunder to land near the lever that Phariseer pulled. Go east, and then south, collecting a Soul Arbiter's Scroll from a nook before stepping outside and entering the Spine.

> **TIP**
>
> Blast the Stonebite on the gate's high window if you haven't already.

SOUL ARBITER'S SCROLL
3

Go south and scale a wall to reach a ledge. Immediately turn around and jump out to grab a floating Boatman Coin. Climb back up the wall afterward, and then scale the next wall ahead to enter a short passage.

Gate Goodies

After exiting the gate, turn around to spy a peg and hoop running up the exterior wall. Vault from the peg and Deathgrip the hoop to reach a high hand hold, and then shimmy over to a ledge with a chest. Take aim and blast the nearby Stonebite before dropping back down to the dusty trail below.

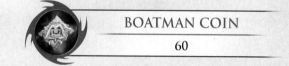

BOATMAN COIN
60

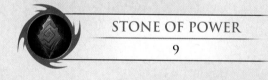

STONE OF POWER
9

Northwest Valley

Dispatch the Skeletal Warriors that roam the Spine's northwest valley as you advance toward a great stone bridge. The bridge connects to the Spine's southeast valley, and also leads to the City of the Dead. Though the northwest valley's north ruin can be entered and explored, it leads to a nefarious maze that you're not prepared to solve quite yet.

> **CAUTION**
>
> It's not worth attempting the Soul Arbiter's Maze until you've found all of the Soul Arbiter's Scrolls, which provide the secrets to navigating the maze. See the "Side Quests and Areas" chapter for complete details on how to solve this deadly labyrinth.

Though the Soul Arbiter's Maze is beyond Death's present skills, approach it anyway, if only to discover the nearby Relic of Etu-Goth that's tucked away near the edge of the east cliff.

RELIC OF ETU-GOTH
7

Stone Bridge

Make for the Spine's southeast valley by crossing the east bridge. Swipe a missing page of the Book of the Dead from the bridge's east lookout, and then head south to continue your journey toward the Judicator's Tomb.

> **NOTE**
> The City of the Dead lies to the north, but you can't enter this great citadel at present.

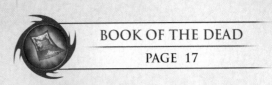

BOOK OF THE DEAD
PAGE 17

Southeast Valley

RELIC OF RENAGOTH
3

The entrance to the Judicator's Tomb lies directly south of the bridge. Before entering the dreadful place, search around the valley's rock clusters to locate a Boatman Coin.

BOATMAN COIN
61

East Tower

Venture east of the Judicator's Tomb to explore one final ruin. Bear right at the fork in the trail and head uphill. Before scaling the tower's south wall, find a Relic at the edge of the nearby cliff. Climb the tower's south wall after claiming this prize, navigating hoops, hand holds, and growth until you reach the top. Then, slide down a post to explore the tower's interior.

Blast the Stonebite inside the tower and slide down another post to reach a lower tier, where a portal you currently can't activate is found. Drop through a nearby hole to reach a lookout, and then aim and Deathgrip the nearby hovering Boatman Coin. That's all you can accomplish here for now; leap from the lookout and then head into the Judicator's Tomb to carry on with your quest.

STONE OF POWER
10

BOATMAN COIN
62

Judicator's
Tomb

The second Dead Lord is known as the Judicator and resides within this forboding stronghold.

1ST FLOOR

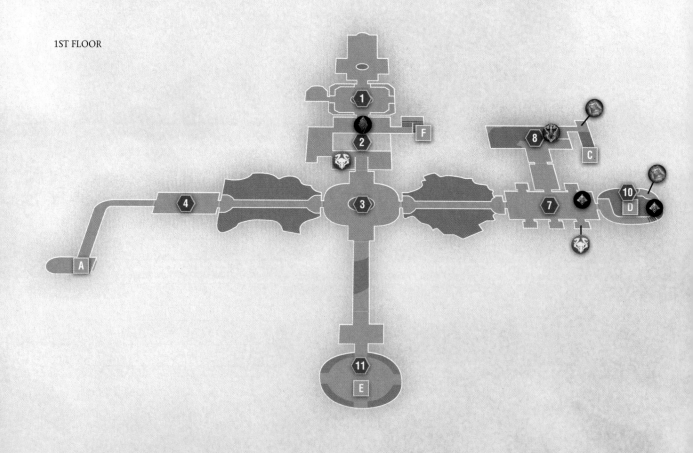

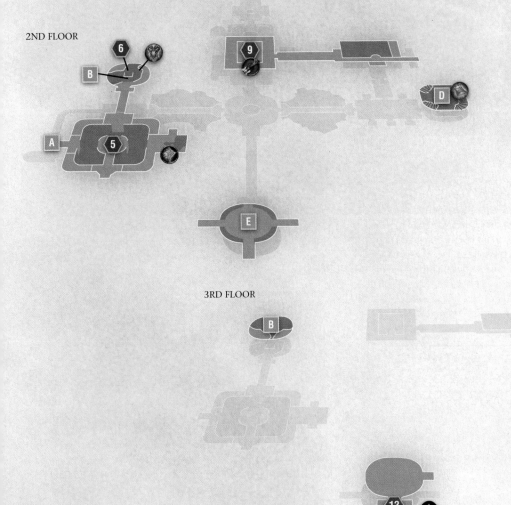

2ND FLOOR

3RD FLOOR

4TH FLOOR

BASEMENT

Area 1: Entry Chamber

A caged lever draws your eye to the center of the keep's first room. Explore the west passage to discover a Summoning Circle, and then use Interdiction to summon Phariseer. Enter aiming mode and direct the Dead Lord to pull the central lever. The south door then becomes unbarred.

Area 2: Dungeon

A large pit dominates the center of this sizeable chamber. First, look up and shoot the Stonebite in the overhead cage. Then turn right and explore the west passage to discover another Summoning Circle. Call forth Phariseer once more and team up to slay the deadly Undead Prowlers and Skeletal Champion that ambush you here. Cut down the Prowlers first to simplify the battle, and then turn your attention to felling the stalwart Champion.

Pull the lever at the passage's south end to raise a platform within the central pit. Order Phariseer to move through the nearby gate afterward and trigger the pressure plate beyond to raise a second platform.

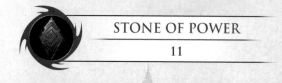

STONE OF POWER
11

With both platforms raised, backtrack out of the passage and drop into the pit. Grab the tall pillar you find here and slide it between the two raised platforms. Climb out of the pit and leap across the platforms and pillar to join Phariseer on the room's south balcony. Rip open the chest to the east and find a Soul Arbiter's Scroll behind the west pillar before proceeding through the south door.

ENEMY: UNDEAD PROWLER

Class: Minion

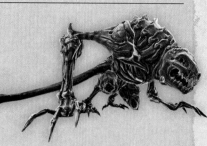

Crossing over to the Kingdom of the Dead hasn't tamed the Prowler—in fact, these creepy beasts are even more menacing in their undead form. Undead Prowlers attack with great fury and aggression, using their speed to quickly surround the Reaper, avoid his attacks, and counter with swift, leaping strikes.

> **NOTE**
> You can't claim the two chests that surround the pit just yet. You'll get them on your way out of the tomb.

SOUL ARBITER'S SCROLL
4

Area 3: Circle of Judgment

No need to seek out the Judicator—he awaits you in this circular area. Unlike Phariseer, this Dead Lord doesn't wish to fight—instead, he pleads with Death to seek out and return three lost souls to him, which are being held prisoner in this very fortress. Once all three souls have been brought to the Judicator, he'll pass judgement on them, and in doing so he will help them find their way to the City of the Dead. Only then will the Judicator agree to follow the Pale Rider.

THE FIRST SOUL

Area 4: Lich's Lair

After speaking with the Judicator, proceed through the west door and cross a bridge that leads to this chamber, where a devious Lich assaults you. The Lich isn't particularly powerful, but it has the bothersome ability to summon undead minions to aid it in battle. Focus on killing the Lich, and then mop up any skeletal stragglers.

ENEMY: LICH

Class: Elite

Liches have the power to call forth hordes of spectral Skeletons, seeking to overwhelm Death with an endless torrent of undead. Use abilities such as Exhume and Murder to keep a Lich's minions occupied while you focus on slaying the undead summoner itself. Liches are not powerful, so unleash your most lethal attacks to quickly cut them down. Evade away from their ground-pound attacks, and use the Deathgrip to pull Liches toward you and temporarily stun them.

After the Lich has been defeated, go through the west door and sprint upstairs. Summon Phariseer at the Summoning Circle you discover near the door to the next area.

Area 5: Statue Room

A familiar statue stands in the center of this chamber, but it lacks a light-emitting lantern. You'll need to solve this puzzling room in order to progress.

Order Phariseer to trigger the pressure plate near the statue. It takes a moment for the Dead Lord to get there.

Cross the bridge that extends when the plate is triggered. Now order Phariseer to trigger another pressure plate near the east Corruption crystals.

Only half of the bridge extends; the crystals are causing an obstruction. Leap toward Phariseer, then Deathgrip the Dead Lord to zip over to the east ledge.

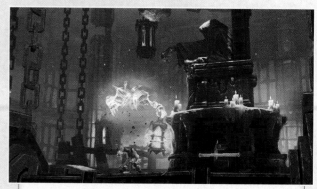

Deathgrip the lantern that lies beyond the east pit and carry it back to the central statue.

Collect a Shadowbomb from the east ledge's north nook and use it to destroy the Corruption crystals. Now the bridge may fully extend.

With the lantern in place, spin the statue so that its beam fires south. Now you may loot the room's south chest.

Open the chest in the east ledge's south nook to claim the Dungeon Map.

Spin the statue so that the beam faces north to unbar the north door. Order Phariseer to stand on the north ledge's pressure plate, and then cross the bridge after it extends.

DUNGEON MAP

Area 6: West Tower

Make your way to this tall tower, where the first imprisoned soul is held. The stairs here are broken, but you must find your way to the top of the tower in order to free the soul.

Again, the Rider scampers up to a high hand hold. Perform one last 180 leap to reach the tower's apex.

Before beginning your ascent, dive underwater to discover a hidden Relic.

RELIC OF KHAGOTH

2

Scale the east wall to reach a high hand hold, and then perform a 180 leap and Deathgrip the hoop behind you.

Death grabs a higher hand hold. Shimmy to the left, around the corner, and then perform another 180 leap to Deathgrip another hoop.

Lost Soul I

The first lost soul lingers in a cage atop the tower. Approach it and press the Action button to collect the soul—but be ready to battle another vicious Lich and two Skeletal Champions afterward! Make good use of the Deathgrip throughout this trying fight.

TIP

If you possess a weapon that restores health after each kill, allow the Lich to summon its lowly minions and simply cut them down to heal up.

Tower Treasure

When the battle is over, peer over the tower's southwest edge to spy a chest on the ledge below. Carefully drop down to the ledge and crack open the chest, and then jump to another nearby ledge to raid a second chest.

You're all finished here. Return to the Judicator and allow him to pass judgment on the soul you've claimed. The east door then unbars—hurry through and begin your search for the second soul.

THE SECOND SOUL

Area 7: Prison

Death is waylaid by a hoard of Undead Prowlers and Skeletal Champions upon entering this area. Fight hard to cut down this mob of fiends, but beware: an even more powerful foe emerges once you do!

BOSS BATTLE: TORMENTOR

A monstrous villain known as the Tormentor appears after the Prowlers and Champions have been slain. Strive to evade this hulking terror's fast and devastating blows, and strike hard from behind while it slowly turns to face you. Use your best abilities to bring down the Tormentor as quickly as possible. Teleport Slash is particularly effective, helping you slip past the brute just before he strikes.

Prison Prizes

When the Jailor is no more, open the chest in one of the south cells, and then search the southeast cell to discover writing on the wall that bestows a Soul Arbiter's Scroll. Smash the northeast crates as well to claim a hidden Boatman Coin. The east door is locked, so proceed through the north door instead.

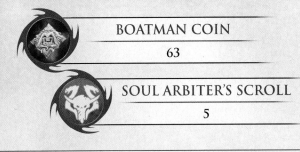

	BOATMAN COIN
	63
	SOUL ARBITER'S SCROLL
	5

Area 8: East Wing

Acrobatic antics are required for the Pale Rider to reach the tower that houses the second lost soul.

Use the Summoning Circle to call forth Phariseer as you enter the room.

Plunder the chest and equip the Deathgrip before wall-running toward Phariseer, vaulting off of another peg.

Go right and order Phariseer to stand atop the pressure plate that lies beyond the gate. This causes two pegs to appear on the surrounding walls.

Jump off the wall as you near Phariseer, and then Deathgrip the Dead Lord to zip over to solid ground.

Return to the room's entrance and run along the outside wall. Jump the corner and vault from a peg to reach a small ledge with a chest.

The passage that follows features a long pit. Collect the Book of the Dead page from atop the north bone pile.

Two Treasures

Run and jump out over the pit. Quickly Deathgrip the distant hoop to zip across and scale the far wall.

Your map reveals a chest in a nearby passage, directly above Phariseer. Go east from the lever and scale a few hand holds to enter the passage. Make your way over to the far chest.

Sprint upstairs and pull a lever to lower a gate and reveal another wall hoop.

Next, carefully drop down into the nearby hole to land in a lower passage where a lost Relic is found.

RELIC OF ETU-GOTH
8

Drop down into the hole after claiming the Relic and fall to the bottom passage. Immediately look up and Deathgrip the overhead hoop to soar up to the top passage's hand hold and shimmy back out of the passage. Sprint past the lever you recently pulled and head through the west door.

Area 9: Dungeon Balcony

You've made your way back to the Dungeon area, but you're now on a high balcony. Go north and loot a small chest, and then head south and crack open a larger chest to acquire a Skeleton Key. You'll encounter a Skeletal Champion and a few Undead Prowlers along the way.

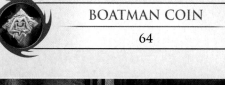

SKELETON KEY

With the key in hand, backtrack to the previous area and drop down through a small hole in the floor near the lever. You land near the East Wing's entry door; continue backtracking to the Prison area, and then use your newfound key to unlock its east door.

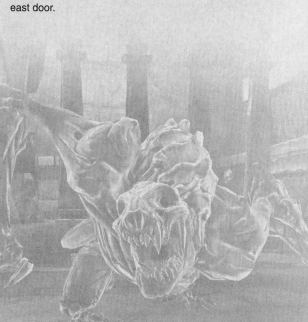

Area 9: East Tower

At last, you've reached the tomb's East Tower. As before, you'll need to work your way up to the imprisoned lost soul at the tower's apex. Before beginning your ascent, dive into the water and collect an underwater Boatman Coin.

BOATMAN COIN
64

Scale the first flight of stairs, and then Deathgrip the central hoop to bound up to a hand hold.

Climb up to the central platform, and then Deathgrip the Book of the Dead page from the tip of the broken staircase. Run, jump, and Deathgrip the north hoop afterward to reach another hand hold.

BOOK OF THE DEAD
PAGE 19

Perform a 180 leap from the hand hold and Deathgrip an overhead hoop to swing toward the south wall.

Quickly Deathgrip the south wall's hoop before you fall. Death will then scamper up the south wall; jump off and Deathgrip another hoop behind you to reach a high hand hold.

Shimmy around the corner and 180 leap toward a final hoop. Deathgrip this to scale the west wall, and then 180 leap to the tower's apex.

Lost Soul II

Beware: Collecting the second imprisoned soul causes two Skeletal Champions and a horrific Undead Stalker to materialize behind you. The Stalker is one of the most deadly opponents you've encountered to this point, becoming increasing fierce as the battle wages on. Cut down the Skeletal Champions first, and then focus on slaying the Stalker.

ENEMY: UNDEAD STALKER

Class: Brute

These ultimate renditions of the Stalker are by far the most deadly. At first, their attacks largely resemble those of previous Stalkers—however, as the Undead Stalker suffers more and more damage, it begins to unleash longer and more furious claw strike combinations. These lengthy claw combos can quickly spell the Reaper's demise, so it's wise to slay all other present adversaries before facing off against an Undead Stalker. This prevents the fiend from unleashing its longer claw combos until it's the only threat left to deal with.

When the last of the undead have fallen, carefully drop down from the tower's southeast corner to land on the broken stairs below, not far from a chest. Claim your plunder, and then exit the tower and find your way back to the Judicator. Return the second soul for judgment, and the south door unbars. Only one soul left to go!

THE THIRD SOUL

Area 10: South Tower

Wall-run across the broken passage that leads to the final tower. Summon Phariseer at the Summoning Circle just before the tower's spacious elevator platform, and then step aboard.

A monstrous Undead General storms forth to attack you on the elevator platform. Allow Phariseer to keep the General occupied while you assail it from its unguarded rear. The Dead Lord won't last long against this powerful foe, and the summoning circle is sealed off during this fight, so take full advantage of Phariseer's support while you can.

> ⚬ **TIP**
>
> Remember, heavy secondary weapons can reach past the General's shield. Ghouls raised with the Exhume skill can also help you flank the brute.

Elevator Games

Summon Phariseer again, if need be, and then strike the crystal with the number "II" etched before it to begin your ascent. Unfortunately, a large crop of Corruption crystals prevents the elevator from reaching the tower's second floor. You'll need to find a way to remove this obstruction.

Order Phariseer to trigger the pressure plate beyond the west gate. This lowers another gate on the high east ledge.

Enter the east passage, ignore its pressure plate, and scale the east wall to reach a hand hold. Wall-run and shimmy around the corner.

Continue wall-running around the tower, vaulting from several pegs to preserve your run.

You land on a small ledge above Phariseer's position. Look down at the east passage's pressure plate and order Phariseer to trigger it. This lowers a gate on the highest east ledge, exposing a Shadowbomb pod.

Grab the nearby hand hold, shimmy around the corner, and vault off of the two pegs above to reach a higher hand hold.

Wall-run around the tower again, heading for the high east ledge.

Collect a Shadowbomb from the east ledge's pod and hurl it at the Corruption crystals to obliterate them. Wait for the elevator to rise, and then cross the platform and enter the south room.

Area 11: Stairwell

Plunge into the water up here to discover a sunken Boatman Coin. Pocket the prize, and then surface and scale the stairs. Deathgrip the north hoop to reach an upper balcony, and then circle around and claim a lost page from the Book of the Dead. Proceed into the north candlelit chamber afterward.

BOATMAN COIN
65

BOOK OF THE DEAD
PAGE 20

Area 12: Room of Wax

The final soul is kept in this quiet chamber. Equip Redemption before collecting it, for you'll soon have need of Death's faithful sidearm.

A gate rises as you attempt to leave with the lost soul, and the Skeleton that hangs from the ceiling begins to writhe in misery. This summons a host of Skeletons that soon swarm you. Before cutting them down, target the hanging skeleton and quickly destroy it with Redemption. The hanging skeleton will repeatedly summon minions until you destroy it, and you don't have energy to waste on those when an even deadlier fiend must be faced...

BOSS BATTLE: BONE GIANT

A monstrous Bone Giant materializes in the room's center after the hanging Skeleton has been destroyed. The hulking brute stalks about with lethal intent, and then swipes twice with its razor-sharp claws when Death draws near. The Bone Giant can also lash out with its skull when Death remains at a distance, and occasionally stomps its massive feet to crush Death underfoot.

Evade in a circle around the Bone Giant, seeking to dodge its favored one-two combo. Deathgrip close to the monster after you dodge and unleash your most lethal combo to pile on the damage. This is the tomb's final battle, so feel free to call upon Death's Reaper Form if you wish.

Stonebite on High

After reducing the Bone Giant to dust, look up and blast the high Stonebite near the ceiling.

STONE OF MYSTICS

22

Recruiting the Judicator

Make the uneventful trip back to the Judicator and present the Dead Lord with the third and final soul. True to his word, the Judicator agrees to heed his master's call. Surprisingly, the third and final Dead Lord, Basileus, also makes a brief appearance—he challenges Death to brave the Psychameron, a twisted labyrinth where the Horseman's resolve will be put on trial yet again.

Last of the Loot

You haven't forgotten about those two chests back near the Dungeon area's pit, have you? After speaking with Basileus, make your way back to the Dungeon and use the west Summoning Circle to call forth Phariseer and the Judicator. Lead the Dead Lords down the northeast stairs, order Phariseer to trigger one of the two pressure plates, and have the Judicator activate the other. Now you can open the two chests down here.

⊘ TIP

After plundering the pit, fast travel back to the *Eternal Throne* and trade with Ostegoth before returning to the Gilded Arena, where Basileus has hinted that the entrance to the Psychameron can be found.

Court of Bones III: Basileus

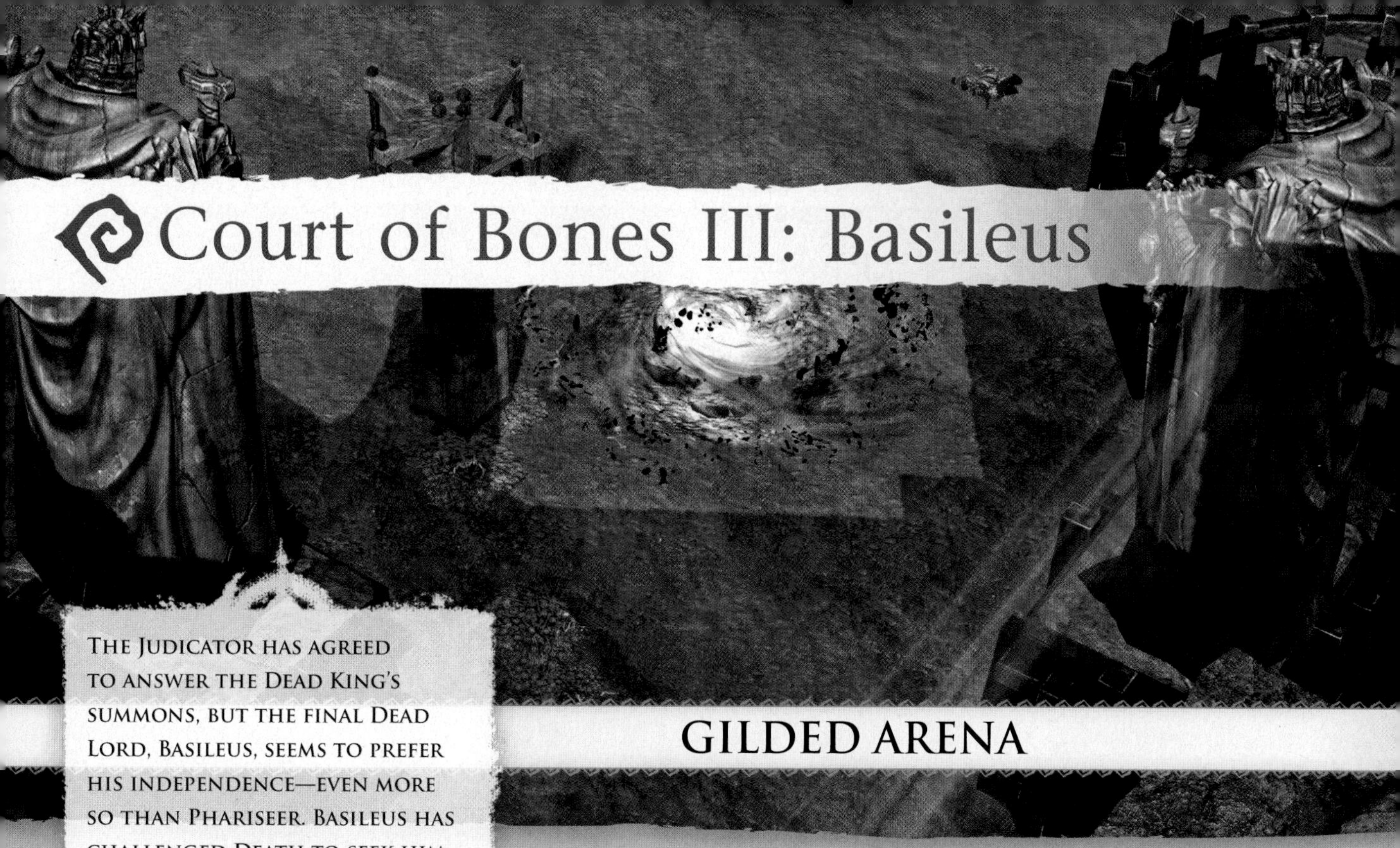

The Judicator has agreed to answer the Dead King's summons, but the final Dead Lord, Basileus, seems to prefer his independence—even more so than Phariseer. Basileus has challenged Death to seek him out within the Psychameron: a lethal labyrinth that's home to all manner of horrific beings. If the Pale Rider can survive the Psychameron's twisted depths, the final Dead Lord will be his to command...

GILDED ARENA

Return to the Gilded Arena and speak with the voices that once beckoned to Death within the arena proper. They agree to allow the Rider passage into the Psychameron, and waste little time in opening a portal, which Death quickly enters.

The Keeper of Secrets
The Fire of the Mountain
The Tears of the Mountain
To Move a Mountain
The Heart of the Mountain
The Tree of Life
The Kingdom of the Dead
The Toll of Kings
Court of Bones I: Phariseer
Court of Bones II: Judicator
Court of Bones III: Basileus
The City of the Dead
The Key to Redemption
The Rod of Arafel
Stains of Heresy
The Lord of the Black Stone
The Well of Souls

INTRODUCTION
EXPLORATION AND COMBAT
SKILLS AND COMBOS
WALKTHROUGH
SIDE QUESTS AND AREAS
APPENDIX
BEHIND THE SCENES

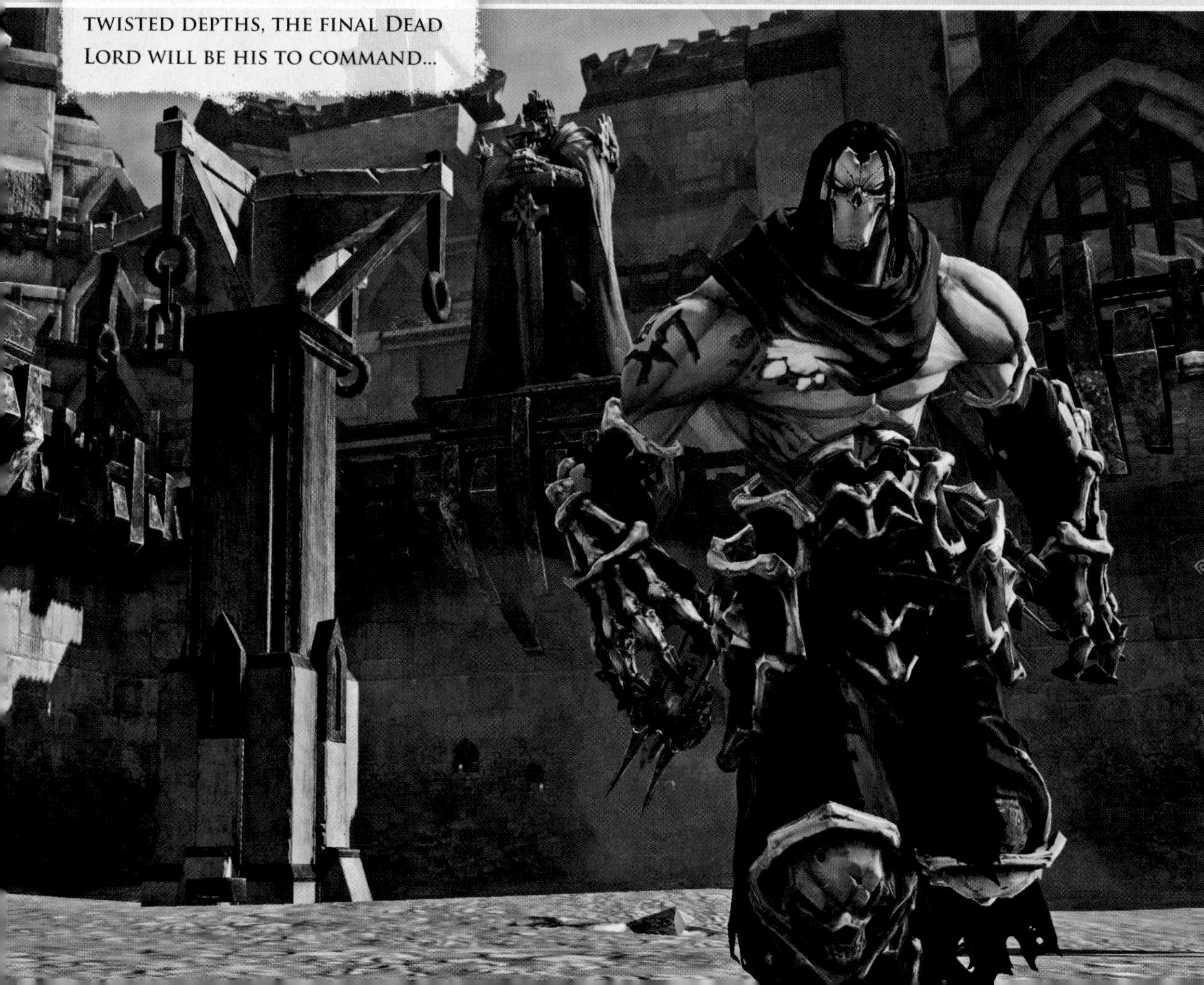

Few would dare to brave the epic depths of this twisted underworld maze.

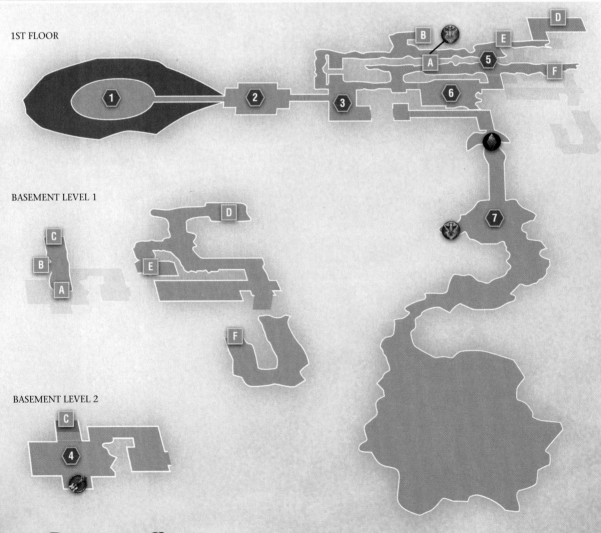

1ST FLOOR

BASEMENT LEVEL 1

BASEMENT LEVEL 2

Area 1: Arena

As soon as the Reaper enters the Psychameron, he's plunged into a frantic battle against not one, but *two* Undead Stalkers. This is the most challenging battle Death has faced thus far, so don't hold back. Focus on slaying one of the Stalkers, and then work at cutting down the other. Remember that Undead Stalkers attack with great ferocity as they near death, so avoid weakening both creatures at once. Strive to damage only one at a time.

> **CAUTION**
>
> Undead Prowlers appear after the first Stalker falls. Kill them all, and then focus on slaying the remaining Stalker.

Area 2: Lift

If you survive the undead ambush, proceed through the east door to reach a small chamber with a Summoning Circle. Call forth the Dead Lords and then climb the south wall to reach a chest on the ledge above.

Next, stand in the east nook and order your remaining Dead Lord to trigger the north pressure plate. This causes the floor beneath you to rise, delivering Death up to a higher passage. Proceed through the east door.

Area 3: Puzzling Passages—West

Slay a few Scarabs as you enter these mind-bending passages. Use the Summoning Circle near the entry to summon your Dead Lords, and then begin the process of navigating this confusing area.

Order one Dead Lord to stand on the nearby pressure plate, extending a bridge to the north.

Cross the bridge and order the other Dead Lord to trigger the pressure plate beyond the north gate. This removes the gate, allowing Death to advance.

Pass through the gate, and then order both Dead Lords to step off of their pressure plates. Run east and order one Dead Lord to trigger the pressure plate across the chasm, which exposes a chest.

TIP

If you make a mistake beyond this point, simply scale the west wall and take the west passage back to the Summoning Circle at the entry.

Leap toward the Dead Lord and Deathgrip him to zip over to the chest. Claim your plunder, and then look down into the chasm you've just crossed and notice a low gate.

With the low gate gone, leap toward the Dead Lord and Deathgrip him to zip into the lower passage.

Look for the pressure plate beyond the low gate and command your remaining Dead Lord to activate it. He'll do so after a bit of traveling.

Explore the passage, cross a Banishing Field, and leap to the wall post beyond. Slide down to an even lower passage that leads into a new area.

Area 4: Key Chamber

Summon your Dead Lords at the circle in this chamber, and then order one to trigger the middle of three switches on the high east balcony. Trigger the right switch next, followed by the left, in order to gain access to the room's ornate chest. Rip it open to acquire a Skeleton Key.

SKELETON KEY

CAUTION

Activating the switches in the wrong order causes skeletal enemies to materialize all around you.

NOTE

You can't reach the other two chests in this area without the ability to travel through portals. You won't gain this ability for quite some time.

Back to the Passages

Backtrack out of the chamber and scale the wall post to return to the passages above. Glance up to notice a high hoop, and Deathgrip it to vault up to a small ledge where a lost Relic awaits. Drop down from the ledge to land near a locked door, and then head through it.

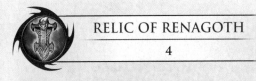

RELIC OF RENAGOTH

4

Area 5: Puzzling Passages—East

Call forth your Dead Lords at the circle beyond the locked door, and then order one to trigger the nearby pressure plate. This extends a nearby bridge.

With the Dead Lord in place, wall-run to a hand hold, and then shimmy to the right. Perform a 180 leap from the final hand hold to reach a hanging post.

Run east and spy another pressure plate on the south passage. Order your remaining Dead Lord to trigger this plate, and the nearby gate will open.

Slide down the post, and then 180 leap toward the Dead Lord. Deathgrip the Lord to zip into the lower passage.

Before exploring beyond the gate, order the first Dead Lord to step off of his pressure plate. Move past the gate and order the Lord to trigger a lower, distant pressure plate to the north.

Command the Dead Lord to step off of the pressure plate, and then explore the passage. Raid a pair of chests on your way to another pressure plate.

Order the Dead Lord to trigger the plate, and move beyond the gate it lowers. Push the switch there to extend a bridge across the nearby chasm.

Cross the bridge and cut down Scarabs as you climb the stairs. You emerge near the second Dead Lord; leave him be and enter the nearby south door.

Area 6: Brutal Ambush

The door leads into a square chamber. Ensure you're prepared for a challenging battle before using the central Summoning Circle to call forth your Dead Lords, for doing so triggers a deadly ambush. First, you face four Skeletal Warriors, followed by a lone Bone Giant, and then finally, a pair of Undead Scarab Hulks. It is fortunate that you have the aid of the Dead Lords to help you battle these dangerous brutes!

> **TIP**
>
> Summon the Dead Lords again each time they're slain. Use Harvest to clear foes away from the central Summoning Circle, or distract them with Exhume's ghouls.

ENEMY: UNDEAD SCARAB HULK

Class: Brute

Scarabs don't come any bigger or deadlier than this. Use extreme caution when fighting an Undead Scarab Hulk, for they have far greater health and attack power than their purple-shelled peers. Their fast, far-reaching attacks remain largely the same, but land with even greater impact. Do your best to avoid each strike, and be quick to counter with effective skills and combos.

Proceed through the west door after cutting down the Undead Scarab Hulks. You find yourself back at the west side of the Puzzling Passages. Wall-run across the south pit to reach a switch, and then push it to extend the nearby bridge leading back to the entry. There's no need to cross the bridge, however. Advance through the east door instead.

> **TIP**
>
> Consider fast traveling to the *Eternal Throne* and restocking your potions at this point. The Psychameron's final battle lies ahead, and it will put Death's skills to the ultimate test.

Area 7: Path of Shadows

After navigating a hallway and passing through a door, turn around and blast the Stonebite above the door's opposite side. Cross the bridge ahead afterward, and then search the landing on the right to discover a lost Relic. Continue following the passage until you reach a large, dark cavern where the final challenge awaits.

STONE OF MYSTICS
23

RELIC OF ETU-GOTH
9

BOSS BATTLE: BASILEUS AND ACHIDNA

The final Dead Lord makes his stand against Death within this shadowy cavern. Basileus's attacks are difficult to predict and evade, so focus on doling out fast damage instead. Skills such as Unstoppable can aid you in this effort, while Aegis Guard can help you withstand Basileus's aggressive onslaught.

After losing significant health, Basileus calls upon a monstrous ally: an overgrown spider known as Achidna. Although the creature is enormous, Achidna's attacks aren't as powerful as Basileus's. Leap to avoid damage when the monster slams the ground, and evade its lunging strikes as you look for openings through which you can pile on the damage.

It's not long before Death manages to rip Basileus off of Achidna's back, reverting the battle to its initial stage. Face off against the Dead Lord again, doing your best to avoid his lightning-fast attacks as you unleash powerful skills at every chance. This is a good time to call upon Death's Reaper Form if you haven't already.

◈ CAUTION

Achidna will periodically drop in and slam the ground in a surprise ambush. Listen for her chittering and be prepared to jump and avoid this nasty attack.

When Basileus is left with only a fraction of his health, he summons Achidna once more. Go on the offensive and finish off the eight-legged fiend, and Basileus will be left with no choice but to yield. Pleased with his handiwork, Death takes a moment to fashion a powerful new weapon from the remains of his latest quarry.

ACHIDNA'S FANGS

◈ SIDE QUEST ADVANCED: ◈
"FIND AND KILL ACHIDNA"

The Dead King's Wrath

With nothing left to accomplish within the Psychameron, fast-travel back to the *Eternal Throne* and present the Lord of Bones with his three wayward servants. The Dead King is not merciful toward his subjects and wastes no time in reducing the Dead Lords to ashes. Pleased to have his revenge, the Lord of Bones keeps his word to the Rider. He informs Death that one with knowledge on how to reach the Well of Souls lies beyond the City of the Dead, and grants Death the power he needs to enter and explore his kingdom's greatest citadel.

SOUL SPLITTER

TIP

If you've previously visited the City of the Dead, simply fast travel there to carry on with Death's quest. If you haven't been to the city's gates, fast travel to the Judicator's Tomb instead, and then ride north across the bridge.

SOUL SPLITTER EXCURSIONS

Now that you've acquired the Soul Splitter, you're able to revisit a few areas and claim some bonus loot before tackling the Kingdom of the Dead's final dungeon. Here's the rundown—refer to the "Side Quests and Areas" chapter for further details:

The Fjord's East Keep: Travel back to the Forge Lands and use the Soul Splitter to divide Death into two souls. Use his physical form and one soul to trigger the keep's two pressure plates, then use the remaining soul to claim a Book of the Dead Page from the upper balcony, along with a special chest that appears after you smash all four of the balcony's pots.

Leviathan's Gorge Underbelly: Fast travel to the Breach's north entrance and go west toward the gate that connects to Leviathan's Gorge's west valley. Don't pass through the gate, but navigate the nearby wall's hand holds and posts instead to reach the Gorge's underbelly. Destroy the Corruption crystals and traverse the overhead hoops to reach a pair of pressure plates, then trigger them to access a chest. Blast a Stonebite on the high wall near the chest afterward.

Breach Chest: Return to the Breach and raid the chest in the pressure plate passage. Split Death's soul and leave one on the plate, then use the other soul to loot the chest.

The Maw's Northwest Ruin: Return to the Maw's northwest ruin (across from Sentinel's Gaze) and split Death's soul to trigger the pressure plates and access the chests here.

Sentinel's Gaze and Boneriven: Now's a good time to revisit Sentinel's Gaze, located just southeast of the Maw's T-shaped bridge. This underground ruin leads to a sizeable side dungeon called Boneriven, and the Soul Splitter is required to get there. See the "Side Quests and Areas" chapter for a complete walkthrough.

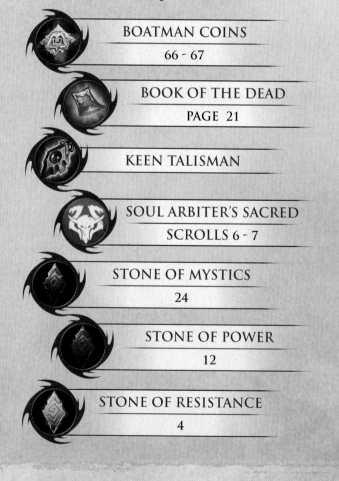

BOATMAN COINS
66 - 67

BOOK OF THE DEAD
PAGE 21

KEEN TALISMAN

SOUL ARBITER'S SACRED
SCROLLS 6 - 7

STONE OF MYSTICS
24

STONE OF POWER
12

STONE OF RESISTANCE
4

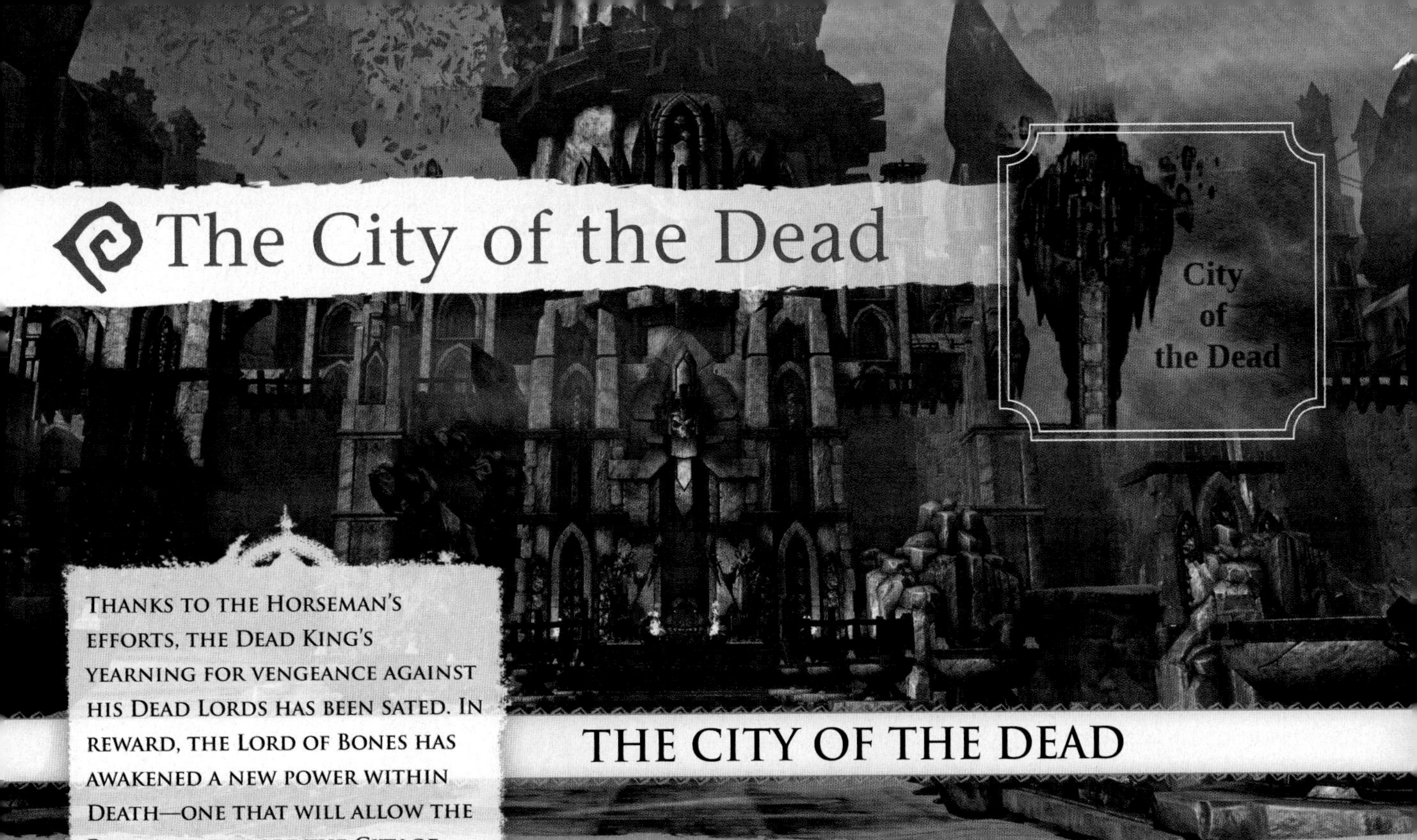

The City of the Dead

THANKS TO THE HORSEMAN'S EFFORTS, THE DEAD KING'S YEARNING FOR VENGEANCE AGAINST HIS DEAD LORDS HAS BEEN SATED. IN REWARD, THE LORD OF BONES HAS AWAKENED A NEW POWER WITHIN DEATH—ONE THAT WILL ALLOW THE REAPER TO EXPLORE THE CITY OF THE DEAD. THE ANSWERS DEATH SEEKS ARE RUMORED TO BE FOUND WITHIN THIS ANCIENT CITADEL... BUT SO ARE COUNTLESS HORRORS.

THE CITY OF THE DEAD

This sprawling underworld city must be explored, for the secrets of accessing the Well of Souls lie somewhere within.

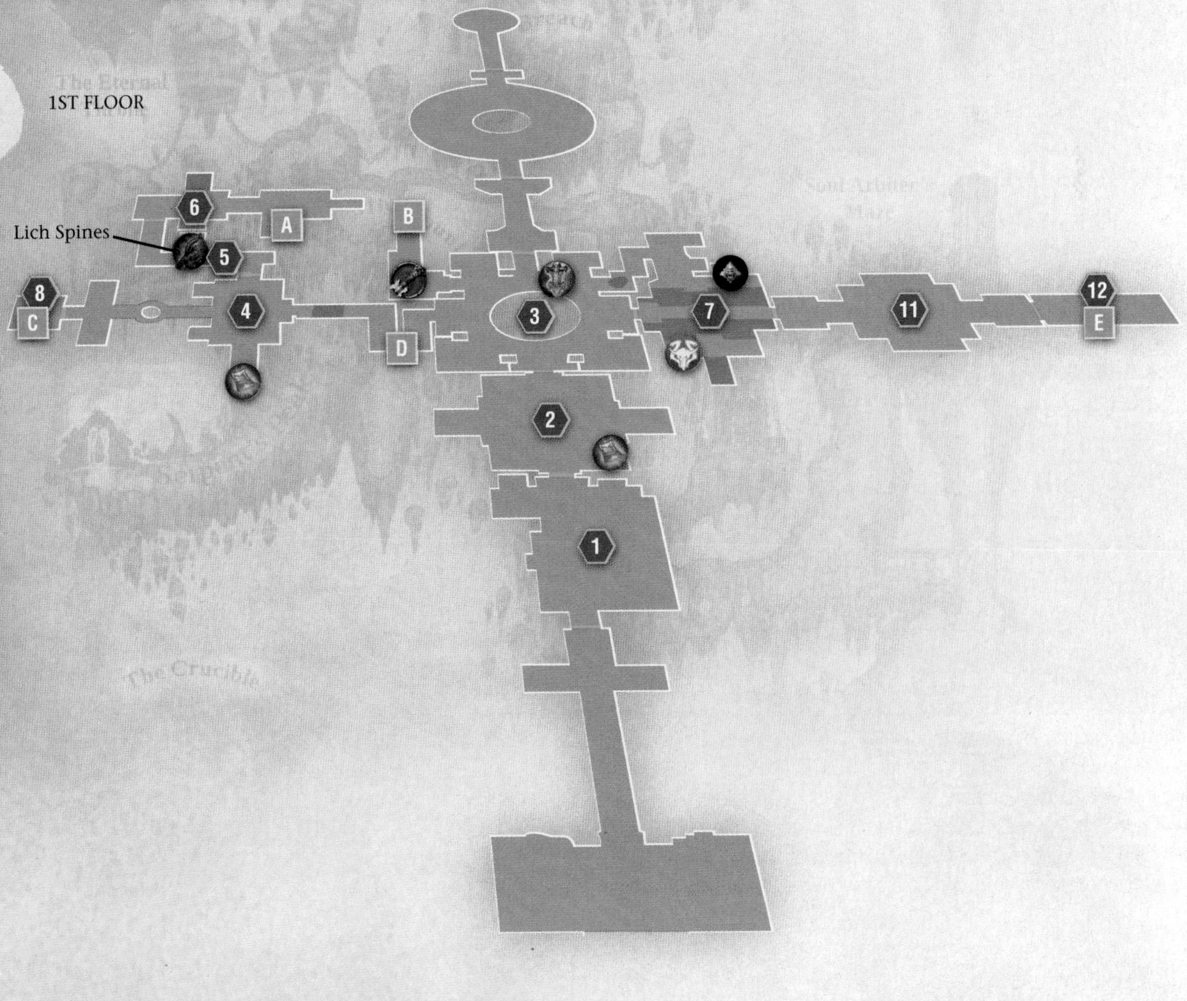

1ST FLOOR

Lich Spines

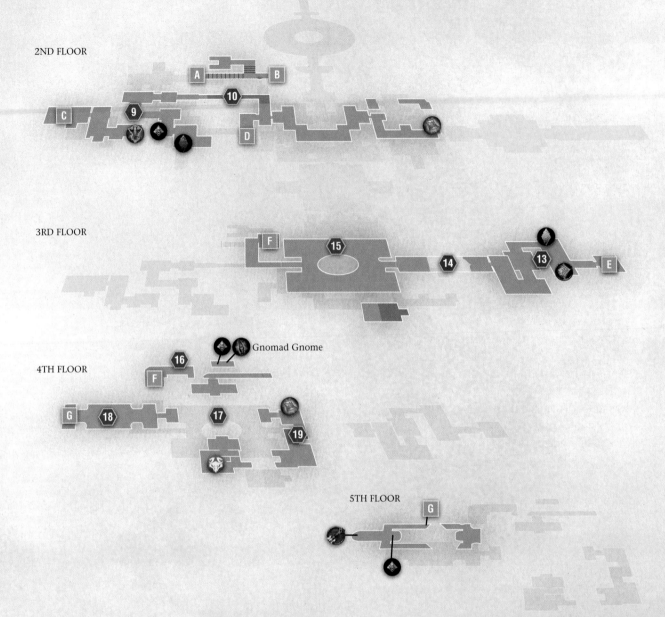

2ND FLOOR

3RD FLOOR

Gnomad Gnome

4TH FLOOR

5TH FLOOR

Entering the City

Approach the city's front gate, and use your newfound Soul Splitter ability to split Death into two ghostly spirits, with his physical form remaining in place as a stone statue. Grab one of the nearby statues with one soul and slide it away from the gate, and then hold the Action button to assume control of the second soul. Slide the remaining statue away from the gate as well to open the way forward.

Area 1: Entry Plaza

Squash Scarabs in the area beyond the main gate, and then raid the northwest chest before proceeding through the north door.

Area 2: Champion Square

Slay a pair of Skeletal Champions in this square, and then face off against the Undead General that appears after the first Champion falls. Claim a Book of the Dead page from the area's southeast corner. Then, split Death's soul and have one spirit stand on the northeast pressure plate. Doing so lowers the gate that was surrounding the northwest pressure plate. Now switch to the other soul and stand on the northwest plate. This lowers an overhead gate. Switch to the other soul and scale the west wall to reach the switch that opens the north door.

BOOK OF THE DEAD

PAGE 22

Area 3: Central Plaza

Cut down a few ghostly Skeletons in this spacious plaza, which features a large central pit. Search near the sealed north door to discover a lost Relic. The east door is locked, so proceed into the west passage, smashing a few more Skeletons and wall-running past a pit on your way to the next area.

> **CAUTION**
> Beware of smashing crates in the city—
> some contain angry Scarabs!

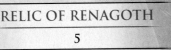

RELIC OF RENAGOTH

5

Area 4: Statue Room

A lantern-less statue greets you in this area, but there's little to accomplish here at present. Venture on through the north door.

Area 5: Crumbling Corridor

Scale this hall's hand holds and wall-run to reach a post. 180 leap to another post, and then circle around and wall-run over to a tantalizing prize. This unique pair of weapons are known as the Lich Spines. Advance through the door at the passage's end after claiming your new gear.

LICH SPINES

Area 6: Lever Puzzle

Split Death's soul in this room, and then use one spirit to spin the central lever and lower the east gate.

Turn the lever again, and then switch to the other soul and pull the platform past the east gate to bypass this obstacle.

Switch to the other soul and run past the gate, collecting a Shadowbomb from the room's east side.

Backtrack through the gate and toss the bomb at the north switch to trigger it. This exposes a nearby moveable platform.

Return to Death's physical form and jump onto the platform. Split his soul once more, so that his statue form stands atop the platform.

Chest Quest

Return to Death's physical form and stand on one of the two pressure plates beyond the gate before splitting Death's soul again. Move one spirit onto the neighboring plate to lower the east gate, and then use the other spirit to raid the chest beyond.

Proceed up the nearby stairs and raid another chest, and then drop down through a hole in the stairwell to reach a lower passage, where two more chests are located. One of these contains a Skeleton Key.

 SKELETON KEY

Press the switch near the key chest to open the nearby gate, and then pass through to return to the Central Plaza. Use your newfound key to open the east door.

Area 7: Rotating Bridge

Move to the middle of this room's central bridge and split Death's soul there. Deathgrip the nearby wall hoop afterward to spring up to a hand hold and shimmy around the corner.

Collect a Book of the Dead page from the balcony's east end, and then spin the central lever to rotate the bridge below.

Drop down to solid ground and examine the writing on the nearby wall to gain a Soul Arbiter's Scroll.

BOOK OF THE DEAD
PAGE 23

Switch to Death's other soul and sprint north across the bridge. Claim a Boatman Coin from an alcove, and then climb the nearby wall growth and swing from a ceiling hoop to reach a chest.

SOUL ARBITER'S SCROLL
6

Next, use another hand hold to enter the south passage, which has no floor. Leap between the passage's narrow walls to reach the balcony above.

BOATMAN COIN
68

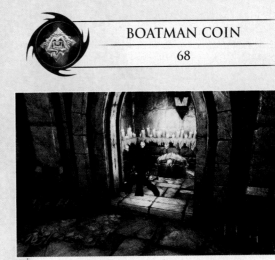

Drop down to the ground and smash the Scarabs in the north passage. Raid a chest in an alcove before continuing on your way to a switch. Push it to remove a gate in the Central Plaza, exposing a lantern.

Lantern Run

Return to your physical form and backtrack to the Central Plaza. Deathgrip the lantern in the northeast alcove, and then carry it through the west passage, heading back to the Statue Room. Set the lantern down when you reach the passage's pit, wall-run across, and Deathgrip the lantern from the other side.

Place the lantern in the statue's hand, spin the statue, and use its beam of light to open the south passage. Claim a Book of the Dead page from within, and then spin the statue to the west to extend a bridge. Cross over and proceed through the west door.

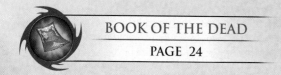

BOOK OF THE DEAD

PAGE 24

Area 8: Exterior Rampart

Climb the wall growth, and then wall-run between the nearby hand holds.

Perform a 180 leap from the final hand hold, and then Deathgrip the distant hoop to reach more growth.

Climb around the corner and wall-run to a post, jumping the corner along the way.

Drop down from the post to reach solid ground, and then crack open the nearby chest before advancing through the east door.

Area 9: Wraith Gates

A pair of deadly Wraiths guard this gate-filled area. Slay them both, split Death's soul at the corner of the L-shaped bridge, and then work at solving this area's puzzle.

Have one spirit scale the nearby wall and land on a pressure lever. The lever lowers, banishing the east gate.

Have one soul pull the south lever to rotate the L-shaped bridge. Be sure to collect the Relic that's tucked away near the south wall, opposite from the lever.

Switch to the other soul and collect a Shadowbomb from the west pod.

RELIC OF ETU-GOTH
10

Head east and toss the bomb at the northeast switch to lower the gate near the pressure lever.

Return to the Reaper's physical form, and then immediately split Death's soul again to regroup his two spirits.

Run south until you reach a small balcony where two Wraiths guard a chest and Stonebite. Secure the area, and then claim your valuables.

STONE OF POWER
13

Backtrack a bit and scale the south passage's growth. Perform a 180 leap from the end of the growth to snatch a hovering Boatman Coin. Return to physical form and proceed through the northeast door.

BOATMAN COIN
69

Area 10: Pitfall Passage

Make a daring wall-run to navigate this bottomless passage, leaping between its narrow walls to extend your run around the corner. Push the switch at the passage's end to open the nearby door, and then head through.

> **NOTE**
> Dropping down into the south pit returns you to the Central Plaza's west passage, but there's no need to do so right now.

Balcony Antics

Cross the Central Plaza's upper balcony, and smash the clutter you pass on your way to the east door. Go through to find yourself back at the Rotating Bridge's upper level. Press the switch here to lower the nearby gate and unbar the lower east door. Descend the nearby stairs and jump the broken railing near the lever to quickly drop down to the bridge. Then, proceed east.

Area 11: Square of Torment

Death must survive a trying battle in this square. First, a trio of Wraiths ambush the Rider—slay two of these to summon an Undead General. Bring down the brute and a monstrous Tormentor will challenge you next. This hulking horror is similar to the Jailor you battled back at the Judicator's Tomb. Cut him down, and another Tormentor will enter the fray, followed by a third after the second Tormentor falls. Open the two east chests after you emerge victorious, and then proceed through the east door.

> **CAUTION**
> Stay evasive during this intense battle, but beware of becoming pinned in any of the square's four corners.

ENEMY: TORMENTOR

Class: Brute

Tormentors are huge, horrific, and capable of lashing out with surprising speed and ferocity. They commonly strike with their massive hooked arm first, and then follow up with a crushing shoulder blow. Evade in a circle around Tormentors to avoid their swift attacks, and then counter sharply after you dodge. These hulking brutes can dish it out, but they can't take it—use powerful skills to bring them crashing down fast.

Area 12: Furnace

Scale this chamber's north wall and wall-run to the right until you reach a pressure lever. Landing on this lever causes a fiery floor to rise from the depths below, giving Death only a brief window to scale the room and reach the ledge above.

> **CAUTION**
>
> There's no room for error while climbing this chamber, so try not to make any mistakes!

Immediately wall-run up to a hand hold, and then wall-run again to the left and shimmy around the corner.

Wall-run to the left again and jump the corner to reach another hand hold. Vault off of the two pegs above to gain some height.

Again, wall-run to the left and jump the corner to reach a hand hold. Drop down from this one to reach the hand hold below it, and then shimmy around the corner and wall-run to the left peg.

Vault from the peg to reach another hand hold, and then quickly vault off of the peg above it to reach a higher hand hold.

Wall-run to the neighboring hand hold on the right, and then Deathgrip the hoop above to bound up to a higher hand hold.

Make a long wall-run to the right, shimmy around the first corner, jump the second corner, and shimmy around the third corner.

Deathgrip another overhead hoop to soar up to a high hand hold before shimmying to the left and climbing out of the pit. Catch your breath and pull the nearby lever to unlock the west door and proceed through it.

Area 13: Exterior Walkways

Death's respite doesn't last long, for an Undead Stalker and several Undead Prowlers ambush the Rider in this area. Slay the Prowlers first, and be very careful not to become cornered during this battle—especially once the Stalker goes berserk as its health nears depletion.

Shoot the Stonebite on the tall north tower after the battle, and then wall-run to the tiny south ledge. Open the ornate chest to at last obtain the Dungeon Map.

STONE OF RESISTANCE
5

DUNGEON MAP

Wall-run back to the walkways and scale the stairs. Two hulking Abominations assault you on your way to the west door. Unleash Death's skills to speedily cut down these dangerous adversaries, as their attacks are quite powerful.

ENEMY: ABOMINATION

Class: Brute

Although these grotesque fiends move slowly, they wield a number of deadly ranged attacks. Abominations commonly spew poisonous vomit that inflicts significant damage—evade in a circle to dodge these deadly attacks. These brutes also emit a short-range aura that poisons Death when he draws near. Keep away from Abominations and use skills such as Teleport Slash and Exhume to damage them from a safe distance. Should their poisonous auras fade, Deathgrip into close range and let loose with lethal combos.

Just beyond the Abominations, a trio of Liches materialize and strike. Make liberal use of the Deathgrip to stun these summoners, and focus on cutting down each one in turn. Proceed through the west door after surviving this third and final encounter.

Area 14: Pit of Bone

Drop into this chamber's central pit and raid the far chest before using the east wall growth to climb back out. Wall-run to a corner post, and then perform a number of 180 leaps to cross the pit via the posts. Proceed through the west door.

Area 15: Upper Plaza

A light-emitting statue catches Death's eye as he enters this wide area, but the statue's hanging platform is too high to reach. There's nothing else of interest here, so simply advance through the west door.

Area 16: Northwest Balcony

Deathgrip this small room's south hoop to soar up the wall and jump at the height of your climb to reach a hanging post.

Wall-run to the right twice, crossing another hand hold and landing near a switch. Push it to unbar the south door.

180 leap to the next post, jump over to the hand hold on the east wall, and run to the left to reach a high balcony.

Wall-run back across the hand holds. Stop on the first one, and then switch to the other soul and step off of the pressure plate. This causes the hand hold to flip around, delivering the hanging soul to a secret area.

Split Death's soul, leaving one of them on the balcony's pressure plate. Have the other soul Deathgrip the north hoop to soar up to a hand hold.

When entering this passage, smash the crates in the alcove near the stairwell to expose a hidden Boatman Coin. Navigate the passage on your way to a large chest. Collect the Gnome figurine as well, which pertains to a side quest.

BOATMAN COIN
70

GNOMAD GNOME
1

SIDE QUEST ACQUIRED:
"GNOMAD'S GNOMES"

Revert to physical form after looting the secret passage, split Death's soul again, and then leave one spirit on the pressure plate. Have the other soul cross the south wall's hand holds to reach a chest. Return to physical form afterward and proceed through the south door.

Area 17: Upper Plaza Ledges

Push a switch to lower the nearby gate, and then Deathgrip the overhead hoop to swing to the central hanging platform. You've reached the light-emitting statue, but Corruption crystals are preventing you from activating its switch. Grab and spin the statue, angling its light westward to unbar the west door. Deathgrip another overhead hoop to swing over and head through.

Area 18: Scarab Den

This spacious chamber is home to a host of Scarabs, including a fearsome Undead Scarab Hulk. Evade and use anti-group attacks and skills to slay the swarming Scarabs, but focus mainly on cutting down the larger Undead Scarab Hulk. Two more Undead Scarab Hulks materialize after the first one falls; use evasive maneuvers to avoid damage as you tackle this deadly duo.

Grab a Shadowbomb from the south pod after the battle and use it to obliterate the north Corruption crystals. Scale the exposed wall growth to reach a higher balcony, and raid the west chest to obtain a Skeleton Key.

SKELETON KEY

Deathgrip across the overhead hoops afterward to reach the east chest, and then swing back across the hoops to claim a floating Boatman Coin. Backtrack to the Upper Plaza Ledges afterward, and drop down to the Upper Plaza area below. Scale the east wall's pegs to return to the Upper Plaza Ledges, and use your newfound key to open the locked east door.

BOATMAN COIN
71

Area 19: Burial Passages

Smash the crates as you enter this winding passage to discover a lost page of the Book of the Dead.

Before rounding the next corner, turn and wall-run back the way you came. Shimmy around a corner to reach a small ledge with a chest.

BOOK OF THE DEAD
PAGE 25

Shimmy around a corner and wall-run across the pit that follows.

Wall-run back through the passage until you reach a post, and then slide down to solid ground. Notice the moveable platform just beyond a gate, and then drop to a lower area containing two pressure plates.

Scale the north wall when you reach the next pit and wall-run to the left. Round a corner, and then wall-run and jump to the hand hold on the opposite wall.

Stand on one of the plates and split Death's soul. Move one soul onto the other plate and scale the wall with the remaining soul.

You can now reach the moveable platform. Inspect the nearby wall to obtain a Soul Arbiter's Sacred Scroll, and then slide the platform as far east as possible.

Use the remaining soul to slide the platform to the west until another gate blocks your progress. Toggle back to the lower soul and move him onto the right plate to lower this final obstacle.

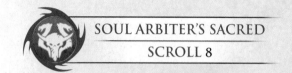

SOUL ARBITER'S SACRED SCROLL 8

Return to physical form and climb onto the moveable platform. Split Death's soul again and send one soul back down to trigger the left pressure plate.

Shove the moveable platform onto the pressure plate beyond the second gate to unbar the nearby door. Revert to physical form and go through.

Upper Plaza Ledges, Revisited

Push the south ledge's switch to lower its gate, and then grab a Shadowbomb from the nearby pod. Hurl the bomb at the light-emitting statue's Corruption crystals to at last destroy them. Then, swing from the overhead hoop to reach the central platform.

Press the statue's switch to cause the hanging platform to lower like an elevator. The platform comes to a rest back in the Central Plaza; angle its beam to the north to unbar the north door, and then go through to advance to the final battle.

 TIP

As always, consider returning to the *Eternal Throne* and stocking up on potions before engaging the boss.

BOSS BATTLE: THE WAILING HOST

A titanic fiend awaits the Horseman in the city's final area. This great devourer of souls must be defeated before the Reaper can uncover the secrets he seeks.

The Wailing Host commonly attacks by slamming the ground with its massive fist, and then swiping back and forth with its arm. The first swipe will hit Death if he's too close to the monster, while the second will hit him if he's too far away. Tap the Evade trigger to backflip away from the Host and avoid the first blow, then evade into close range to dodge the second before returning to attacking the boss.

Sometimes the Wailing Host will smash the ground before it with both forearms. Again, tap the Evade trigger to backflip and avoid this punishing attack, and then quickly close in and attack the arms to score damage before they rise.

The Host will periodically vanish and summon a horde of ghostly Skeletons. This is the perfect time to fill up Death's Wrath meter, along with his health bar if you possess gear that heals the Reaper after each kill. Slaughter all of the Skeletons to make the Host reappear, and then repeat your previous strategies.

When the Host collapses, quickly close in and press the Action button to deliver a nasty attack that rips its mask off. It won't be long now before the great fiend meets its demise.

Having slain the Wailing Host and conquered the City of the Dead, the Rider is surprised to find none other than the Crowfather awaiting him in the following chamber. He informs the rider that two keys are needed to enter the Well of Souls—one possessed by the Angels, and the other kept by the Demons. The Crowfather also reveals information about the spread of Corruption, and tells the Reaper to meet him at the Tree of Death when he's ready to begin his search for the first key.

When you've finished speaking with the Crowfather, fast travel to the Tree of Death to meet him there and speak with the specter yet again. Proceed through the northeast portal afterward to begin your search for the Angel's key.

DEATH TOMB II

If you've been following this walkthrough carefully, then you've already acquired over 20 Book of the Dead pages. This means you're able to trade the second Book of the Dead chapter to Vulgrim for a special key that grants access to the second Death Tomb. Obtain the key from Vulgrim, and then make your way down to the bottom of the Lair of the Deposed King by simply descending its long, spiral staircase. Use Vulgrim's key to open the colorful basement door, enter the Death Tomb, and claim its hoard of plunder.

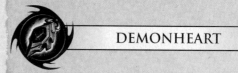

DEMONHEART

THE CRUCIBLE, PART II

You receive a new Tarot Card after you defeat the Wailing Host. Use this to participate in the next 25 stages of the Crucible. Clear them all and you'll receive a special prize.

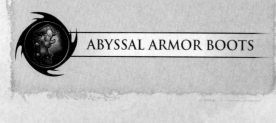

ABYSSAL ARMOR BOOTS

The Key to Redemption

The Ivory Citadel

The Crystal Spire

The Crucible

Though it was not his original intent, the Horseman has purged the Forge Lands of Corruption and passed through the Kingdom of the Dead unscathed. Now, the Rider must journey to the realm of angels in search of a special key—one of two keys needed to gain entry to the Well of Souls.

This tranquil realm is home to angels, but it has known turmoil in recent times.

To the Crystal Spire

Chat with the Crowfather as you exit the Tree of Life, and then ride north toward a distant tower known as the Crystal Spire. Along the way, explore a side passage to your right where you can raid a chest and visit with the demonic merchant, Vulgrim. Search behind the brush near Vulgrim to discover a lost Relic.

RELIC OF ETU-GOTH
11

You soon reach a long stone bridge that leads to the Crystal Spire. Collect a Book of the Dead page from the nearby ruin to your right (south) before venturing across.

BOOK OF THE DEAD
PAGE 26

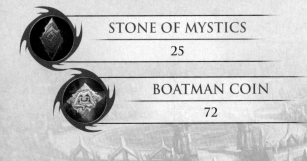

Return to the main trail and notice the colorful door of a Death Tomb farther north. You don't have enough Book of the Dead pages to open this door, but don't let that stop you from shooting the Stonebite above it. Snag the Boatman Coin that's tucked away behind the brush to the left, as well.

STONE OF MYSTICS
25

BOATMAN COIN
72

Fallen Angels

A host of Corrupted Angels ambushes Death after he crosses the stone bridge. Beware of their vicious melee blows and ranged attacks as you fight to cut them all down. Call upon abilities and use potions as you see fit—you'll soon be able to replenish your supply.

Speak with Nathaniel after the battle to learn more about the plague of Corruption that has befallen Lostlight. The honored Hellguard also wishes to aid Death in his quest by offering him a small selection of fine wares. Nathaniel also bestows you with a side quest that involves bringing a special scroll back to the Kingdom of the Dead.

ENEMY: CORRUPTED ANGEL

Class: Soldier

These once holy souls have fallen victim to Corruption and now seek to destroy anything that threatens the insidious substance's spread. Corrupted Angels move with swift grace and strike with great fury, and they're also able to fire from afar. This makes them particularly dangerous in groups. Stay mobile to avoid being surrounded, and focus on slaying each Angel in turn.

NATHANIEL'S SCROLL

SIDE QUEST ACQUIRED: "THE LOST SOUL"

Angelic Aid

More Corrupted Angels appear after the first few fall, but Death is also aided by the timely appearance of a powerful Hellguard named Nathaniel. Corruption has not touched this noble warrior. Fight hard at Nathaniel's side and slay the Corrupted host.

Scouring the Grounds

Begin exploring the Crystal Spire's grounds after speaking with Nathaniel. Collect the Boatman Coin that hovers close by.

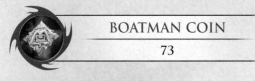

BOATMAN COIN

73

ENEMY: VENGEFUL SPIRIT

Class: Fodder

These small, spiteful spirits hover around the Horseman before striking with surprising speed. Keep your distance and make short work of these lowly foes with Redemption.

Circle around the tower afterward, heading southeast. Shoot the Stonebite affixed to a statue's sword.

STONE OF MYSTICS

26

Continue past the chest and search the far east nook to discover a lost Relic.

RELIC OF RENAGOTH

6

Continue circling around the tower and raid the far chest. Beware: a number of Vengeful Spirits materialize after you rip the chest open.

Backtrack toward Nathaniel and explore to the north. Shoot another Stonebite attached to a statue's sword.

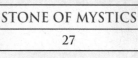

STONE OF MYSTICS

27

This holy tower is home to the Archon, a mighty angel who peers into the darkness and records all that he sees.

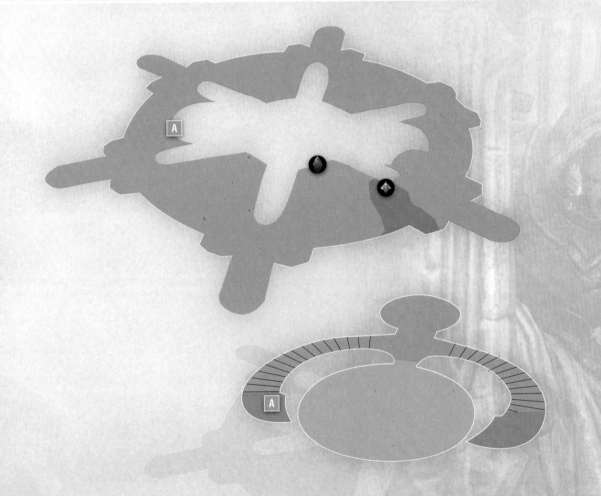

Exploring the Spire

After fully plundering the outer grounds, enter the Crystal Spire and pull the interior lever to ride up to its first floor. Slay a few Corrupted Angels on the balcony, and then circle around the north Corruption crystals to discover a chest.

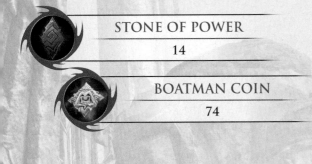

Circle back around the balcony and blast the Stonebite above a statue on the tower's wall. Drop down into the nearby crevasse afterward to snag a Boatman Coin.

STONE OF POWER
14

BOATMAN COIN
74

Catch the Shadowbomb

Climb out of the crevasse and split Death's soul. Have one spirit scale the nearby wall and shimmy around the hand hold to cross the crevasse.

Collect a Shadowbomb from the pod on the other side, and then enter aiming mode and toss it over to Death's other spirit.

Switch souls and run north. Use the Shadowbomb to obliterate the crystals, and then scale the wall they were covering to reach the tower's apex.

The Archon

Death finds the Archon awaiting him at the top of the Spire. The mighty angel agrees to give the Rider the key he keeps, but only after Death journeys to Earth and obtains a powerful artifact known as the Rod of Arafel. This sacred item has the power to clear a path to the Ivory Citadel, where the Archon's key is kept. With little choice, the Horseman agrees to seek out the Rod.

Step outside after speaking with the Archon and descend the east stairs to locate a chest. Consider tackling Nathaniel's side quest at this point before plunging into the portal that the Archon has opened (see the sidebar).

NATHANIEL'S QUEST

Before going to Earth, you may wish to do a bit of fast-traveling to complete Nathaniel's side quest. This involves bringing his scroll to the Chancellor at the Eternal Throne, and then taking it to Muria at Tri-Stone. The Chancellor will ask you to retrieve an artifact from the Soul Arbiter's Maze, but the task is too difficult at this point in your journey and is better left until later. Muria, on the other hand, will ask Death to visit a side dungeon in the Forge Lands and defeat a powerful enemy there. This dungeon is called the Scar, and now is a good time to accomplish this task for the Forge Lands' humble shaman. See the "Side Quests and Areas" chapter for further details.

BOATMAN COINS
75 - 76

BOOK OF THE DEAD PAGE
27

STONE OF POWER
15

SIDE QUEST COMPLETE:
"LOST SOUL"

SIDE QUEST COMPLETE:
"SPARK OF LIFE"

SIDE QUEST ACQUIRED:
"THE CHANCELLOR'S QUARRY"

The Rod of Arafel

The Ivory Citadel

The Crystal Spire

The Crucible

DEATH HAS FOUGHT HIS WAY TO THE CRYSTAL SPIRE ONLY TO LEARN THAT THE KEY HE SEEKS ISN'T KEPT THERE. WORSE, CORRUPTION HAS TAKEN HOLD OF LOSTLIGHT, AND ONLY A MYSTERIOUS ARTIFACT CALLED THE ROD OF ARAFEL CAN CLEAR A PATH TO THE IVORY CITADEL, WHERE THE ARCHON'S KEY IS KEPT. WITH ONLY ONE PATH LEADING FORWARD, THE HORSEMAN TRAVELS TO EARTH BY WAY OF MAGIC PORTAL AND BEGINS HIS QUEST TO LOCATE THE LOST ROD...

EARTH

The advanced triggering of the apocalypse has left Earth in ruins. Angels and demons now wage war over possession of this fallen world.

1ST FLOOR

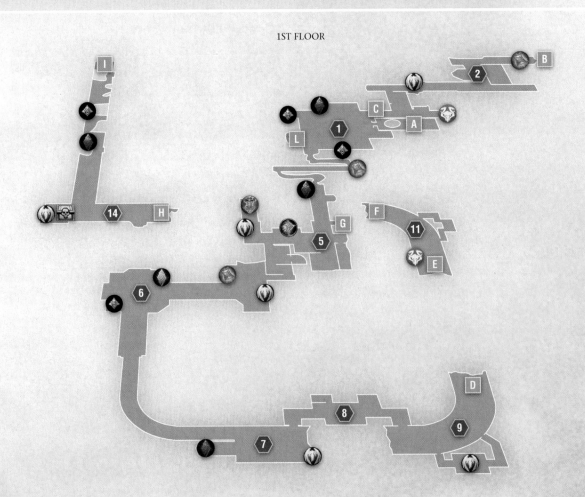

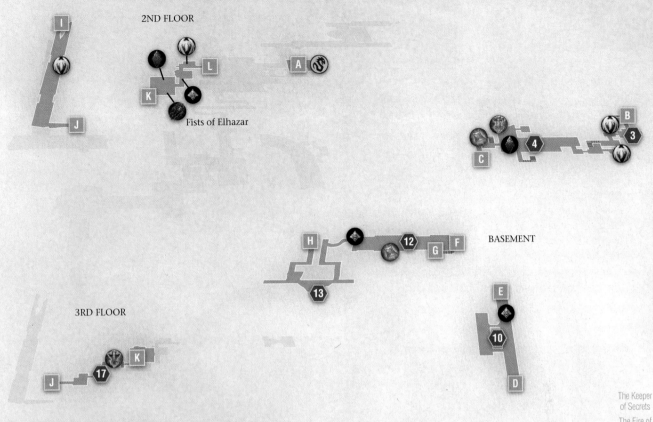

2ND FLOOR

Fists of Elhazar

BASEMENT

3RD FLOOR

Area 1: Courtyard

Death arrives on Earth just in time to help a Hellguard angel named Uriel battle a host of demons known as the Swarm. Hurry and collect the golden weapon in the southwest corner of the courtyard, which functions like a machine gun. The weapon is called Salvation. Simply press and hold the Special Item trigger to unleash rapid-fire lightning rounds against the Swarm.

CAUTION

Beware of overheating Salvation. Fire in controlled bursts and keep an eye on the upper-right heat gauge.

TIP

Press the Focus trigger to unleash more powerful blasts from Salvation. These are ideal for use against larger targets, such as Fleshbursters, as the impact staggers such foes.

ENEMY: THE SWARM

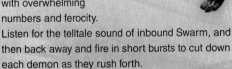

Class: Fodder

The Swarm is the generic term given to the demonic undead that have overrun Earth. The name is fitting, for these mindless, unarmed minions simply swarm their victims with overwhelming numbers and ferocity. Listen for the telltale sound of inbound Swarm, and then back away and fire in short bursts to cut down each demon as they rush forth.

ENEMY: FLESHBURSTER

Class: Soldier

These lethal demons pursue Death with the same single-minded fervor as the Swarm. Fleshbursters are far more dangerous, however, because they explode when they get close to the Reaper, inflicting massive damage. Don't let these fiends draw near; back away as you blast them with Salvation's powerful charged shots to keep them staggered.

Blast a car in the northwest alley to expose a Boatman Coin.

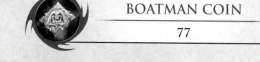

BOATMAN COIN

77

Uriel provides Death with information about the Rod of Arafel after the battle, revealing that it has been shattered into three pieces. Death must brave the city in order to locate all three and restore the Rod. Uriel also bestows a side quest on Death that involves slaying ten trapped angels around the city, thereby granting them peace.

Look up after claiming the coin and notice the Stonebite on a nearby building. Shoot this with Salvation to draw in the stone.

SIDE QUEST ACQUIRED:
"LIGHT OF THE FALLEN"

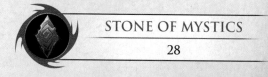

STONE OF MYSTICS

28

Courtyard Loot

Make a thorough sweep of the Courtyard area after speaking with Uriel, raiding a chest to the north and another to the south. A third chest lies on the second floor of the east building; use the stairs near the portal to find it.

Another Boatman Coin is found in the southern building, not far from the south chest.

BOATMAN COIN
78

Beware of the Swarm as you venture northeast. Slay them all, and then drop into the northeast pit to find a Soul Arbiter's Scroll. Enter the nearby building afterward to proceed north to the next area.

SOUL ARBITER'S SCROLL
7

Area 2: Northern Streets

Cut down more Swarm in the northern streets, and shoot the angel trapped on the side of the building as you enter. You can't save these tormented souls, but you can at least grant them the mercy of death.

TRAPPED HELLGUARD
1

Beware: as you progress east down the street, a hulking beast known as a Suffering will storm forth. Back away and blast this overgrown demon with charged Salvation shots to keep it staggered until you can manage to kill it.

ENEMY: SUFFERING

Class: Brute

The Suffering are monstrous demons that rush the Reaper with terrifying speed and ferocity. Hold nothing back when battling one of these brutes—unleash Salvation's powerful charged shots to slow their advance and drop them with all speed.

Proceed to the northeast passage after slaying the Suffering and crack open a chest along the way. Search around the nearby red Corruption crystals to discover a missing page of the Book of the Dead, and then enter the passage to reach the next area.

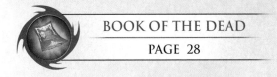
BOOK OF THE DEAD
PAGE 28

Area 4: Subway Station

Dispatch another monstrous Suffering as you enter this spacious area. Fight your way westward and blast the strange demonic growth on the far west wall to obtain the Staff of Arafel.

STAFF OF ARAFEL

Area 3: Subway Entry

Descend the stairs beyond the northeast passage to enter a subway. When you reach the bottom of the stairs, check the west nook near a light to find another trapped angel.

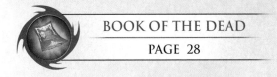
TRAPPED HELLGUARD
2

Subway Secrets

Before continuing westward, detour north from the demonic growth to discover a Relic hidden behind some red Corruption crystals.

RELIC OF RENAGOTH
7

Cut through the Swarm as you advance down the next flight of stairs. Go east and find a trapped angel in a nook.

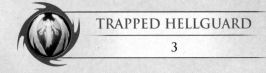
TRAPPED HELLGUARD
3

Backtrack to the east a bit and cross a bridge to reach the station's north side. Scan the ceiling over here for a Stonebite. Shoot the stone, and then enter the north room to loot a pair of chests.

STONE OF MYSTICS
29

Proceed west, past the demonic growth, to find stairs that lead back out to the Courtyard area. Deathgrip the Book of the Dead page that sits on a high pipe as you ascend the stairwell.

BOOK OF THE DEAD
PAGE 29

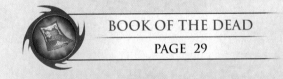

Area 1, Revisited

Take the subway's west stairs to return to the Courtyard area. The Hellguard have taken position near the southwest passage. Speak with Uriel to advance your quest, and the angel will open the way forward. Proceed through a large tunnel to reach the city's southern streets, collecting a Book of the Dead Page from the tunnel's east end as you enter.

BOOK OF THE DEAD
PAGE 30

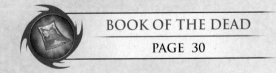

Area 5: Southern Streets

A new brand of weapon lies just outside of the tunnel. This one is similar to a rocket launcher, which makes it ideal for use against larger threats. However, its slow reload time isn't well suited to handling the Swarm. Choose your weapon, and then advance and kill a host of demons, including another ferocious Suffering.

 As you approach an overpass, turn and look for a Stonebite on the side of the nearby building. Continue south after shooting it, cross the overpass, and then enter a ruined building to raid the chest within.

TIP
Ignore the stairs that lead down to the area beneath the overpass; you'll have to travel down there later on.

STONE OF MYSTICS
30

Take the west street and raid the ornate chest on the nearby stairs to score the Dungeon Map.

DUNGEON MAP

When you reach the street corner, sprint to the north dead end and collect a lost Relic that sits near a car. As you backtrack south, blast the trapped angel that's stuck to the side of a nearby building.

	RELIC OF RENAGOTH
	8

	TRAPPED HELLGUARD
	4

Head south and enter the south building. Blast more demonic foes as you make your way through the building and into the next area.

Area 6: Noss Ambush

The streets widen beyond the building. Go west and claim a Book of the Dead page from inside a nearby building. Turn around afterward and scan the tops of the east buildings to locate another trapped angel in need of Death's mercy.

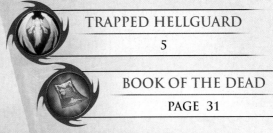

TRAPPED HELLGUARD

5

BOOK OF THE DEAD

PAGE 31

BOSS BATTLE: THE NOSS

Continue moving westward. Drop down into a lower plaza where a towering fiend known as the Noss attacks. Largely ignore the Stingers that the Noss spawns and rush forward, unleashing Salvation's charged shots from medium range to inflict maximum damage.

The Noss will periodically unleash terrible screams that push Death backward—this is because it doesn't fare well against close-range Salvation blasts. Keep enough distance to avoid being smashed by the Noss's melee blows, but stay close enough to inflict heavy damage with each charged Salvation blast.

Plaza Prizes

Claim a Boatman Coin from the plaza's southwest corner after defeating the Noss, and then blast the Stonebite on the north building before proceeding into the south tunnel.

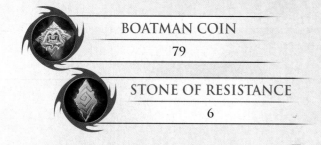

BOATMAN COIN
79

STONE OF RESISTANCE
6

Area 7: Car Tunnel—West

Eradicate more Swarm as you delve into this spacious car tunnel. Loop around and search a side tunnel to raid a chest after the main tunnel bends eastward, and then look up and blast the Stonebite on the tunnel's roof.

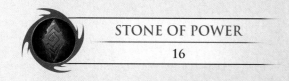

STONE OF POWER
16

Scale some broken pavement to reach a narrow walkway, where more Swarm assault you. Cross the broken section of walkway to reach another trapped angel. Free the poor soul before advancing into the north tunnel.

TRAPPED HELLGUARD
6

Area 8: Access Tunnel

Obliterate more demons in this small side tunnel. Raid a chest in one of the north alcoves as you pass through, reentering the main car tunnel on the other side of some blockage.

Area 9: Car Tunnel—East

Shoot the cars in this stretch of tunnel to create explosions and thin the Swarm's ranks. Several Fleshbursters and a hulking Suffering engage you here. After things quiet down, explore the south access tunnel to discover another trapped angel. Delve into the north sewage tunnel afterward.

TRAPPED HELLGUARD
7

Area 10: Sewage Tunnel

Beware of Fleshburners in this tight tunnel—drop them fast with charged Salvation shots. Snag a Boatman Coin as you exit the side passage, and continue heading north to reach the next area.

BOATMAN COIN
80

Area 11: Car Tunnel—North

Bring down another Suffering in the car tunnel's final stretch. Search the west alcove to discover a scrawl on the wall near the doorway—this bestows a Soul Arbiter's Sacred Scroll.

SOUL ARBITER'S SACRED
SCROLLS 9

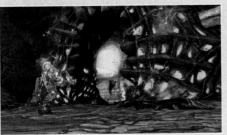

A demonic growth is found in this tunnel as well. Blast it to obtain the second piece of the Rod of Arafel, and then use the side passage beyond the growth to circumvent the tunnel's rubble and return to the surface.

EYE OF ARAFEL

Area 12: Overpass—Lower Area

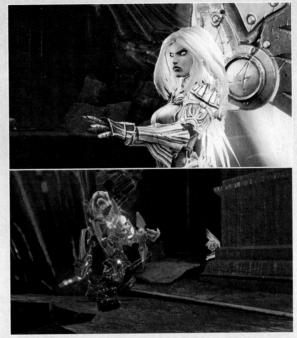

Uriel awaits Death at the far end of this area, which runs beneath Area 5's overpass. Speak with her to advance your quest, and then claim a Book of the Dead page from near the south wall, along with a Boatman Coin from the northwest nook. Enter the west passage afterward to begin your search for the Rod's final fragment.

BOOK OF THE DEAD
PAGE 32

BOATMAN COIN
81

Area 13: Access Tunnel 2

Despite what you might expect, there's nothing of interest to be found in this winding passage. Simply make your way through to the next area.

Area 14: Noss Ambush 2

Another formidable Noss stalks you in this wide street. As before, rush the monster and bombard it with charged Salvation blasts, ignoring the Stingers it summons. The Swarm will periodically rush you during this encounter—back off and blast these demons as needed before returning to ripping into the Noss.

When the mayhem finally subsides, sweep the street and destroy four postboxes to make a secret chest appear at the street's west end. Raid the chest, and then peer over the street's west edge to discover another trapped angel. Set its soul free with Salvation before venturing across the north bridge.

TRAPPED HELLGUARD
8

Area 15: Lower Bridge

Lay waste to the Swarm and Suffering that assault you on this stretch of bridge. When you reach the first broken section, peer down at the bridge's support column and blast the Stonebite on its north side.

STONE OF MYSTICS
31

Continue moving northward and search a small side room to the left (west) to discover a Boatman Coin. Press onward and scale the north slope of broken pavement to reach the bridge's upper half.

BOATMAN COIN
82

Area 16: Upper Bridge

Death is forced to battle another towering Noss on the bridge's upper area. Cut down the Swarm as you advance on this distant foe, and work at felling the Noss with charged Salvation blasts as you've done before.

Fight your way southward until you reach a small passage that leads east. Before crossing, turn around and backtrack a bit to blast an angel that's stuck to the south side of bridge's tall arch.

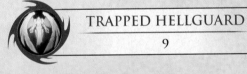

TRAPPED HELLGUARD
9

Cross the east passage to reach the third and final demonic growth. Destroy it to obtain the Rod of Arafel's last missing piece. Now that Death has acquired all three pieces, the Rod is made whole once more.

ROD OF ARAFEL

Area 17: Hotel

Advance past the growth and loot a chest as you maneuver through a ruined hotel. Search the dark hole in the wall across from the chest to discover a Relic.

RELIC OF ETU-GOTH
12

Press onward and descend a slope of debris. Shoot the Stonebite on the room's high north wall.

STONE OF POWER
17

Scale the debris slope again and carefully jump to a nook in the south wall. Here you discover a unique secondary weapon known as the Fists of Elhazar.

FISTS OF ELHAZAR

Advance into the next room and snag a Boatman Coin from a large hole in the left (west) wall.

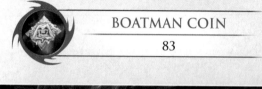

BOATMAN COIN

83

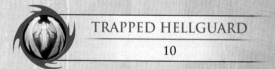

Blast the trapped Hellguard in the hall that follows to free the final angel. Exit the hotel via the hole in the wall to return to the Courtyard area.

TRAPPED HELLGUARD

10

Area 1, Third Visit

Uriel awaits the Reaper in the Courtyard. Inform her of your success in both restoring the Rod and freeing all ten of the trapped Hellguard. There's little left to accomplish here on Earth, so leave the Hellguard to their fate and use the portal in the east building to return to Lostlight.

SIDE QUEST COMPLETE: "LIGHT OF THE FALLEN"

SUNDER

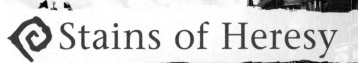

Stains of Heresy

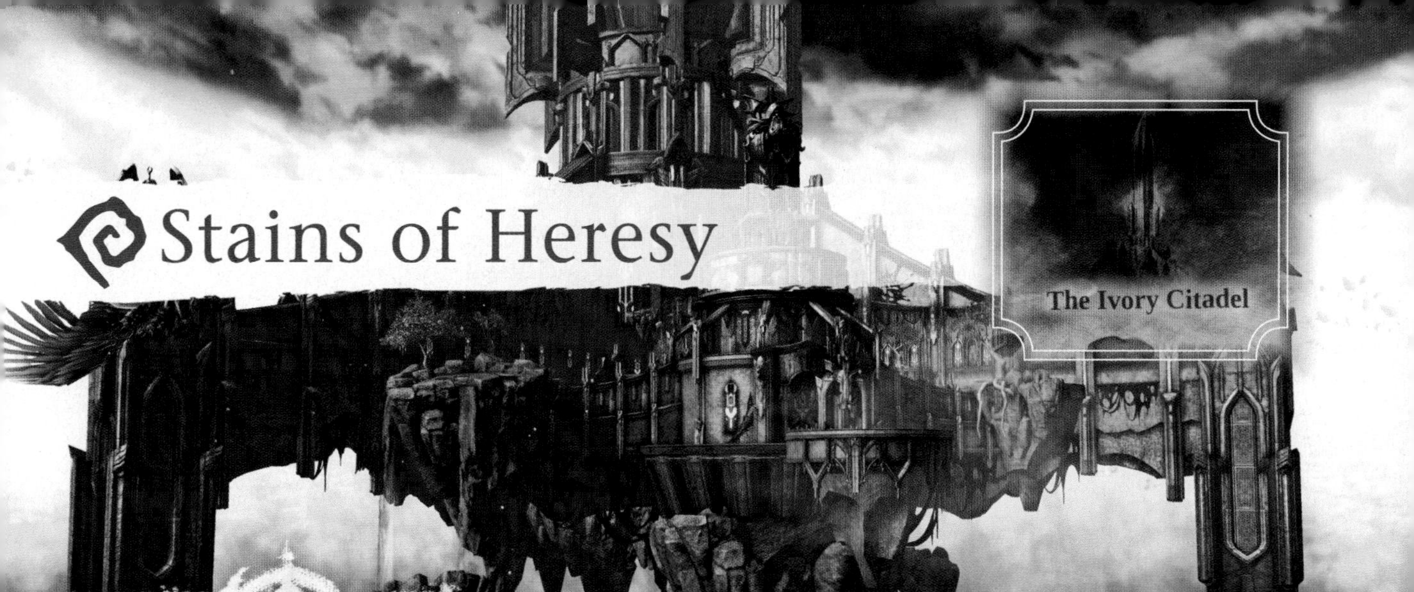

The Ivory Citadel

THE ROD OF ARAFEL HAS BEEN RESTORED. TRUE TO HIS WORD, THE ARCHON USES THE MIGHTY ARTIFACT TO CLEAR A PATH THROUGH THE DENSE WEB OF CORRUPTION THAT BLANKETS THE IVORY CITADEL. EAGER TO OBTAIN THE ANGEL'S KEY TO THE WELL OF SOULS, THE HORSEMAN WASTES NO TIME IN VENTURING TO THEIR FALLEN CITY...

THE IVORY CITADEL

This labyrinthian stronghold contains a library that's vast beyond imagining, but Corruption now owns this once holy place.

1ST FLOOR

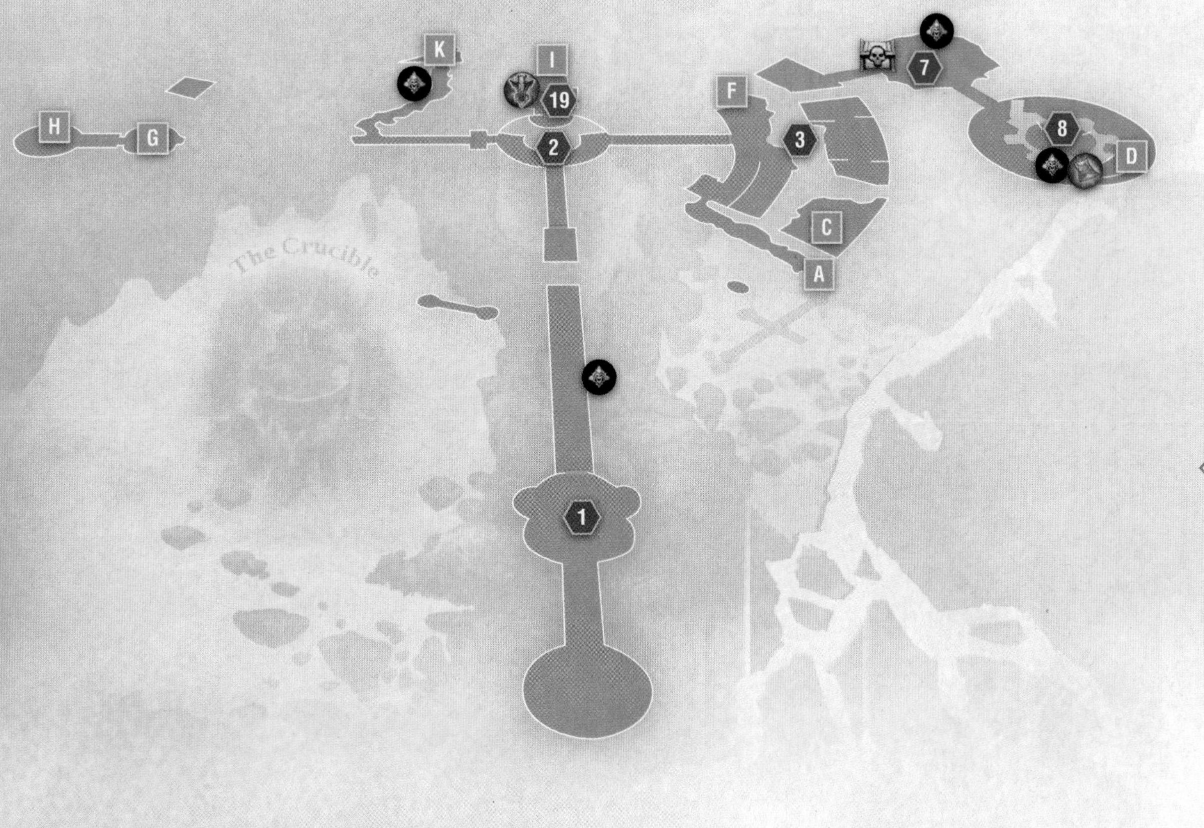

The Crucible

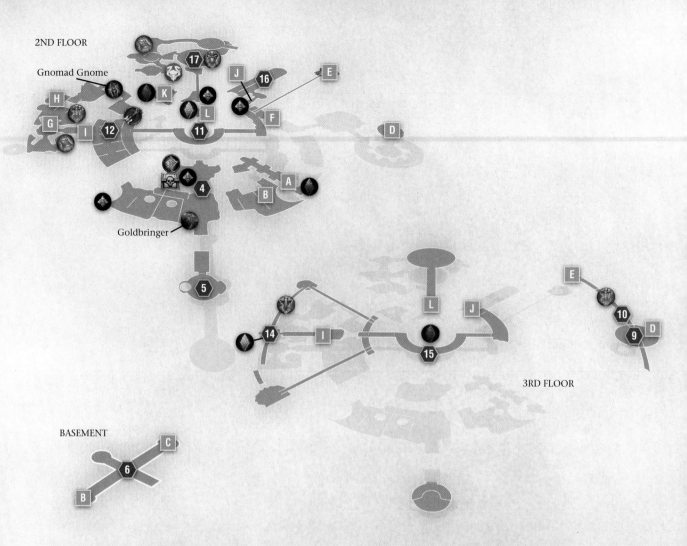

2ND FLOOR

Gnomad Gnome

17

J   16   E

H   K

G   L   F

I   12   11   D

4   A

B

Goldbringer

5

E

L   J   10

14   I   15   9   D

3RD FLOOR

BASEMENT

C

6

B

Area 1: Entry Hall

Death begins on an exterior landing. Advance through the north door to reach a small room with an unusual golden orb—a Holy Fire Node. Carefully avoid the inky Corruption ooze on the floor and scale the northwest wall to reach the room's second floor.

⌖ CAUTION

Oozing pools of Corruption will quickly drain Death's health. Avoid them at all costs.

DEATH TOMB III

If you've been following this walkthrough carefully, then you obtained your thirtieth Book of the Dead page on Earth. Consider fast-traveling to the Tree of Life at this point and riding north to trade your pages to Vulgrim in exchange for another special key. Ride north and use the key to unlock Lostlight's Death Tomb. You'll find a hoard of loot inside, including two Boatman Coins and a unique talisman.

BOATMAN COINS

84 - 85

HOARDSEEKER TALISMAN

Cleansing Fire

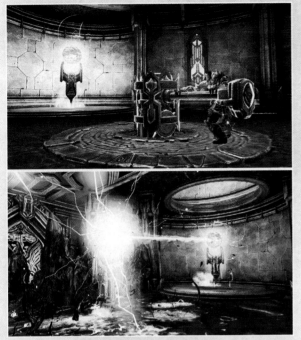

Spin the crank you discover on the entry hall's second floor to lower another Holy Fire Node down to the first floor. When both Nodes draw close to one another, they emit a powerful blast of cleansing fire that eradicates the Corruption ooze. Drop down to the first floor and proceed through the north door.

You can't obliterate the high Corruption crystals in the Entry Hall's north stretch, but you can slip around the wall to the right and claim a hidden Boatman Coin from a small ledge. Proceed north afterward and Deathgrip an overhead hoop to swing over to a door that leads to the next area.

> **CAUTION**
>
> Beware of Vengeful Spirits that emerge from the corpses of fallen angels in the city. Cut them down fast with Redemption.

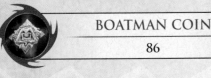

BOATMAN COIN

86

Area 2: Corruption Pool

A large pool of Corruption ooze has filled this chamber and blocks access to the north door. The west door is sealed, so head through the east door instead.

Area 3: East Courtyard

Travel south, loot a chest that sits behind a tree, and then scale the nearby stairs to reach an earthen passage. Run to the end and climb the far wall to reach the passage's second floor.

After climbing up to the second floor, turn around and wall-run over to a chest. Shoot the nearby Stonebite as well, and then wall-run back to the main passage and follow it to the next area.

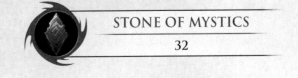

STONE OF MYSTICS

32

Area 4: South Courtyard

Swing across an overhead hoop to reach this area's northern island. Cut down a few Corrupted Angels after you land, and then collect the Boatman Coin that sits between a fallen column and a broken wall.

BOATMAN COIN
87

Inspect the northwest wall and notice a peg which hints that you need to wall-run across. Before doing so, spy a hand hold on the edge of the island and carefully drop down to a lower ledge where an ornate chest is found. Crack it open to claim the Dungeon Map.

DUNGEON MAP

Climb back up from the low ledge after looting the chest and make a long wall-run to reach the South Courtyard's

south island. Find a Boatman Coin tucked into the west corner.

BOATMAN COIN
88

Under Pressure

Notice the south island's circular pressure plate, which opens the nearby aqueduct gate. Stand on the larger circular pattern to the north and split Death's soul there.

Move one soul onto the circular pressure plate, and then switch to the other soul and proceed east through the aqueduct gate.

Turn left (north) after passing through the aqueduct gate and scale the low wall to reach a ledge. Stand on the circular pressure plate up here to open the floor where Death's physical form is standing.

Death's body lands in a lower passage. Return to physical form and scale the passage's far wall to reach the south island's east side.

Crystal Cracker

Beat down more Corrupted Angels on the south island's east side, and then Deathgrip a Shadowbomb from the nearby pod and use it to obliterate the southern Corruption crystals. Toss another bomb at the crystals to the northwest to destroy those, as well.

> **NOTE**
>
> Have no fear of the black residue left behind by destroyed Corruption crystals—it's harmless.

Before swinging from the south hoop, backtrack to the west and climb the low wall that leads to the second pressure plate. Now that the corruption crystals are gone, you can pull a lever up here. This opens another aqueduct gate to the east.

Drop down from the lever ledge and follow the aqueduct to its end. Loop around the debris to your right to discover a unique weapon.

GOLDBRINGER

Make your way back to the south walkway and swing from the hanging hoop to clear the gap. Proceed through the south door.

> **NOTE**
>
> Now that the southern Corruption crystals have been destroyed, you can quickly move between the Entry Hall and South Courtyard areas by scaling the wall.

Area 5: Voidwalker Chamber

Drop into this chamber and smash the chained object to obtain the Voidwalker—a gun-like tool used to activate warp portals. Test out this new item by firing it at the two portals in the room. Pass through the lower portal to pop out of the upper one, and then make your way back out to the South Courtyard.

VOIDWALKER

Area 4, Revisited

Slay a few more Corrupted Angels back at the South Courtyard before using the Voidwalker to activate the nearby portal. Aim and fire another blast at the distant portal to the north, but don't travel through just yet. Instead, Deathgrip another Shadowbomb and toss it through the nearby portal to obliterate the north island's corruption crystals, exposing a hidden chest. Now, pass through to warp over to the north island and claim your loot.

Wall-run back to the south island and return to its east side. This time, use the Voidwalker to activate the distant portal to the east. Only two portals can be open at once, so fire another blast at the south island's portal if need be, and then step through to reach the east island.

Area 6: Basement

Pull a nearby lever to open a trap door. Drop through the hole to reach a small basement passage. Activate the west portal down here and raid a chest, and then hold the Special Item trigger to charge up the Voidwalker before releasing it and activating the portal on the floor to the north. Death rockets out from charged portals at high velocity; step through the west portal and see for yourself!

Area 3, Revisited

Death bursts up from the Basement area's portal and lands in a new section of the East Courtyard area. Deathgrip the nearby hoop to swing across a gap and land on the area's eastern walkway.

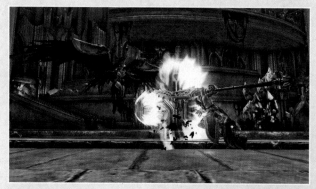

Advance until you're trapped in an area with a dangerous new enemy called an Ayfid. Avoid this winged warrior's swift attacks and counter until it can withstand no more. Slay the pair of Ayfids that appear after the first Ayfid falls.

ENEMY: AYFID

Class: Soldier

Ayfids are agile, winged creatures that glow with power before unleashing their swift, far-reaching strikes. Watch for this telltale glow, evade to one side, and then quickly counter with powerful skills and combos. Ayfids can withstand more punishment than Corrupted Angels, so don't hold back. Deathgrip Ayfids to keep them from mounting much offense.

Area 7: East Tower Access

Proceed north after slaying the Ayfids and use the Voidwalker to travel through the north portal. After you emerge, cut down the Corrupted Angel and cross the east bridge to reach an island with a Holy Fire Node.

Dispatch more Corrupted Angels near the Node, and then circle around behind the nearby standing wall and smash the four vases behind it to cause a secret chest to appear. Search behind the north tree as well to discover a hidden Boatman Coin.

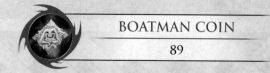

BOATMAN COIN
89

Activate the standing wall's portal, and then look south to notice another Fire Node. Open the portal near this distant node, and the two Fire Nodes will ignite and wipe out the black Corruption that blocks the southern bridge.

Area 8: East Tower

Cross the bridge and circle around the tower, heading for its southern staircase. Drop down into the hole on the side of the tower before you reach the stairs and activate the two portals there, using a charged Voidwalker blast to open the portal on the wall.

Climb out of the tower and advance toward its exterior stairs. Claim a Boatman Coin along the way, and shoot the Stonebite on the stairs' archway before heading up.

Cut down an Ayfid and several Corrupted Angels within the tower, making good use of the Deathgrip to draw in enemies and simplify the challenging fight. Split Death's soul in the center of the room afterward, and then have each soul trigger the pair of pressure levers that stick out from the walls. With both levers lowered, the floor opens, causing Death's physical form to plummet through the portals you opened below and soar out to the tower's north side.

Area 9: East Tower Apex

Scale the tower's outer wall to reach its top, where a Holy Fire Node hovers over a pool of deadly Corruption ooze. Activate the portal up here, and then peer over the tower's north edge and open the portal near the previous Fire Node. With both portals opened, the Nodes resonate and purify the pool, sending clean water flowing through the nearby aqueduct.

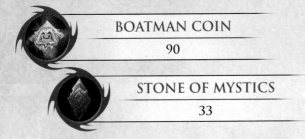

BOATMAN COIN

90

STONE OF MYSTICS

33

Area 10: East Aqueduct

Jump into the aqueduct and follow the water's flow. Drop down to the lower channels. After making your second drop, turn around and claim a Relic hidden behind the waterfall.

RELIC OF RENAGOTH
9

Keep going until you reach the aqueduct's end. Deathgrip a Shadowbomb from the nearby pod and hurl it at the Corruption crystals. Now you can easily return to the East Courtyard's entry, but don't do so at present. Instead, scale the wall growth that the crystals were blocking to reach a narrow balcony.

A curious creature called a Sycophant appears when you reach the balcony, but quickly vanishes. You'll catch up to this little devil soon enough. For now, proceed through the south door to reach the next area.

Area 11: Corruption Pool—Second Floor

As Death enters the Corruption Pool's second floor balcony, he notices that pure water is now flowing into the lower pool. It's not enough to purify the pool, but it's a start. Smash vases for minor items on your way to the west door, which leads back outside.

Area 12: West Courtyard

Corruption crystals block this area's north balcony, and the door above the west stairs is locked. Go west anyway and drop down from the north edge of the walkway just before the stairs to reach a small ledge with a chest. Climb back up afterward, and run south along the balcony.

Drop down from the balcony's south end to reach a lower walkway. Head north until you're trapped and forced to battle a mighty Corrupted Champion. Another Champion and two Corrupted Angels appear after the first foe falls.

ENEMY: CORRUPTED CHAMPION

Class: Soldier

These armored angels rank among the most powerful in the Hellguard, and yet even they cannot withstand Corruption's vile influence. Beware their powerful sword strikes and dive-bomb attack, the latter of which sends out a shockwave of damaging force. Evade to one side to avoid their linear sword charges, and counter with Death's best skills and combos at every chance.

Area 13: West Tower

After defeating the Corrupted Champions, venture north, and then west to enter the West Tower. Before dropping through the cracked floor, head south and claim a Book of the Dead page that's tucked away near some black Corruption just outside the tower.

BOOK OF THE DEAD

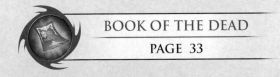

PAGE 33

Return to the tower's interior and drop down through the cracked floor to reach a lower chamber. Ignore the portal and Holy Fire Node down here. Instead, step outside to combat a trio of Corrupted Angels.

A hoop lowers after the Angels have fallen. Deathgrip it to swing over to a hand hold, and then make a long wall-run to reach another hand hold. Vault off of the peg above to return to solid ground.

You're now exploring the West Tower's north grounds. Two cranks can lower a pair of portals here, but leave them be for now and run east to locate a switch. Press this to lower the nearby gate; now you can easily travel into and out of the tower. Turn around and claim the Relic that sits just north of the switch, and then backtrack to solve the portal puzzle you passed earlier.

RELIC OF RENAGOTH

10

Portal Puzzle

Open the portal near the switch first.

Approach the cranks and split Death's soul. Have one soul turn the south crank to lower the south portal.

Switch to the other soul and stand atop the lowered south portal. Fire the Voidwalker to open the raised north portal.

Switch back to the other soul and release the south crank to raise the south portal again. Next, fire a charged Voidwalker blast through the portal near the switch, and it will pass through the north portal and open the south one.

Now, spin the north crank to lower the north portal. Switch souls again and reopen the portal near the switch, and then step through.

Death rockets through the south portal and lands near a lever. Pull this to raise the gate behind you, and then return to physical form and pass through.

Key Seeker

Beware the river of Corruption ooze that flows into the north passage beyond the portals. Ignore the passage and wall-run along the north wall to reach the West Courtyard's north end, where a few Corrupted Angels guard an ornate chest. Crack open the chest after securing the area to obtain a Skeleton Key.

SKELETON KEY

Scale the east wall and grab a Shadowbomb from the pod on the balcony. Use this to destroy the Corruption crystals that previously blocked your path. Go south, and then west afterward, scaling the long stairs and unlocking the door to the West Tower's upper floor.

Area 14: West Tower Apex

The tower's top floor houses a Holy Fire Node and a warp portal. Shoot the interior Stonebite above the doorway, and then open the portal and backtrack downstairs. Drop from the south end of the balcony to return to the lower walkway, and then enter the West Tower again and drop down through the cracked floor to reach the lower Node and portal you noticed before. Open this portal to ignite the Nodes and cleanse the tower's flow of water.

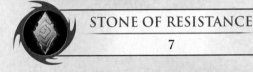

STONE OF RESISTANCE
7

Aqueduct Run

Step through the tower's lower portal to return to its top floor, and then jump into the water channel. Go south and Deathgrip across a pair of hoops to reach a platform with a chest.

Area 15: Corruption Pool—Third Floor

Return to the tower's apex one last time and follow either aqueduct to its end. Scale the wall and enter the high east door to reach the Corruption Pool area's third floor balcony. Again, Death notices that pure water is flowing into the lower pool, but it's still not enough to cleanse the dense Corruption ooze.

Follow the south aqueduct to its end and scale the wall, but don't enter the east door just yet. Instead, drop down to the lower balcony and return to the tower's top floor. Go north this time, following the north aqueduct. After you drop down to a lower channel, turn around and collect a Relic that's hidden behind the waterfall.

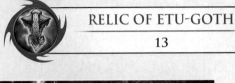

RELIC OF ETU-GOTH
13

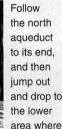

Follow the north aqueduct to its end, and then jump out and drop to the lower area where you discovered the Skeleton Key. With the West Tower's water cleansed, the Corruption ooze is no longer present in the north passage. Step through and claim the Gnomad Gnome hidden within.

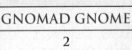

GNOMAD GNOME
2

Cut down the handful of Corrupted Angels that attack as you cross the balcony, and then blast the Stonebite on the north statue's chest before advancing through the east door. Cross the outdoor balcony and descend a wall to reach a small, watery passage that leads out to the next area.

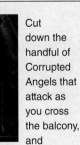

STONE OF POWER
18

Area 16: Exterior Stairs

Grab the Boatman Coin from the bottom of the watery passage's shallow pool, and then step outside. Descend the wide staircase and crack open a chest on the way down. The Sycophant appears and taunts you again, but flees before battle can be joined.

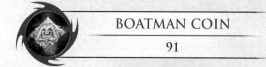

BOATMAN COIN

91

Death automatically wall-runs to a distant ledge. Collect the Boatman Coin in the corner before activating the portal on the curved wall ahead. Open the distant portal below with a charged shot.

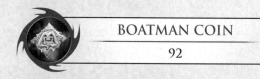

BOATMAN COIN

92

Portal Hopping

Open the two south portals when you reach the end of the stairs, and then Deathgrip a pair of overhead hoops to swing into one portal and emerge from the other.

Wall-run along the curved wall, and Death will enter its portal and rocket out from the lower one. Climb onto the ledge that Death grabs and begin exploring the new area.

Turn around and look up to spy another portal above you. Open this one with a charged Voidwalker blast, and then step through the nearby portal to rocket out of the one above.

Prima Official Game Guide   www.primagames.com

Area 17: North Courtyard

At last, the Rider catches up with the Sycophant in this final courtyard. The agile demon is tough to approach, so use the Deathgrip to halt his dodging and bring it near. More Sycophants appear after the first one falls—show them no mercy.

Go south to locate a crank. Split Death's soul and turn the crank to rotate the nearby circular wall so that an opening appears. Put on your thinking cap, because some serious puzzle solving skills are required here.

Cranky Portals

> Leave one soul holding the crank while the other pulls a moveable platform out from beyond the circular wall.

ENEMY: SYCOPHANT

Class: Soldier

These nimble troublemakers have the power to teleport, making them tough for Death to track. Sycophants can't withstand much punishment, but their attacks are quite powerful. Deathgrip these pesky devils to pull them toward the Reaper, and then unload.

> Return to physical form and the wall will reset. Stand atop the moveable platform and split Death's soul again.

Progress past the Sycophant ambush to discover a Holy Fire Node and a warp portal. Ignore them both for the moment and step out onto the west landing to claim a Book of the Dead page.

BOOK OF THE DEAD
PAGE 34

> Turn the crank to rotate the wall once more, and then switch souls and pull the moveable platform back through the circular wall. Return to physical form once you're inside the wall, and take note of a Fire Node and a portal to the east that's covered by black Corruption.

Go south to locate another crank. Before turning it, blast the distant Stonebite to the south, and then drop down onto the nearby ledge and claim a Soul Arbiter's Sacred Scroll. Open the nearby portal as well down here.

Split Death's soul and turn the crank again. Switch souls and step through the lower portal, and Death will fly out from the charged portal, landing inside the circular wall. Notice the Fire Node here and raid the west chest before returning to physical form.

STONE OF POWER
19

SOUL ARBITER'S SACRED
SCROLL 10

You're nearly finished! Backtrack to the north and split Death's soul while standing inside the first rotating wall. Drop to a lower ledge and scale the north cliff to return to the first crank.

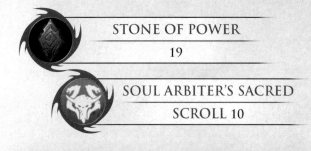

Climb back up to the crank and split Death's soul. Turn the crank to rotate the nearby circular wall and expose a portal. Switch souls and open the circular wall's portal.

While standing near the first crank, look north and fire a Voidwalker blast through the hole in the north wall to open the portal near the northern Fire Node.

Return to physical form and allow the wall to reset back to its original position. Drop to the lower ledge again and fire a charged Voidwalker blast through the lower portal. The blast exits through the circular wall's portal and activates another portal to the south.

Head back to the southern crank and turn it to rotate the wall again. Once fully rotated, the northern and southern Fire Nodes will resonate, and the southern Fire Node will become charged with energy.

Moving On

Excellent work! Before sprinting along the water channel, search behind a nearby web of Corruption to discover a Relic.

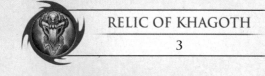

RELIC OF KHAGOTH
3

Now simply return to physical form to release the crank. When the circular wall returns to its original position, the southern and central Fire Nodes will resonate, obliterating the Corruption near the central Node.

Now, simply run along the water channel, hopping over the side to raid a chest on your right as you go. Return to the channel, follow the water to its end, and wall-run over to a ledge with a portal.

Go east to find a fourth Fire Node, and then look up and open the portal above it. The central and western Nodes will then resonate, purifying the pool of Corruption ooze near the central Node.

Open the ledge's portal, and then peer through the hole in the nearby wall to spy another portal. Open this one by shooting through the wall's hole. Travel through and drop down into the hole in the ground to reach the next area.

Area 18: Waterway

Death lands in a narrow watery passage. Dive into the blue and claim an underwater Boatman Coin, and then return to the passage and head south. Keep going until you reach a barred door. Pull the nearby lever to unbar the door so that you may advance.

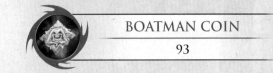

BOATMAN COIN
93

Area 2, Revisited

The Horseman has found his way back to the Corruption Pool room. With all three aqueducts purified, the Corruption ooze here is finally cleansed. Proceed through the north door.

Area 19: Portal Platforms

Claim a Relic from behind a statue as you enter this small chamber. Open the north portal, and then look up and activate the portal directly above with a charged blast.

Death pops out near the chest. Claim your plunder. Then, look up at the portal above and blast the Stonebite that's cleverly hidden on the broken wall near the portal.

RELIC OF ETU-GOTH
14

STONE OF RESISTANCE
8

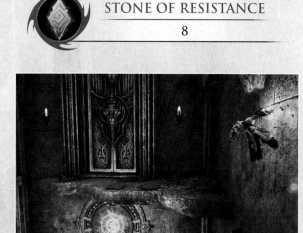

Step through the lower portal to rocket out of the higher one. Look up again and fire a charged blast at the high portal on the south wall. Drop down to the lower portal and reopen it, and step through to rocket out of the high south portal.

Drop from the chest ledge and open the bottom portal once more. Step through to rocket out of the high south portal again. This time, simply wall-run over to the north door and proceed through to reach the final battle.

Look west after you land to find a chest in a nearby nook. Open the portal above the chest, and then reactivate the south portal with another charged blast and wall-run into it.

BOSS BATTLE: JAMAERAH THE SCRIBE

A mighty angel known as the Scribe resides within the Ivory Citadel's towering library. Corruption has taken control of the Scribe's min presenting Death with a challenging foe.

Death can attempt to close in and strike the Scribe, but Jamaerah will counter by lashing out with a grotesque tentacle. Instead, keep your distance and open one of the many portals around the ground floor. Then open the opposing portal directly across the room.

The Scribe glows with golden light before unleashing a powerful, linear energy blast. Stand before one of the portals you've opened and evade to one side to avoid this deadly strike. If you time it right, Jamaerah's energy blast will pass through the portals and strike him from behind.

> ⚑ **TIP**
>
> Jamaerah spreads his arms just before unleashing his energy attacks. Evade the moment you see his arms spread open.

It's not long before the Scribe becomes stunned by his own attacks. Race forward and unleash Death's most lethal skills and combos while Jamaerah is slumped in his chair.

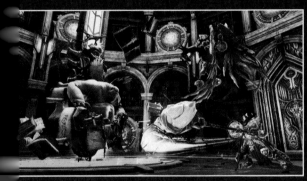

After suffering significant damage, Jamaerah will take to the air, power up, and then come crashing back down. Keep near the outside wall and jump to avoid the resulting shockwave. The Scribe then summons a few Corrupted Angels to aid it. Quickly slay these threats, and then work at setting Jamaerah up to blast himself again via the portal trick.

When Jamaerah is near death, he takes to the air once more, and a portal appears beneath him. Use a charged Voidwalker blast to open any of the room's upper portals, then open the one beneath the Scribe. Switch to the Deathgrip and drop through.

Death rockets out of the upper portal. Quickly Deathgrip the Scribe to close in, and then unleash a midair combo once you're in range. Repeat this as needed until you finish off Jamaerah.

Having had more than his fill of the angels' games, Death interrogates Jamaerah regarding the whereabouts of their key. Surprisingly, the Scribe reveals that the Archon possesses it—the once-noble angel has apparently gone quite mad. Question Jamaerah further if you wish before fast-traveling back to the Crystal Spire.

> **TIP**
>
> Consider visiting Nathaniel at the Spire's base and replenishing your potions before confronting the Archon.

BOSS BATTLE: ARCHON

The Archon attempts to explain his motives for tricking Death, but his excuses fall on deaf ears. Only the Reaper's wrath will be enough to wrest the key from its twisted guardian.

Armed with the Rod of Arafel, the Archon is a force to be reckoned with. He unleashes a number of blistering energy attacks that inflict heavy damage, and he can withstand vast amounts of punishment. Make use of skills such as Unstoppable and Aegis Guard to lend Death extra strength throughout this trying battle.

The Archon commonly takes flight during the fight, and often maintains an impenetrable shield while airborne. Simply evade to dodge his rhythmic energy attacks at these times.

Attacking the Archon in midair will eventually stun him and cause him to fall. When this occurs, close in and strike hard until an Action button prompt appears. Then, press the Action button to chop off the Archon's wings.

After casting several energy blasts from midair, the Archon raises his Rod, lowers his shield, and begins to build up power. Quickly jump and Deathgrip the Archon to zip close, and then unleash a midair combo to score damage.

Now the Archon is forced to battle Death on the ground. Do your best to avoid his wide energy blasts as you close in and pile on more damage. When the Archon begins to block, quickly tap the Evade trigger to backflip away from him before he unleashes a concussive blast that knocks Death backward.

The Archon soon comes crashing back down, sending out a wide shockwave of damaging force. Leap to avoid this attack, performing a midair combo to maintain height if need be.

When the Archon is near death, he'll sprout wings of Corruption and take to the sky once more. Dodge his linear flying charges, and then Deathgrip the Archon and assault him until he begins to block. Again, backflip away to avoid his defensive blast, and then dodge his next flying charge. Repeat this sequence until you're at last able to finish off the Archon with a press of the Action button.

Into the Shadows

With the mighty Archon slain, Death has finally managed to acquire the Angel Key. Fast-travel back to the Tree of Life and speak with the Crowfather to learn of your next destination: the demonic realm of Shadow's Edge. It is there that the Horseman will find the Demon Key, but obtaining it won't be easy. Proceed through the portal that the Crowfather opens to begin your search for the final key.

VOIDWALKER VENTURES

Now that you've obtained the Voidwalker, a number of optional side areas can be fully explored. Here's the rundown—refer to the "Side Quests and Areas" chapter for more details:

The Weeping Crag: Armed with the Voidwalker, you can now fully explore this optional side area. If you've yet to explore the Crag, you can slay a special enemy here to complete one of Thane's side quests. Even if you've previously run through the Crag, use the Voidwalker to open a pair of portals that lead you to a special treasure room, where plenty of loot and a Gnomad Gnome are found.

The Fjord: Swim to Vulgrim's area in the Fjord harbor and travel through the portals to claim a Book of the Dead page and a rare Stonebite. You'll need to toss a Shadowbomb through the portals to clear out some Corruption crystals.

The Nook: Return to the Nook and use the Voidwalker to open the portals in the basement, which lead to a pair of treasure chests. If you haven't revisited the Nook since your initial trip to the Lost Temple, you can also use the Deathgrip to claim a Book of the Dead page from the lower courtyard area, as well as a Boatman Coin from the lava cavern, where another special enemy can be defeated as part of Thane's side quests.

Breach Portals: Return to the Breach and use the Voidwalker to open the portals in the area with the switch and bridges. Travel through the portals to reach a pair of chests.

The Spine's East Tower: Scale the tower to the east of the Judicator's Tomb and use the Voidwalker to travel through the portals and raid more chests.

Psychameron Portals: Fast travel to the Psychameron and open the basement portals in the room with the three switches and Skeleton Key. The portals lead to a pair of chests.

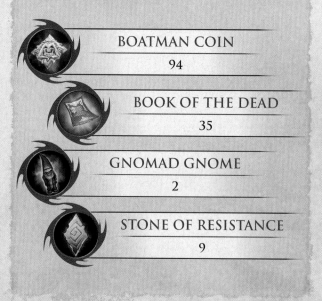

	BOATMAN COIN
	94
	BOOK OF THE DEAD
	35
	GNOMAD GNOME
	2
	STONE OF RESISTANCE
	9

The Lord of the Black Stone

Shadow's Edge

THE PALE RIDER'S QUEST NEARS ITS END. HAVING FOUGHT HIS WAY THROUGH THE FALLEN REALM OF ANGELS, THE HORSEMAN HAS MANAGED TO ACQUIRE ONE OF TWO KEYS NEEDED TO GAIN ENTRY TO THE WELL OF SOULS. NOW, THE REAPER MUST BRAVE THE DEMONIC REALM OF SHADOW'S EDGE AND OVERCOME INSURMOUNTABLE ODDS TO OBTAIN THE DEMON KEY...

The Crucible

The infernal realm of demons is a dark and foreboding place. Ash and shadow are prevalent in this unholy land.

To the Black Stone

The Crowfather awaits the Reaper just outside of the Tree of Death. Speak with him to learn of this sinister new realm, and then proceed north into a small keep.

Veer left at the fork in the keep's hall and follow the west passage to its end. Before exiting the keep, turn right and scale the nearby wall to reach a small ledge with a pressure plate. Collect the Book of the Dead page that sits near the pressure plate, and then stand atop the plate and split Death's soul.

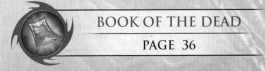

BOOK OF THE DEAD
PAGE 36

Backtrack to the fork in the hall and explore the east passage. With the pressure plate depressed, this passage's gate is now open. Claim the Relic at the end of the passage, and then return to physical form and exit the keep.

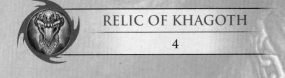

RELIC OF KHAGOTH
4

A Familiar Face

Death finds Ostegoth lingering just outside the keep. The savvy merchant suspects something is amiss with the Black Stone's lord, a powerful demon named Samael—for Corruption has ravaged even this unholy realm. Question Ostegoth for more information and trade with him before entering Samael's stronghold.

The Black Stone

This once mighty stronghold has fallen to ruin. Corruption has taken hold of the fortress, but Death must still find a way to confront its master.

PRESENT

1ST FLOOR

Gnomad Gnome

2ND FLOOR

BASEMENT

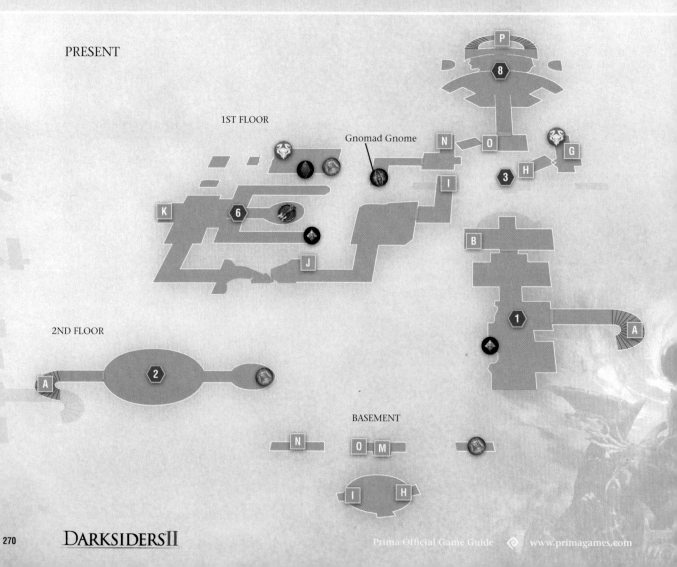

PAST

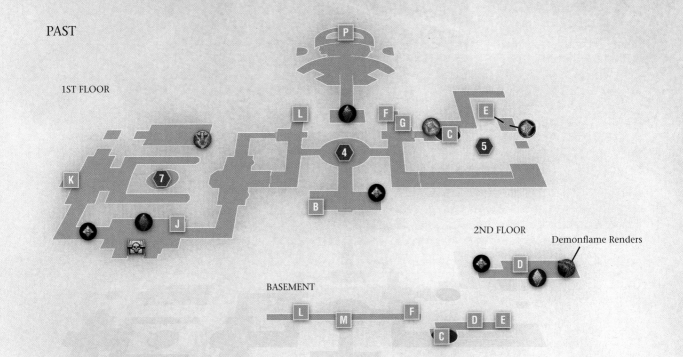

1ST FLOOR

2ND FLOOR

Demonflame Renders

BASEMENT

Area 1: Entry Hall

Ostegoth was right: something is very wrong here. Circle around the black Corruption to the left as you enter and claim a hidden Boatman Coin. Go through the east door afterward and scale some stairs to reach the stronghold's second floor.

BOATMAN COIN
95

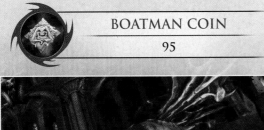

Area 2: Lilith's Chamber

Here, Death encounters a seductive demon named Lilith: the one who was responsible for creating the Horseman and his brethren, the Nephilim. Lilith informs the Rider that Samael has left the Black Stone, and that the Demon Key has left with him. All is not lost, however: Lilith imbues Death's Voidwalker with the power to open portals through time—a trick that will allow the Horseman to explore the Black Stone in the past, before its fall.

PHASEWALKER

Question Lilith further if you wish, and then sprint east and claim a Book of the Dead page from the far

end of the room. Backtrack downstairs afterward and proceed through the north door to reach the next area.

Area 3: Great Foyer (Present)

This massive chamber has fallen to ruin; there's no way of exploring it in its present state. Use your newfound Phasewalker on the nearby time portal to open a window to the past. Step through to travel back in time.

Area 4: Great Foyer (Past)

Death emerges from the portal to find himself in familiar surroundings, but the Great Foyer is no longer a ruin. Search behind the east pillar to discover a Boatman Coin before advancing north to explore the area.

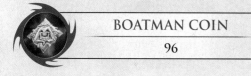

BOATMAN COIN
96

> **NOTE**
>
> Many of the Black Stone's collectibles only appear in either the past or the present. This Boatman Coin couldn't have been claimed in the present, for example.

Beware: mighty demon warriors known as Legion Champions and Legion Soldiers ambush Death as he moves to the Foyer's central platform. This is a deadly attack, so don't hold back: unleash Death's best skills to quickly cut down the demons, and dodge often to avoid becoming overwhelmed. Proceed through the southeast door after the battle.

ENEMY: LEGION CHAMPION

Class: Soldier

These ancient demons vanished after Corruption claimed the Black Stone, but Death must contend with them when he travels back in time. Legion Champions wield heavy maces that double as far-reaching whips. These devious tools can be used to pull the Reaper toward them, setting Death up for further damage. Strive to avoid these dangerous whip lashes while quickly defeating Champions with powerful skills.

ENEMY: LEGION SOLDIER

Class: Soldier

These formidable demons make up the bulk of the infernal army. They often attack in groups and are commonly found alongside Legion Champions. Soldiers are not as powerful or resilient as Champions, so cut them down first when faced with mixed groups. Anti-group attacks can be quite effective when these nimble demons begin to swarm.

Area 5: East Wing (Past)

Open the treasure chest here before heading downstairs to reach a long passage filled with lava. Wall-run to the first platform, and then wall-run again, jumping between the narrow walls to extend your run to a distant hand hold. Wall-run to the next hand hold, and then climb up to the northern ledge.

Don't Deathgrip the hoop at the passage's end. Instead, look for another hoop high on the south wall inside the passage. Deathgrip this hoop and make your way up a narrow shaft.

An ornate chest to the south tantalizes you, but you can't claim it just yet. Instead, go west and slay a couple of Legion Soldiers in a passage that leads to a large circular pit.

East Wing Secrets

Battle a Legion Champion in the secret room above the passage, and then claim the nearby Boatman Coin. Face South afterward and blast the distant Stonebite on the ceiling.

Leap out and Deathgrip the pit's south hoop to bound up to a hand hold. Rather than climbing out of the pit, drop from the hand hold afterward to slip past the hoop and grab a lower hand hold.

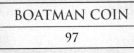

BOATMAN COIN
97

STONE OF RESISTANCE
10

Scale the east stairs and claim a powerful unique weapon. Drop back down to the lower passage after claiming this final prize.

Shimmy around the low hand hold and climb up to enter a secret passage.

DEMONFLAME RENDERS

Now, Deathgrip the hoop on the east wall at the end of the secret passage. Death bounds up the wall; quickly jump back and forth until you reach the ledge with the ornate chest you noticed before. Open this to obtain the Dungeon Map.

DUNGEON MAP

Wall-run to the north ledge after claiming the map, and then make your way back to the circular pit. Deathgrip the hoop again, and this time, scale the wall and climb out of the pit. Claim the nearby Book of the Dead page before proceeding through the west door.

BOOK OF THE DEAD

PAGE 38

Area 4: Great Foyer (Past), Revisited

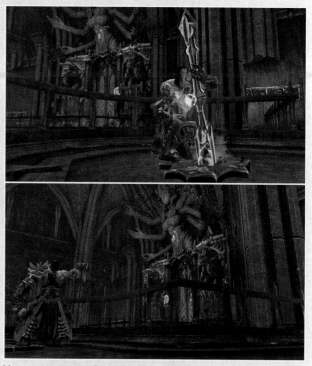

You emerge on the Great Foyer's northeast balcony. Pull the lever to lower the nearby gate, and then battle the Legion Champion that materializes. Shoot the Stonebite on the belly of the large statue to the north after the fight.

STONE OF POWER

20

Before opening the nearby time portal, grab the north wall's hand hold, shimmy to the left, and then drop down to the walkway below. Cut down the Legion Soldier here, and then open the chest in the nook. Climb back up the hand holds to return to the northeast balcony.

Area 3: Great Foyer (Present), Revisited

Now, open the balcony's time portal with the Phasewalker and step through to return to the present. Raid the chest and collect the nearby Soul Arbiter's Scroll, and then leap off the balcony to reach the Foyer's collapsed central platform.

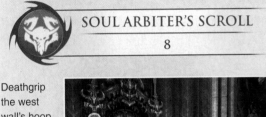

SOUL ARBITER'S SCROLL
8

Deathgrip the west wall's hoop and climb up to the Foyer's west balcony. Sprint up the south stairs and proceed through the southwest door.

Area 6: West Wing (Present)

Take note of a locked door as you enter this area, and then make your way downstairs. Turn around when you reach the bottom of the stairs to see a time portal. Open this and step through to travel back to the past.

Area 7: West Wing (Past)

Open the nearby chest after you emerge from the portal, and then smash everything in the vicinity to make a secret chest appear. Loot this larger chest before traveling back through the time portal to return to the present.

Area 6: West Wing (Present), Revisited

Press onward and descend another staircase. Ignore the west time portal for the moment and climb the east stairs to claim a Boatman Coin from the end of the south walkway. Loop around to the north walkway afterward and blast the Stonebite high up on the north wall. Return to the west time portal and pass through to travel back in time.

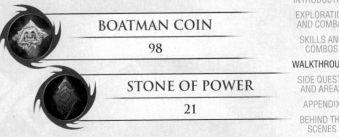

BOATMAN COIN
98

STONE OF POWER
21

Battle a number of Legion Soldiers and a new enemy known as a Maelstrom after emerging from the portal. Use anti-group attacks and skills to hasten these fiends' demise.

Descend the nearby stairs to reach a low walkway where another Maelstrom lurks. Slay this fiend, and then solve this area's portal puzzle in order to destroy the central Corruption crystals.

Blast from the Past

ENEMY: MAELSTROM

Class: Soldier

These fiery demons prefer to keep out of reach as they lob large fireballs at Death from afar. Maelstroms add an unwelcome layer of chaos to battles waged against Legion Soldiers and Champions, but they can't withstand much of the Reaper's wrath. Deathgrip these drifting devils to pull them close, where the Horseman can quickly eviscerate them.

Split Death's soul while standing atop the north walkway's circular pressure plate.

With the pressure plate depressed, a gate is lowered to the west. Loop around and enter the west passage. Wall-run to its hand holds and climb up.

With the demons destroyed, run south and claim a Boatman Coin from atop the southern stairs. Backtrack and climb the east stairs afterward, and then shoot the Stonebite on the far south wall.

BOATMAN COIN	
99	

STONE OF POWER	
22	

Wall-run again to reach a small side room where more demons ambush you. Show them no mercy, and then collect the Relic in the southeast corner before opening the nearby warp portal.

Return to physical form and open the west time portal. Step through to return to the present.

Switch souls, run east from the pressure plate, and open the north warp portal. Stand directly in front of the portal, where the walkway's railing is broken, and then switch back to the other soul.

Collect a Shadowbomb from the side room's pod and use it to destroy the nearby Corruption Crystals. Grab another bomb and then peer into the portal you've opened. Aim and toss the Shadowbomb through the portal, so that Death's other soul catches it.

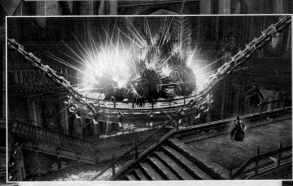

Switch souls and loop around to the southern walkway. Toss the Shadowbomb at the central Corruption crystals to obliterate them.

Area 6: West Wing (Present), Third Visit

Go west and leap up to a hand hold. Shimmy around the corner, drop down to a small ledge, and wall-run over to another ledge with a chest. Claim your plunder before wall-running south, heading upstairs, and using the southern time portal to return to the past.

Destroying the Corruption crystals in the past has also eliminated them from the present. Walk onto the broken central platform and crack open the ornate chest to claim a Skeleton Key.

SKELETON KEY

Loot Before You Leave

With the Skeleton Key in your possession, you're ready to move on. Before you do, remain in the present and head north, and then open the two north warp portals again. Deathgrip the hoop near the lower portal to swing into it and emerge in the side room.

Search behind the black Corruption in the side room's southeast corner to discover a Book of the Dead page. Then, inspect the scrawl on the wall where the Corruption crystals formerly stood in the past to acquire a Soul Arbiter's Scroll. (If you don't see the scrawl, return to the past and destroy the side room's Corruption crystals.)

BOOK OF THE DEAD
PAGE 39

SOUL ARBITER'S SCROLL
9

Area 7: West Wing (Past), Third Visit

After popping out of the time portal, go upstairs and slay the band of demons that ambush you near the locked door. Open the door afterward and make your way back to the Great Foyer.

Area 4: Great Foyer (Past), Third Visit

Back at the Great Foyer, pull the lever you discover on the northwest balcony to open the nearby gate. Descend the north wall's hand holds afterward to reach a lower walkway. Slay the Legion Soldier down here and open the chest in the west nook before using the nearby time portal to return to the present.

Area 3: Great Foyer (Present), Third Visit

Climb back up the north wall to return to the northwest balcony. Enter the west door to revisit the passage beyond the West Wing's locked door.

Area 6: West Wing (Present), Fourth Visit

GNOMAD GNOME
4

SIDE QUEST COMPLETE:
"GNOMAD"

GNOMAD SCYTHES

Now that you're in the present, you can collect the fourth and final Gnomad Gnome from this small passage. Backtrack to the Great Foyer afterward.

> ⬡ **NOTE**
>
> Now that you've found the final Gnome, visit a Tome to find a special weapon waiting for you. The nearest Tome is found at the small keep that stands between the Tree of Death and the Black Stone.

Area 3: Great Foyer (Present), Fourth Visit

Descend the Foyer's north wall again to reach the lower walkway. This time, open the west warp portal, then stand on the northeast corner of the walkway, aim carefully, and open the warp portal on the side wall to the east. Pass through the west portal to emerge from the east one and claim a Book of the Dead page.

Travel back through the warp portals, and then notice a peg on the central wall. Scale this wall to reach the Great Foyer's north balcony and proceed through the north door.

BOOK OF THE DEAD

PAGE 40

> ⬡ **TIP**
>
> The confrontation with Samael is at hand, and it's anything but pleasant. Consider fast-traveling to replenish your potions with Ostegoth before progressing any farther. Also, if you've followed this walkthrough to the letter, you can open the fourth and final Death Tomb at this point and claim valuable gear before the coming clash—but you'll need to visit another realm to obtain the key from Vulgrim.

Area 8: Samael's Throne Room (Present)

This spacious chamber is eerily quiet—Samael has indeed vanished from his fortress. He's sure to be here in the past, however. Steel yourself for an epic battle before passing through the north time portal.

The Lord of the Black Stone is a mighty tyrant, and he is unwilling to part with the Demon Key. The Horseman must take it from him by force.

Samael has many powerful attacks and abilities. He often teleports before striking. Remain focused on the villain, evade the moment he teleports near, and then unleash a damaging skill or combo before evading out of harm's way again.

Each time Samael suffers significant damage, he flees to his throne and summons a number of energy orbs, and then casts them toward the Rider. Evade to one side and then the other to dodge these dangerous projectiles.

TIP

Don't hesitate to down Wrath potions during this trying battle. Skills are your best friends when fighting Samael.

TIP

Wait to activate timed skills such as Unstoppable and Aegis Guard until after Samael returns from his throne. Activating them too early or too late is a waste of precious Wrath.

Phase II

Samael's most dangerous attack is a rare foot stomp that sends out a shockwave of lethal energy. Tap the Evade trigger to backflip away from the Blood Prince the moment you see him raise his left leg in preparation to stomp.

The pace of the battle changes after Samael uses his demonic power to draw the main arena closer to his throne. Now, the tyrant unleashes far more powerful attacks. Maintain Aegis Guard at all times, and do your best to avoid Samael's devastating blows.

The third time Samael flees to his throne, a bridge appears, allowing Death to advance on him. Sprint over to the demon lord and pound away until he tosses the Reaper back to the main arena.

Samael will continue to flee to his throne after suffering significant damage. Instead of lobbing energy orbs, however, the villain summons columns of flame beneath Death's feet. Run to avoid being scorched, and evade the moment you see a circular pattern appear on the ground, which heralds the arrival of each flame column.

> ### TIP
> Unleash Reaper Form the moment Samael leaves his throne—it's the perfect time to pile on the damage!

As he nears defeat, Samael will begin to spew out searing flames. This is one of his longest and least effective attacks, so if you have plenty of health potions, stand before him and capitalize by unleashing your most powerful combos. Don't relent until the Blood Prince has been dethroned.

Demon Key Acquired

Beaten and broken, Samael has no choice but to admit defeat. He hands the Horseman the Demon Key, and then departs. Perhaps it was the Reaper who caused the Lord of the Black Stone to vanish all along? In any case, the way to the Well of Souls can now be opened!

Open the large chest that appears after Samael departs. There's nothing left for you to accomplish here; fast travel back to the Tree of Death to find the Crowfather awaiting you.

THE LAST OF THE LOOSE ENDS

If you've been following this walkthrough, then there are only three things left for you to accomplish prior to entering the Well of Souls. See the "Side Quests and Areas" chapter for additional details.

Death Tomb IV: You've found the fortieth and final Book of the Dead page within the Black Stone's walls. Travel to any other realm and obtain the final Death Tomb key from Vulgrim, and then return to Shadow's Edge and ride north from the Tree of Death to find the entrance to the final Death Tomb near Ostegoth's position. Inside you'll find the largest hoard of valuables yet, including two Stonebites, the final lost Relic, and two unique pieces of gear.

The Soul Arbiter's Maze: You've now found every Soul Arbiter's Scroll and Sacred Scroll, except for the few that are found within the Maze itself. Go there now and complete this final side area to enter the Well of Souls at maximum power.

Blackroot: After obtaining the final Stonebite from within the Soul Arbiter's Maze, return to the Fjord's most voracious construct and complete his side quest.

The Crucible, Part III: Defeating Samael earns you the third Tarot Card, allowing you to delve deeper into the Crucible. Clear the 75th wave to claim another excellent prize.

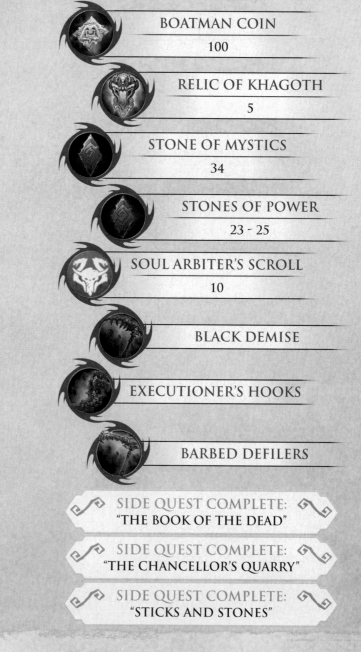

BOATMAN COIN
100

RELIC OF KHAGOTH
5

STONE OF MYSTICS
34

STONES OF POWER
23 - 25

SOUL ARBITER'S SCROLL
10

BLACK DEMISE

EXECUTIONER'S HOOKS

BARBED DEFILERS

SIDE QUEST COMPLETE:
"THE BOOK OF THE DEAD"

SIDE QUEST COMPLETE:
"THE CHANCELLOR'S QUARRY"

SIDE QUEST COMPLETE:
"STICKS AND STONES"

The Well of Souls

THE FINAL BATTLE IS AT HAND. USING THE ANGEL AND DEMON KEYS, THE PALE RIDER IS AT LAST ABLE TO OPEN THE TREE OF DEATH'S DOOR AND ENTER THE WELL OF SOULS. IT IS HERE THAT THE ROOT OF CORRUPTION MAY FINALLY BE RIPPED OUT OF EXISTENCE... BUT ONLY WITH GREAT SACRIFICE.

FINAL BOSS: AVATAR OF CHAOS

The unbridled rage of this twisted Nephilim has manifested itself into the nefarious Corruption that threatens to destroy the realms. Death must defeat his fallen brother in order to save humanity and clear the name of his embattled brother, War.

cont. ❯

Avatar of Chaos wields a massive axe, and the wide arc of his blows makes evading a challenge. Instead, go on the offensive and assault the wicked Nephilim with your most vicious skills and combos.

🜙 **TIP**
Keep Unstoppable and Aegis Guard active throughout this battle to gain a decided advantage.

Phase II

It's not long before Avatar of Chaos drops down to one knee. Advance and pile on the damage until the Action button prompt appears over the Nephilim's head, and then press the Action button to attempt a kill-shot that goes awry.

The battle changes after Death's failed attempt to finish off Avatar of Chaos. Now, the monster becomes covered in thick tendrils of Corruption and lashes out with furious spinning blows that are quite difficult to dodge. Do your best to evade these rhythmic strikes, but remain offensive and unleash Death's best moves to bring Avatar of Chaos to one knee a second time. Again, press the Action button to attempt another fatal blow.

Death's second attempt at finishing off Avatar of Chaos doesn't do the trick, but it does weaken the fiend, banishing his protective vest of Corruption. During this final phase, Avatar of Chaos will periodically slam the ground and send out sinister pockets of Corruption that can ensnare the Reaper, leaving him temporarily helpless. Try to avoid these roaming traps, for Avatar of Chaos will inflict massive damage if he's able to catch Death and capitalize on his advantage. Simply evade until he stops casting out the snares, and rapidly press the Action button to break free if you're caught.

🖝 TIP

The start of Phase III is a perfect time to unleash Reaper Form if you haven't already.

Strive to evade Avatar of Chaos's attacks during this final phase, for his combos can be excruciating. Counter with violent skills and punishing attacks at every opportunity. Pressure the wretched Nephilim until the source of Corruption is at last rooted out.

The Journey Ends

Having slain his greatest adversary, The Reaper has at last succeeded in wiping Corruption from existence. Now, he faces a difficult choice. Should he restore his fallen brethren, the Nephilim? Or should he undo the ravaging of humanity, thereby clearing his brother War's name? The choice is far from easy, for choosing to save one race will forever damn the other. Deep within his soul, the Pale Rider knows what he must do...

🖝 NOTE

Congratulations, you've beaten the game! Clearing *Darksiders II* unlocks Nightmare difficulty, allowing you to play through the adventure again at a higher challenge level. Even more gratuitous loot can be acquired in Nightmare mode, including special pieces of gear that you couldn't obtain during your first playthrough. See the "Appendix" chapter for details!

Side Quests and Areas

⟢ Side Quests

THE CRUCIBLE

DEATH'S ADVENTURE TAKES HIM TO MANY REALMS, BUT NOT EVERY AREA WITHIN THESE WORLDS IS VITAL TO COMPLETING HIS QUEST. THIS SPECIAL CHAPTER HAS BEEN CREATED SPECIFICALLY FOR THOSE WHO WISH TO EXPLORE THE OPTIONAL CONTENT IN *DARKSIDERS II*. EVERY SIDE QUEST AVAILABLE TO THE PALE RIDER IS DETAILED HERE, AND IS PRESENTED BY QUEST-GIVER FOR EASY REFERENCE.

Death receives a special invitation to visit the Crucible after he defeats the mighty Guardian at the end of the Forge Lands. This is not the first side venture that the Pale Rider can explore, but the Crucible is unique in that it can be visited from any realm.

What is the Crucible?

The Crucible is an epic combat arena consisting of four stages. Each stage presents Death with 25 predetermined waves of enemies, and each wave is more challenging than the last. The Reaper receives special rewards for reaching milestones within the Crucible:

Complete Stage I (Waves 1-25): Heartstone Talisman

Complete Stage II (Waves 26-50): Abyssal Armor Boots

Complete Stage III (Waves 51-75): Barbed Defilers

Complete Stage IV (Waves 76-100): Abyssal Spaulders, Assassin Talisman

Complete All 100 Waves in One Sitting: Aftermath

Defeat Wicked Killington: Elemental Talisman

⟢ **NOTE**

See the "Appendix" chapter at the end of this guide for details on these special items, along with others named throughout this chapter.

⟢ **NOTE**

You can opt to open a random loot chest after every 5 Waves. Taking this prize ends your ride through the Crucible, however. You'll have to start again.

Unlocking the Crucible

After defeating the Guardian, you receive an anonymous Tome message. Visit the Tome at Tri-Stone (or any other Tome) to find a special invitation to the Crucible in your inbox. This invite comes with a Tarot Card that serves as a pass, allowing you to challenge the Crucible's first 25 waves. You'll receive additional Tarot Cards as you reach various milestones within the game, as detailed in the following table.

TAROT CARDS

CARD	UNLOCKS	REQUIREMENT
The Fool	Waves 1-25	Defeat the Guardian
The Emperor	Waves 26-50	Defeat the Wailing Host
Strength	Waves 51-75	Defeat Samael
The Devil	Waves 76-100	Advance Death to Level 25
Death	Wave 101 (Wicked Killington)	Beat Waves 1-100 in a single visit to the Crucible
The World	Bragging rights!	Defeat Wicked Killington in Wave 101

⟢ **NOTE**

Once the 100th wave is defeated, the Crucible transforms into an arena ominously called "The End." The keeper of this arena then instructs Death to confront his master. Traverse the columns and navigate to the top of the elevated arena to confront one final adversary.

Clearing the Crucible

As you can see, completing the Crucible is quite a feat. Knowledge is power, so use the following table to help you prepare for each level of the Crucible:

CRUCIBLE: STAGE I (RECOMMENDED LEVEL: 15-20)

WAVE	ENEMY I	#	ENEMY II	#	ENEMY III	#
1	Construct Warrior	3	—	—	—	—
2	Construct Warrior	5	—	—	—	—
3	Construct Adjunct	3	Construct Warrior	3	—	—
4	Construct Champion	1	Construct Adjunct	2	—	—
5	Construct Champion	2	—	—	—	—
6	Stinger	5	Stinger	5	—	—
7	Prowler	4	—	—	—	—
8	Prowler	5	Prowler	4	—	—
9	Stalker	1	Stinger	5	Stinger	5
10	Stalker	2	Prowler	3	—	—
11	Tainted Construct Adjunct	5	—	—	—	—
12	Construct Sentinel	1	Tainted Construct Warrior	3	—	—
13	Tainted Construct Champion	1	Tainted Construct Warrior	5	—	—
14	Construct Sentinel	1	Tainted Construct Champion	2	—	—
15	Gharn	1	Tainted Construct Warrior	4	—	—
16	Stinger	30	—	—	—	—
17	Savage Prowler	2	Tainted Construct Adjunct	4	—	—
18	Savage Stalker	1	Stinger	5	—	—
19	Tainted Construct Champion	1	Savage Stalker	1	—	—
20	Savage Stalker	2	Tainted Construct Champion	1	—	—
21	Tainted Construct Champion	3	—	—	—	—
22	Corrupted Rideable Construct	1	—	—	—	—
23	Gorewood	1	—	—	—	—
24	Gharn	1	Ghorn	1	—	—
25	Gorewood	1	Tainted Construct Champion	2	—	—

CRUCIBLE: STAGE II (RECOMMENDED LEVEL: 20-25)

WAVE	ENEMY I	#	ENEMY II	#	ENEMY III	#
26	Skeleton	3	—	—	—	—
27	Skeletal Archer	5	—	—	—	—
28	Skeletal Warrior	4	Skeletal Archer	2	—	—
29	Skeletal Champion	1	Skeletal Warrior	5	Skeletal Champion	1
30	Skeleton Champion	3	—	—	—	—
31	Nightmare Prowler	5	—	—	—	—
32	Nightmare Stalker	2	Nightmare Prowler	4	—	—
33	Skeleton Champion	1	Nightmare Prowler	4	—	—
34	Skeleton Champion	2	Nightmare Stalker	1	—	—
35	Undead General	2	—	—	—	—
36	Wraith	5	—	—	—	—
37	Lich	1	Wraith	3	—	—
38	Scarab	20	—	—	—	—
39	Lich	3	—	—	—	—
40	Scarab	8	Scarab Hulk	2	—	—
41	Skeletal Champion	4	—	—	—	—
42	Abomination	1	Wraith	3	—	—
43	Abomination	3	—	—	—	—
44	Scarab Hulk	2	—	—	—	—
45	Bone Giant	1	—	—	—	—
46	Undead General	1	Skeletal Champion	2	—	—
47	Tormentor	1	—	—	—	—
48	Bone Giant	1	Skeletal Champion	2	—	—
49	Undead General	1	Tormentor	1	—	—
50	Tormentor	1	Bone Giant	1	—	—

CRUCIBLE: STAGE III (RECOMMENDED LEVEL: 25-30)

WAVE	ENEMY I	#	ENEMY II	#	ENEMY III	#
51	Corrupted Angel	3	—	—	—	—
52	Ayfid	2	—	—	—	—
53	Corrupted Angel	3	Ayfid	1	—	—
54	Corrupted Champion	1	Corrupted Angel	4	—	—
55	Corrupted Champion	3	—	—	—	—
56	Corrupted Construct Warrior	8	—	—	—	—
57	Sychophant	2	Corrupted Construct Adjunct	3	—	—
58	Corrupted Champion	2	Corrupted Angel	4	—	—
59	Corrupted Angel	6	Corrupted Angel	4	—	—
60	Sychophant	3	—	—	—	—
61	Undead Scarab	16	—	—	—	—
62	Undead Prowler	5	Undead Scarab	5	—	—
63	Undead Scarab Hulk	1	Undead Prowler	3	—	—
64	Undead Stalker	3	—	—	—	—
65	Undead Scarab Hulk	2	—	—	—	—
66	Legion Soldier	3	—	—	—	—
67	Legion Champion	1	Legion Soldier	1	—	—
68	Legion Soldier	4	—	—	—	—
69	Maelstrom	1	Legion Soldier	2	—	—
70	Maelstrom	1	Legion Champion	1	Legion Soldier	2
71	Ice Skeleton	12	—	—	—	—
72	Nightmare Prowler	3	Ice Skeleton	5	—	—
73	Maelstrom	1	Nightmare Prowler	3	—	—
74	Maelstrom	1	Nightmare Stalker	2	—	—
75	Argul / The Deposed King	1	—	—	—	—

CRUCIBLE: STAGE IV (RECOMMENDED LEVEL: 30)

WAVE	ENEMY I	#	ENEMY II	#	ENEMY III	#
76	Skeleton Warrior	3	—	—	—	—
77	Undead Prowler	5	Skeletal Warrior	5	—	—
78	Skeletal Champion	5	—	—	—	—
79	Skeletal Champion	3	Undead Prowler	4	—	—
80	Undead Stalker	3	Skeletal Archer	5	—	—
81	Wraith	4	—	—	—	—
82	Abomination	1	Wraith	3	—	—
83	Sychophant	1	Skeletal Champion	3	—	—
84	Sychophant	2	Abomination	1	—	—
85	Tormentor	3	—	—	—	—
86	Corrupted Champion	1	Corrupted Angel	3	—	—
87	Fleshburster	6	—	—	—	—
88	Corrupted Champion	2	—	—	—	—
89	Fleshburster	12	—	—	—	—
90	Ayfid	3	—	—	—	—
91	Corrupted Angel	8	—	—	—	—
92	Maelstrom	2	—	—	—	—
93	Legion Champion	1	Legion Soldier	3	—	—
94	Maelstrom	1	Corrupted Champion	1	—	—
95	Legion Champion	1	Maelstrom	1	—	—
96	Corrupted Custodian	1	—	—	—	—
97	Gorewood	1	—	—	—	—
98	Bone Giant	2	—	—	—	—
99	Suffering	1	—	—	—	—
100	Absalom / Avatar of Chaos	1	—	—	—	—

UBER CRUCIBLE BUILD

The good people at Vigil have recommended the following build to help you reign supreme in the Crucible. Don't worry if you've chosen different skills; simply visit Vulgrim to purchase a Respec for a modest fee, and then select the following skills to gain an advantage in *Darksiders II*'s daunting arena:

Attributes to Boost: Strength and Critical Damage

Secondary Weapon: Heavy Hammer or Axe

Harbinger Skills (13): Teleport Slash (3), Immolation (1), Unending Fury (3), Inescapable (3), Rage of the Grave (3)

Necromancer Skills (12): Exhume (3), Undying (3), Enervation (3), Death Allure (3),

THANE'S SIDE QUESTS

This rugged Maker can offer Death a number of side quests that span multiple realms.

Side Quest: "The Maker Warrior"

Location: Tri-Stone

Reward: More Quests

Recommended Level: 3-5

From the very first time you visit Tri-Stone, you can challenge a burly Maker named Thane to a fight. Defeat Thane and he'll offer you four additional side quests that involve killing some of the realms' most notorious fiends (see the sections that follow). It's unlikely that you'll be able to defeat Thane until after you clear the first dungeon, the Cauldron, but you'll have no trouble besting the Maker if you wait until after you've cleared the Drenchfort.

Side Quest: "Find and Kill Gorewood"

Location: The Weeping Crag

Reward: Gorewood Maul

Recommended Level: 10-15

Thane gives you this side quest after you complete "The Maker Warrior". Gorewood is a giant earth golem that resides within the Weeping Crag; you'll find him in the vale beyond the Stalker's den. The brute's attacks are mighty, so evade and counter with punishing skills until you at last manage to chop Gorewood down to size.

> **NOTE**
> The Weeping Crag is an optional area. See the following "Forge Lands Side Areas" section, which appears later in this chapter, for a complete walkthrough.

Side Quest: "Find and Kill Bheithir"

Location: The Nook

Reward: Bheithir's Talons

Recommended Level: 15-20

You acquire this side quest after completing "The Maker Warrior". Bheithir is a huge phoenix that flies around in the basement area of the Nook. Deathgrip over to the basement's broken walkway, and Bheithir will land and combat you. There's little room to maneuver, so use Teleport Slash to zip past Bheither and strike from behind. Unleash Reaper Form to ensure this great fiend's demise.

> **TIP**
>
> Consult the "To Move a Mountain" walkthrough chapter for help in navigating the Nook.

Side Quest: "Find and Kill Achidna"

Location: The Pyschameron

Reward: Achidna's Fangs

Recommended Level: 15-20

You acquire this side quest after completing "The Maker Warrior". Achidna is a monstrous spider that Death must combat at the end of the Psychameron. This is a mandatory battle and part of the main adventure, so you end up completing this side quest during the course of Death's main quest. Refer to the "Court of Bones III: Basileus" walkthrough chapter for help in navigating the Psychameron and locating this foul creature.

Side Quest: "Find and Kill the Deposed King"

Location: Lair of the Deposed King

Reward: Scepter of the Deposed King

Recommended Level: 20+

You acquire this side quest after completing "The Maker Warrior". Argul is a towering skeletal warrior that resides deep within the bowels of the Lair of the Deposed King. Though Death is able to explore this side dungeon early in his adventures in the Kingdom of the Dead, he lacks the power to contend with Argul until much later in his adventure.

> **NOTE**
>
> The Lair of the Deposed King is an optional area. See the "Kingdom of the Dead Side Areas" section, which appears later in this chapter, for a complete walkthrough.

MURIA'S SIDE QUESTS

This learned Maker can bestow upon Death a handful of side quests in addition to offering him potions and talismans.

Side Quest: "Shaman's Craft"

Location: The Forge Lands (Various Areas)

Reward: Grim Talisman

Recommended Level: None

Muria offers you this side quest when you first speak with her at Tri-Stone. Accept this quest and you'll naturally complete its objectives as you explore the Forge Lands. Here's a rundown of how this lengthy quest is best fulfilled:

✦ Speak with Karn outside of the Cauldron to advance the quest.

✦ Kill the Stalker inside the Cauldron as part of the primary walkthrough. You'll obtain the Stalker's Bone.

✦ Speak with Karn as you leave the Cauldron to advance the quest.

✦ Kill Stingers as you travel through the Fjord on your way to the Drenchfort. You'll obtain Mordant Dew.

✦ Speak with Karn outside of The Lost Temple to advance the quest.

✦ Kill Construct Sentinels as you explore the Lost Temple. You'll obtain a Carven Stone.

✦ Return to Muria and trade in your materials to receive the Grim Talisman—an excellent item that helps Death to quickly build Reaper Energy.

Side Quest: "Spark of Life"

Location: The Scar

Reward: XP and Gilt

Recommended Level: 15-20

After speaking with the angel Nathaniel at Lostlight, bring his scroll to the Chancellor at the Eternal Throne, and then to Muria at Tri-Stone. Both characters will offer you a side quest when you bring them the scroll; Muria's involves braving a side dungeon called the Scar, which is located just south of the Charred Pass in the Forge Lands. Go there and defeat the evil construct, Ghorn, to complete this quest and earn a significant amount of XP and Gilt.

> ⌖ **NOTE**
>
> The Scar is an optional area. See the "Forge Lands Side Areas" section, which appears later in this chapter, for a complete walkthrough.

ALYA'S SIDE QUEST

The Forge Sister asks much of the Rider during his time in the Forge Lands. Speak with her after clearing the Drenchfort and obtaining the Maker's Key, and Alya will ask Death to carry out one final task for the sake of her brother, Valus...

Side Quest: "The Hammer's Forge"

Location: The Shattered Forge

Reward: XP and Gilt

Recommended Level: 8-12

Alya offers Death this side quest after the Reaper clears the Drenchfort and restores the Maker's Forge to full functionality. The Deathgrip is required to complete this quest, however, so don't bother attempting it until after you've cleared the Foundry and defeated the Guardian. Visit the Shattered Forge, which is located just north of the Shadow Gorge, and brave the side dungeon in an effort to claim Valus's lost hammer, Splinter-Bone. Return this item to Alya and you'll be handsomely rewarded.

> **NOTE**
> The Shattered Forge is an optional area. See the "Forge Lands Side Areas" section, which appears later in this chapter, for a complete walkthrough.

VULGRIM'S SIDE QUEST

The demonic merchant, Vulgrim, offers Death more than just a unique selection of goods. The first time Death visits him, Vulgrim entreats the Rider to collect forty lost pages of the Book of the Dead for him...

Side Quest: "The Book of the Dead"

Location: Various Areas

Reward: Access to four treasure-filled Death Tombs

Recommended Level: None

Search high and low for the lost pages of the Book of the Dead. Every ten pages you collect completes a chapter. Return each chapter to Vulgrim and he'll give you special keys that open the Death Tombs found in each of the realms. Every tomb boasts its own spread of precious valuables. The following sections detail what you'll find within each tomb.

> **TIP**
> Refer to the "Appendix" chapter at the end of this guide for a quick-reference table that reveals the locations of all forty Book of the Dead pages.

Death Tomb I

Location: The Nook

Special Item: Blade Master Talisman

The first Death Tomb lies along the Nook's exterior trail, which leads toward the Lost Temple. Fast-travel to the Lost Temple's entrance and then travel south to find the tomb's door. Inside, you'll discover several treasure chests, weapon racks, and the Blade Master Talisman. There's also a hidden chest in a nook behind an object that Death can drag.

Death Tomb II

Location: Lair of the Deposed King

Special Item: Demonheart Talisman

Enter the Lair of the Deposed King and descend its long, spiral staircase to discover the second Death Tomb at the bottom. Move two statues within the tomb to access its secret side rooms and obtain additional plunder.

Death Tomb III

Location: Lostlight

Special Item: Hoardseeker Talisman

The third Death Tomb is found in the angelic realm of Lostlight. It lies along the main trail, about halfway between the Tree of Life and the Crystal Spire. Enter the tomb to find plenty of loot, including two Boatman Coins and a unique talisman. Smash the vases within the tomb to make secret Gilt appear.

Death Tomb IV

Location: Shadow's Edge

Special Item: Spear of Storms

The fourth and final Death Tomb is located in the demonic realm of Shadow's Edge. Its entrance stands just south of the Black Stone. A vast amount of loot is housed within, including a Relic of Khagoth, two Stones of Power (look up near the ceiling), and a unique secondary weapon, the Spear of Storms. Smash all of the breakable objects within the tomb to make a secret chest appear above the stairs.

BLACKROOT'S SIDE QUEST

This ancient Construct lives in the Fjord and has a voracious hunger for special items known as Stonebites.

Side Quest: "Sticks and Stones"

Location: Various Areas

Reward: Guillotine

Recommended Level: None

Speak with an immobile construct named Blackroot during your first trip through the Fjord. The friendly construct will bestow a side quest upon Death that involves the collection of special gemstones called Stonebites, which are hidden all around the realms. Blackroot gives the Reaper a special item called the Lure Stone, which imbues Death's pistol, Redemption, with the power to draw in the energy of these special stones. Shoot all seventy Stonebites to acquire their energy, and then return to Blackroot to receive a mighty pair of scythes in reward.

> ◈ **NOTE**
>
> Refer to the "Appendix" chapter at the end of this guide for a complete listing of all seventy Stonebites, including their locations.

ORAN'S SIDE QUEST

This shattered construct sleeps deeply at the far end of the Fjord's harbor. Once Death receives the Maker's Key as part of the main adventure, he can awaken Oran and gain a special side quest...

Side Quest: "Wandering Stone"

Location: The Forge Lands (Various Areas)

Reward: XP and Gilt

Recommended Level: 5+

Clear the Drenchfort to restore the Maker's Forge and obtain the Maker's Key, and then swim to the end of the Fjord's harbor and use the Maker's Key to awaken the slumbering construct, Oran. The giant grants Death a side quest that involves locating Oran's four lost limbs. Simply ride around the Forge Lands in search of Oran's missing limbs. Approach each one and press the Action button to awaken it and send the limb hopping or crawling back to Oran. Return to Oran after awakening all four limbs, and the newly-repaired construct will hand you a unique talisman in thanks.

Here are where Oran's missing limbs are located:

- ✦ The Fjord, along the path to the Drenchfort.
- ✦ The Shadow Gorge, just beyond the watchtower gate.
- ✦ Baneswood, just before you reach the Charred Pass.
- ✦ The Scar, just outside the dungeon's entrance.

OSTEGOTH'S SIDE QUEST

The Horseman encounters this curious merchant shortly after he sets foot in the Kingdom of the Dead. Ostegoth is a creature of many mysteries, and asks a special favor of the Rider...

Side Quest: "Lost Relics"

Location: Various Areas

Reward: Abyssal Gauntlets

Recommended Level: None

The first time Death encounters Ostegoth, the humble merchant asks him to seek out a number of precious Relics that have been scattered throughout the realms. Find and return all thirty of these lost baubles to Ostegoth, and the savvy trader will reward you with a unique prize of remarkable craftsmanship.

> **NOTE**
>
> Refer to the "Appendix" chapter at the end of this guide for a complete listing of all thirty Relics, including their locations.

THE CHANCELLOR'S SIDE QUEST

This haughty soul has little use for the Reaper when the two first meet. Later in the adventure, however, the Chancellor finds a worthy purpose for Death...

Side Quest: "The Chancellor's Quarry"

Location: Soul Arbiter's Maze

Reward: Pillager

Recommended Level: 20+

Shortly after Death arrives in the angelic realm of Lostlight, he encounters an angel named Nathaniel who asks the Rider to bring a special scroll to the *Eternal Throne*. Place this mysterious parchment in the hands of the Chancellor and he'll ask the Reaper to carry out a special side quest that involves solving the tortuous Soul Arbiter's Maze. Brave the maze, defeat its master, and then bring the Crown of the Dead to the Chancellor in order to receive your reward.

> **NOTE**
>
> The Soul Arbiter's Maze is an optional area. See the following "Side Areas" section, which appears later in this chapter, for a complete walkthrough.

NATHANIEL'S SIDE QUEST

This angelic warrior helps Death fend off a host of Corrupted Angels near the foot of the Crystal Spire. After the battle, he asks a small favor of the Rider...

Side Quest: "The Lost Soul"

Location: The *Eternal Throne*; Tri-Stone

Reward: XP and Gilt

Recommended Level: None

The first time you speak with Nathaniel at Lostlight, the angel asks Death to carry a special scroll to the *Eternal Throne*. Go there, hand the scroll to the Chancellor to advance Nathaniel's quest, and you'll also gain another side quest: "The Chancellor's Quarry." Complete Nathaniel's quest by delivering the scroll to Muria at Tri-Stone. The Maker shaman will grant the Rider a new side quest, as well: "Spark of Life."

URIEL'S SIDE QUEST

When the apocalypse was triggered, angelic warriors known as the Hellguard were dispatched to Earth to combat the demonic hoard. Their leader, the angel Uriel, needs all the help she can get—and the Rider arrives just in time.

Side Quest: "Light of the Fallen"

Location: Earth

Reward: Sunder

Recommended Level: None

When Death arrives on Earth, his first task is to help Uriel and her Hellguard repel a monstrous demonic invasion. After witnessing the Pale Rider's prowess, Uriel asks if he wouldn't mind granting the mercy of a swift death to ten Hellguard who are being held in torturous traps around the city. The Reaper must explore the city in search of pieces to a vital artifact, so there's little reason not to seek out these tormented souls along the way. Simply kill all ten of the trapped Hellguard angels you encounter as you journey across Earth, and then speak with Uriel to complete this straightforward quest.

> **TIP**
>
> Refer to the "Rod of Arafel" walkthrough chapter for a complete step-by-step walkthrough of Earth, in which all ten trapped Hellguard are accounted for.

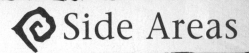

Side Areas

Now that we've touched upon all of *Darksiders II*'s many side quests, let's take an in-depth look at its most prominent side areas. Here you'll find complete step-by-step walkthroughs for every major side dungeon found in the realms.

THE WEEPING CRAG

The Pale Rider's journey to the Cauldron leads him through this ominous cave. Death can simply pass through this area, or he can elect to explore the Weeping Crag more thoroughly. The Deathgrip and Voidwalker (or Phasewalker) are required to fully explore the Weeping Crag.

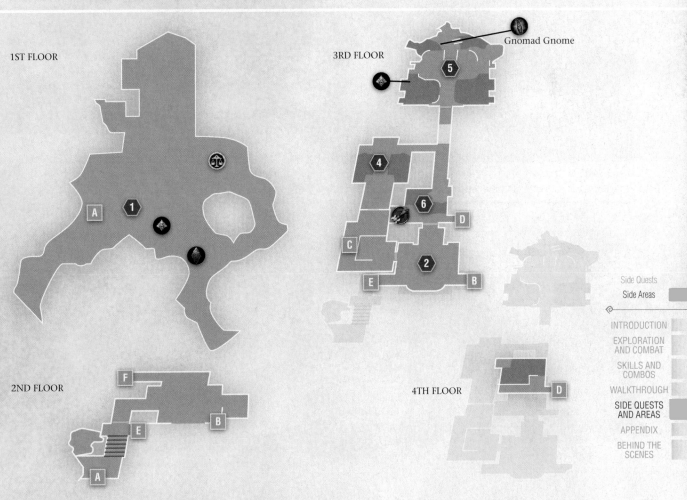

1ST FLOOR

3RD FLOOR

Gnomad Gnome

5

4

A 1

6

D

C

2

E B

2ND FLOOR

F

B

E

A

4TH FLOOR

D

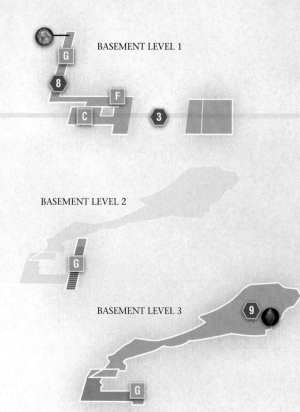

BASEMENT LEVEL 1

BASEMENT LEVEL 2

BASEMENT LEVEL 3

Area 1: Entry and Drawbridge

First, shoot the Stonebite on the stone pillar on the east side of the Weeping Crag's drawbridge. Then, cross the bridge and run up the low wall on the bridge's west side to reach the Crag's second floor.

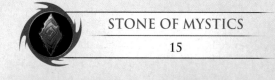

STONE OF MYSTICS

15

When you encounter a locked door, wall-run to a wooden post to the right. Drop down to the hand hold below, and then continue wall-running to the right to reach another post, and then another. Work your way up to the balcony above.

Area 2: Balcony and Stairwell

Cut down the Construct Warriors that ambush you on the balcony. The north door is barred, so enter the west door instead to reach a stairwell. Slay another Construct Warrior, open a chest here, smash the west debris, and explore the nook in the west wall to drop down into a hole and land on a lower level.

Area 3: Lower Ledges

Loot the chest down here, and then Deathgrip the overhead hoop to swing to the east ledge where another chest is found. Drop down into the water afterward and swim south to locate the underwater Boatman Coin that lies beneath the Weeping Crag's drawbridge.

BOATMAN COIN

41

Climb out of the water and return to the Crag's second floor. Again, wall-run across the posts and hand holds to the right of the locked door. This time, however, drop down from the second hand hold and quickly Deathgrip the north hoop as you fall.

Swing across, using a second hoop to reach the grassy ledge with a chest. Drop back down into the water afterward and climb back up to the locked door. Traverse the wall posts and hand holds once again to return to the balcony. Go through the west door, and this time, climb the stairs and proceed through the north door.

Area 4: Pressure Platform

Step on a pressure plate in this room to raise a platform up from the water. Wait for the platform to fully rise, and then step off of the pressure plate. Pause for a brief second before running, jumping, and grabbing onto the platform's hand hold. Quickly climb up and scale the north wall before the platform lowers too far.

Use the Voidwalker (or Phasewalker) to open the warp portal you notice beyond the rising platform. Sprint down the east stairs afterward, and then turn north and open another warp portal on the ceiling. Return to the previous portal and pass through to pop out of the ceiling portal. Proceed through the north door to visit a secret area.

Area 5: Forgotten Treasury

Raid this serene chamber's trio of chests to score loads of loot. Drop down into the southern waters afterward, and swim to the west along the water's surface. Perform a vertical wall-run to grab a Boatman Coin.

BOATMAN COIN
94

Climb back up to the surface and plunge into the room's northern waters. Swim to an underwater alcove, and then surface to discover a hidden Gnomad Gnome. Make your way back out of this room and descend the south stairs to reach the next area.

GNOMAD GNOME
3

Area 6: Skeleton Key Chamber

Wall-run along the north wall and jump the corner to reach an ornate chest which contains a Skeleton Key.

SKELETON KEY

Obtaining the Skeleton key unbars the south door, but don't leave just yet. Instead, enter the southeast nook and jump between the narrow walls to climb up to a balcony.

Wall-run around the room and jump the corner to reach the northwest ledge where a chest is found. Claim your plunder, and then drop back down and proceed through the south door.

Area 3, Revisited

You're back in familiar territory. Drop down from the balcony's southwest edge to land near the locked door you noticed previously. Use your newfound Skeleton Key to open the door and head through.

Area 7: Stalker Den

A menacing Stalker lurks in the small chamber beyond the locked door. Strive to evade its ferocious attacks and strike from advantageous angles. Scour the room for valuables after slaying the Stalker, and crack open the two chests here before dropping down through the northwest hole.

Area 8: Submerged Staircase

You land at the top of a long, narrow staircase. Rather than descending the submerged stairs, make a long wall-run between the staircase's narrow walls, jumping between them as you race toward a high ledge containing a Book of the Dead page. Claim the page, and then plunge into the water below and swim down through a low underwater passage to reach a small, watery cave.

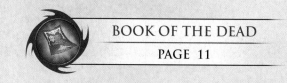

BOOK OF THE DEAD

PAGE 11

Area 9: Gorewood's Lair

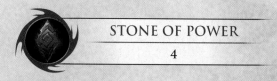

Beware: a vicious monster named Gorewood lurks in this final area. You'll also find a chest here, and there's a Stonebite on the east wall.

STONE OF POWER

4

BOSS BATTLE: GOREWOOD

Gorewood is a monstrous earth golem that values solitude. The creature has little tolerance for trespassers, and attacks Death on sight.

Beware the tangled roots that Gorewood regularly casts out—if you're caught by one, you'll be temporarily immobilized, becoming an easy target for Gorewood's slow but devastating blows. Strive to evade the monster's roaming snares.

Once you learn to avoid his snares, Gorewood becomes fairly easy prey. Circle around his predictable blows and counter with vicious combos—but always be ready to dodge those immobilizing roots. Slay Gorewood to complete a side quest for Thane and receive a unique weapon, the Gorewood Maul.

GOREWOOD MAUL

SIDE QUEST COMPLETE: "FIND AND KILL GOREWOOD"

THE SHATTERED FORGE

This crumbling worksite has been overrun by Corruption. Valus has lost a precious item here, and would be grateful to have it returned to him.

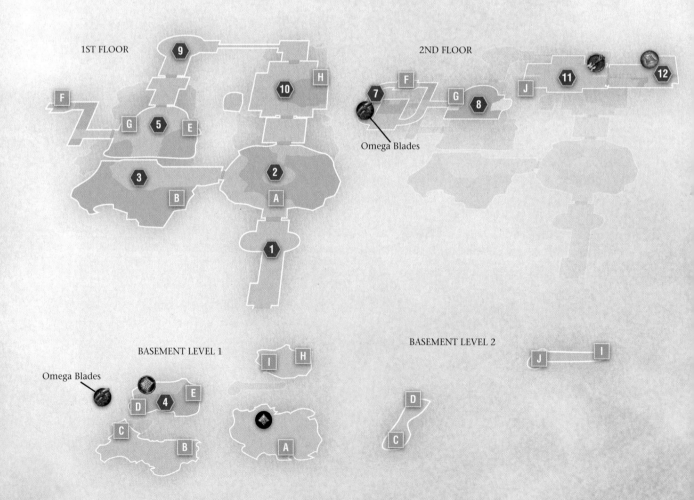

1ST FLOOR

2ND FLOOR

Omega Blades

BASEMENT LEVEL 1

BASEMENT LEVEL 2

Omega Blades

Area 1: Entry Stairs

Turn around when you reach the bottom of the Forge's entry stairs and search behind them to discover a hidden chest. Proceed through the north door after pocketing your plunder.

Area 2: Water Cavern I

A central chest tantalizes Death when he enters this spacious cave, but there's no obvious way to reach it. Plunge into the water, claim an underwater Boatman Coin, and then climb out and head through the west door.

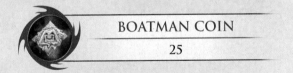

BOATMAN COIN

25

Area 3: Water Cavern II

Drop down into the deep water in this cave, and then swim north and dive into an underwater hole. Continue swimming through the watery passage to reach the next area.

Area 4: Map Cavern

Surface in this cavern and crack open the ornate chest on the low ground to claim the Dungeon Map. Scale the east wall afterward to reach the area above.

DUNGEON MAP

Area 5: Corruption Junction

Eliminate the Savage Prowlers that ambush you in this room. Corruption crystals block the north door, so proceed through the west door instead.

Area 6: Lower Shattered Passage

This watery passage has fallen to ruin. Wall-run to the north ledge, leaping between the walls and jumping the corner to extend your run. If you fall, swim south and scale the hand holds to return to the passage entrance.

When you reach the north ledge, stand in the north alcove and leap between the parallel walls to climb up to a higher passage.

Area 7: Upper Shattered Passage

Wall-run across two pegs in this upper passage, heading south. You soon reach a small room where Corruption crystals block your progress. Drop and scale the platform with the Shadowbomb pod, and then use a bomb to obliterate the crystals.

Before advancing, collect another Shadowbomb and backtrack to the previous passage. Look for a Corruption crystal down below, and toss the bomb to destroy it. Drop down and investigate the nook you've uncovered to discover a unique weapon. Climb out of the passage and proceed east, past the first nest of Crystals you destroyed.

OMEGA BLADES

Area 8: Corruption Junction—Upper Ledges

Pass through a door to find yourself back at the Corruption Junction area, up on a high ledge, Pull the nearby lever to cause pegs and hand holds to appear around the room. Wall-run across the pegs to reach the east ledge and a Shadowbomb pod. Use a bomb to destroy the Corruption crystals below, and then drop down and slay the Savage Stalker that ambushes you. Proceed through the north door afterward.

Area 9: Construct Ambush

Raid a pair of chests on your way into this small chamber, where Death becomes trapped and is forced to battle several waves of Construct Warriors and Champions. Fight hard to slay them all and earn your freedom. Wall-run through the narrow east passage that follows to reach the next area.

Area 10: Locked Door Chamber

Ignore this spacious room's hand holds and plunge into its central pool. Dive and swim into the southwest hole, and keep swimming into the underwater passage. Surface at the passage's far end and scale the wall to work your way up to the room's second floor.

Area 11:
Locked Door Chamber—Upper Ledges

After smashing all of the constructs, break the vases in the room's northeast corner to obtain a hidden Book of the Dead page. Proceed through the west door afterward to return to the previous area.

You emerge near a Shadowbomb pod. Toss a bomb at the east ledge's Corruption crystals to destroy them, and then grab another bomb and drop to the chamber's main floor. Hurl the bomb at the crystals on the northwest ledge to clear it off as well.

BOOK OF THE DEAD
PAGE 7

Area 11, Revisited

Use the room's hand holds to climb up to the northwest ledge. Raid its chest and wall-run around the room, going north and then looping around to the south to reach the east ledge. Proceed through the east door.

You emerge on a ledge with an ornate chest that contains a Skeleton Key. Push the nearby switch to drop the ledge's gate, and then drop to the chamber's main floor. Open the locked south door and go through.

Area 12: Sentinel Ambush

SKELETON KEY

Area 2, Revisited

Wall-run along this room's outer wall and raid a chest on your way to its northeast corner. There, Death becomes trapped and is forced to battle several Tainted Construct Warriors, a Construct Champion, and a Construct Sentinel. Slay one or more of the Warriors to make the Sentinel drop its shield and revive them. Quickly focus on the Sentinel while its shield is down and blast it with Redemption to destroy it.

You've come full circle, finding yourself back in the chamber with the tantalizing chest. Simply cross the walkway and open the chest to obtain Splinter-Bone—the prized hammer that Valus lost long ago. You've nothing more to accomplish here at the Shattered Forge, so find your way back to Tri-Stone. Return Valus's precious hammer and claim your reward.

THE SCAR

This fiery side dungeon can't be entered until the Horseman acquires the Deathgrip. Even then, it's best to wait until you receive the "Spark of Life" side quest from Muria before you probe its searing depths. You receive this side quest after bringing Nathaniel's scroll to Muria as part of his "The Lost Soul" side quest.

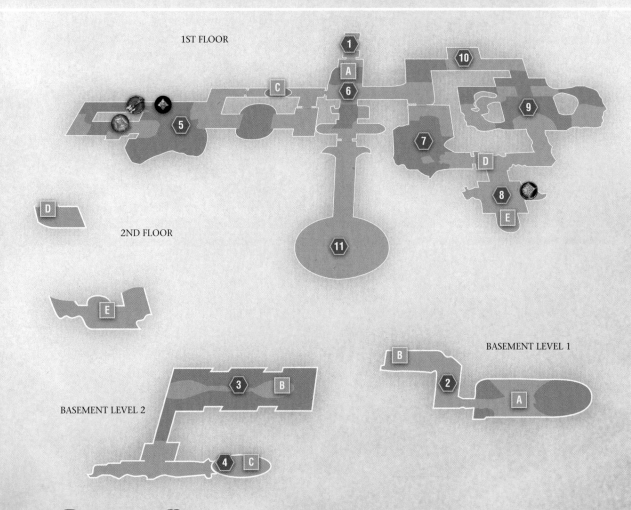

Scar Exterior

To enter the Scar, climb up to its lower balcony and use the Deathgrip to swing across an overhead hoop and grasp a wooden post. 180 leap from the post to claim a floating Boatman Coin, and then go upstairs to reach the Scar's upper balcony. Before heading inside, look up and shoot the Stonebite hidden inside the broken overhead pipe.

BOATMAN COIN	
75	
STONE OF POWER	
15	

Area 1: Entry Stairs

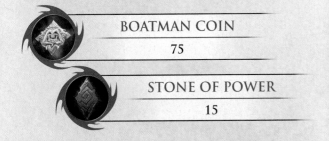

Descend the Scar's entry stairs, and then turn around and wall-run across a pair of pegs to reach a secret ledge behind the stairs where a chest is found. Claim your loot, wall-run back out, and proceed through the south door.

A monstrous construct named Ghorn roars at Death in the next room and smashes the walkway, dropping the Rider in a lower area. Not exactly a pleasant welcome!

Area 2: Basement

Slay the Corrupted Construct Warriors that materialize after you land, and then proceed down the west stairs. Drop down into the hole at the end of the passage to reach the next area.

Area 3: Noxious Nest

A Stinger Hive stands in this lower area. Wipe out the Noxious Stingers it spawns and destroy the hive to prevent more of the pests from emerging. Wall-run through the narrow south passage afterward, jumping between the walls to extend your run.

Area 4: Lava Pit

As Death nears this searing pit, Ghorn begins to pound the ground above. This causes the lava at the bottom of the pit to rise, forcing the Rider to quickly scale the pit before he's burned to a crisp.

Wall-run up to the lowest hand hold, and then circle around the pit and climb up to the hand hold above. 180 leap from this hand hold and quickly Deathgrip the hoop on the opposite wall to bound up higher.

Progress until you vault off of a peg, and then 180 leap again and Deathgrip another hoop to bound upward a second time.

Wall-run to the right to reach the final hand hold, and then vault from the peg above it to climb out of the pit. Proceed through the south door afterward.

Area 5: West Custodian Cavern

Sprint across this room and activate the Maker Custodian, and then unleash its heavy blows against the Corrupted Construct Warriors and Adjuncts that materialize. Roll across the west lava afterward, park the Custodian on an orb slot, fire its chain at the distant target, and tiptoe across.

When you reach the end of the chain, Deathgrip the hoop on the nearby broken pipe and swing to solid ground. Go west, swing across two more hoops, and cut down the Corrupted Construct Warriors that attack you when you land.

Wall-run to the north after slaying the Constructs. Jump the corner and, when your wall-run begins to loose steam, jump off the wall and Deathgrip the hoop ahead to swing over to a hand hold. Climb up to reach a ledge with an ornate chest that contains a Skeleton Key.

SKELETON KEY

After pocketing the key, turn around and wall-run back along the west passage. Navigate a few hand holds to reach a high ledge, where a Book of the Dead page is found. Collect the page, and then shimmy back across the hand holds to return to the Skeleton Key ledge. Carefully jump down from the ledge to land on the Custodian's chain below, grabbing a floating Boatman Coin in the process.

BOOK OF THE DEAD
PAGE 27

BOATMAN COIN
76

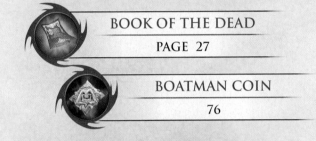

Cross the chain and drop down to solid ground. Use the Custodian to wipe out the Corrupted Construct Warriors that appear, and then smash the Corruption crystals in the nearby passage. Leave the Custodian behind and pass through the east door. Deathgrip the hoop above the lava pit you scaled before, and proceed through the east door to reach the next area.

Area 6: Lava Junction

Cut down the Corrupted Construct Warriors and Adjuncts that ambush you in this area, and then wall-run along the east wall, vaulting off of a peg on your way to a locked door. Use your Skeleton Key to unlock the door and advance.

Area 7: Precarious Pillars

Deathgrip an overhead hoop to swing onto this fiery cavern's northern pillar. The pillar begins to sink under the Horseman's weight; quickly jump toward the pillar to the south and Deathgrip its hoop to ensure you reach it. This pillar also begins to sink; navigate its hand holds with all speed to reach the top, and then leap and Deathgrip over to the next pillar. Repeat this process until you at last reach solid ground, and then advance through the east door.

Area 8: East Custodian Chamber

Slaughter a number of Corrupted Construct Warriors and Adjuncts as you enter this area, and then look for a peg on the wall near the entry door. Vault up off of it to reach a small nook with a chest, and then drop down from the nook and proceed south toward another Maker Custodian.

Death becomes trapped in the room as he nears the Maker Custodian, forced to combat a Corrupted Construct Champion and two Corrupted Construct Adjuncts. Fight hard to destroy these worthy foes, and then scale the north wall and work your way around the room to reach the south balcony. Pull the lever you find there to lower the gate near the Maker Custodian.

Drop down from the ledge, quickly activate the Custodian, and then use it to smash the additional constructs that storm the room. Search the nook from which these final enemies emerged to discover a chest that contains the Dungeon Map. Roll north, and then east afterward, smashing through some Corruption crystals to access a fiery chamber.

DUNGEON MAP

Area 9: East Lava Cavern

Two cranks must be turned within this chamber to raise the north gates. Roll west from the entry to reach a side passage and park the Custodian on the orb slot there to lower the nearby gate. Dismount and wall-run to a hand hold, and then wait for the overhead pipes to stop pouring lava before quickly wall-running past them.

When you reach the final hand hold, climb up to the first crank and turn it to remove one of the two north gates. Enter the nearby passage afterward to discover a chest, and then drop down from the passage's end to return to the Custodian.

Now, roll the Custodian into the chamber's east passage. Park it on another orb slot there, and this time, fire its chain at a target to the north. Mount the chain afterward and tiptoe across, again waiting for overhead pipes to stop pouring lava.

When you reach the end of the chain, turn left and Deathgrip a hoop to swing over to the second crank. Turn this to remove the final gate. Swing back to the chain afterward and avoid the pouring lava as you return to the Custodian. Roll into the north passage.

Area 10: North Passage

Dismount from the Custodian when you reach a tall gate that blocks your progress. Scale the nearby wall to bypass the obstacle. A host of Corrupted Construct Warriors, Adjuncts, and Champions ambush you on the gate's other side. This is a perilous battle because ceiling pipes regularly pour lava into holes in the floor. Evade around these lethal obstacles as you cut down the constructs.

Slaying all of the enemies lowers the surrounding gates, allowing you to return for your Maker Custodian. Do so and roll past the west lava, arriving at a door. Fire the Custodian's chain to destroy the Corruption crystals in the nearby passage, causing a bridge to fall into place. Roll across the bridge to return to the Lava Junction area.

Area 6, Revisited

Park the Custodian on this area's south orb slot, and then fire its chain at the south target. When you're halfway across the chain, turn left and leap into the dark hole in the east wall. Deathgrip the hoop within the hole to ensure you enter it, and then scale the east wall to reach a higher ledge.

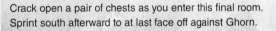

Area 11: Ghorn Showdown

Swing from another hoop to reach the opposite ledge and plunder the chest you discover there, and then carefully drop back down to the chain. Cross it, scale the south wall, and proceed through the south door to reach the final area.

Crack open a pair of chests as you enter this final room. Sprint south afterward to at last face off against Ghorn.

BOSS BATTLE: GHORN

At last, the Pale Rider has caught up to his quarry. There's no place left for this crazed construct to run. Time to teach Ghorn some manners.

At first, Ghorn's attacks are slow and easy to evade. Simply circle around his fist drill, and tap the Evade trigger to backflip away from Ghorn whenever he begins to glow with energy. This means that he's about to unleash a deadly close-range explosion.

Ghorn will eventually begin to pound the ground, causing flames to bubble up from the lava bed beneath the porous arena. Stay mobile during this attack to avoid damage, and then get back to hacking away at Ghorn.

When Ghorn is reduced to half his health, he begins to summon Corrupted Construct Warriors to his aid. Cut them down if they get in your way; otherwise, focus on slaying their master. Return to Muria after the battle and inform her of your success.

LAIR OF THE DEPOSED KING

This underground ruin is home to a menacing skeletal giant named Argul. The door to the second Death Tomb is also located at the bottom of this ruin, and can be easily accessed by descending the main stairwell all the way to the bottom. Argul is a mighty adversary, and likely too much for Death to handle until the Rider nears the end of his quest.

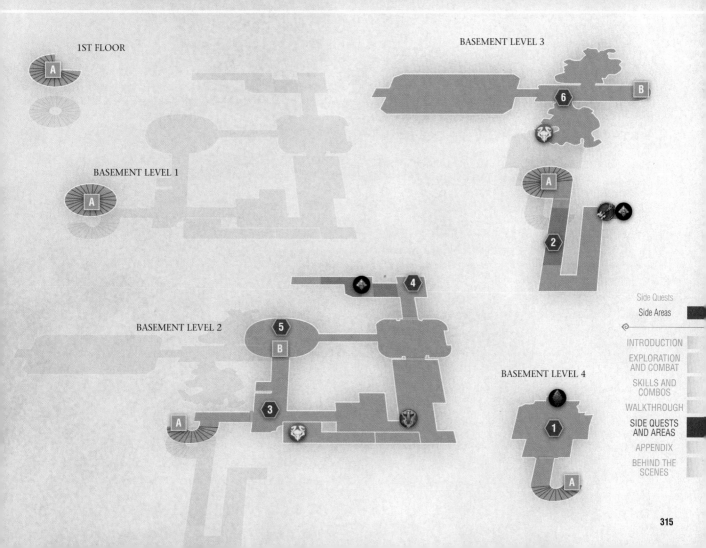

1ST FLOOR

BASEMENT LEVEL 1

BASEMENT LEVEL 2

BASEMENT LEVEL 3

BASEMENT LEVEL 4

Side Quests
Side Areas

INTRODUCTION
EXPLORATION AND COMBAT
SKILLS AND COMBOS
WALKTHROUGH
SIDE QUESTS AND AREAS
APPENDIX
BEHIND THE SCENES

Area 1: Death Tomb Access

Descend the Lair's main stairwell, continuing ever downward until you reach the chamber at the very bottom of the stairs. The door to the second Death Tomb is located here, along with a Stonebite that's lodged atop the door. After collecting twenty Book of the Dead pages, obtain a special key from Vulgrim that allows you to enter this Death Tomb and claim the valuables housed within.

> **TIP**
> See the previous "Side Quests" chapter for details on what you'll find within this Death Tomb.

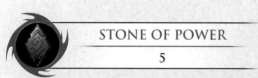

STONE OF POWER

5

Area 2: Skeleton Key Passage

Enter the stairwell's second door to reach this narrow passage. Hang from the entry ledge and drop down past several pegs to reach a low beam.

Jump from the end of the beam and Deathgrip a hoop to swing over to another beam. Scale the wall to reach the passage above.

Sprint up the long flight of stairs to reach an ornate chest that contains a Skeleton Key. Run up the nearby wall after claiming the key, and then jump from the height of your vertical wall-run in order to reach a floating Boatman Coin. Backtrack to the main stairwell afterward, return to the first door you encountered, and then head through.

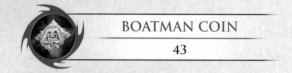

BOATMAN COIN

43

Area 3: Main Ruin

The stairwell's first door leads to the main ruin. Descend the ruin's east stairs, and then look for a pair of hand holds on the south wall. Climb up, wall-run to a third hand hold, and then shimmy around two corners.

Wall-run past a peg to reach another hand hold, and then Deathgrip the hoop above to soar up to a ledge. Collect the Soul Arbiter's Sacred Scroll you find on the ledge before dropping down to return to the east stairs.

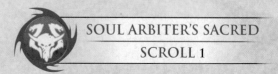

SOUL ARBITER'S SACRED

SCROLL 1

This time, descend the east stairs and drop down off the end of the broken stairs that follow. Turn around and collect the Relic that's hidden beneath the broken stairs, and then open the chest to the north. Proceed through the north door afterward.

RELIC OF ETU-GOTH
1

Area 4: Pitfall Passage

Pass through an empty room to reach this passage, which features two lethal pits. Wall-run past the first pit, and then smash the crates you find on the ledge beyond to discover a Boatman Coin. Deathgrip an overhead hoop to flip past the second pit and land near a chest. Backtrack out of this passage after claiming your plunder, and use the Skeleton Key you found in Area 1 to unlock the empty room's west door.

BOATMAN COIN
44

Area 5: Elevator

Scale this small chamber's south wall to reach a ledge with a lever. Pull the lever to open the nearby gate, allowing for easy travel back to the Lair's main stairwell. Drop down from the ledge afterward and strike the room's central crystal to make the floor lower like an elevator.

Area 6: The Deposed King's Court

The elevator ferries Death to a frigid section of the ruin. Wipe out the Ice Skeletons in the north and south side caverns, and then search the south cavern's southwest corner for a scrawl on the wall that bestows a Soul Arbiter's Sacred Scroll. Backtrack out and proceed west to face off against the Deposed King, Argul—but only if you're prepared for an extremely difficult challenge.

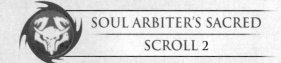

SOUL ARBITER'S SACRED
SCROLL 2

BOSS BATTLE: ARGUL

This towering skeleton is known as the Deposed King, and it wields a massive mace that's capable of freezing Death cold in his tracks. Slaying Argul will advance one of Thane's side quests and earn you an excellent weapon, but the task is easier said than done.

Argul commonly lashes out with his giant mace, attempting to crush the Reaper with a single blow. Circle around

the Deposed King to avoid this lethal strike, and then counter with a devastating combo when his mace becomes stuck in the ground.

> ### ⚑ CAUTION
> Don't attack Argul unless his mace is stuck; he's good at blocking your strikes with his shield and countering with a punishing shield bump.

If Argul's mace doesn't become stuck, then beware: he'll quickly follow-up with a second strike. Evade again to avoid this second

blow and wait for your chance to counter when the Deposed King's mace becomes lodged in the ground.

> ### ⚑ CAUTION
> Being struck by Argul's mace may cause Death to become frozen solid, setting him up for further unpleasantness. Rapidly tap the Action button to break free of the ice before the Deposed King can capitalize on the Rider's immobility.

Sometimes Argul will slam his shield into the ground and then rush forward a short distance in an effort to

ram you. Either backflip away from this attack or evade in a circle around it. Again, don't counter—wait for Argul's mace to become stuck.

After suffering significant damage, Argul adds a new attack: he spins around and races toward Death with

lethal intent. Tap the Evade trigger three times to perform a trio of backflips and ensure you avoid this far-reaching assault. Continue the game of cat-and-mouse against the Deposed King until he finally falls and his exceptional weapon becomes yours.

SCEPTER OF THE DEPOSED KING

SIDE QUEST COMPLETE:
"FIND AND KILL THE DEPOSED KING"

SENTINEL'S GAZE

Descend the stairs at the Maw's north end, just south of the three-way bridge, to visit a small underground keep that serves as the entrance to another side dungeon called Boneriven. The Soul Splitter is required to fully explore Sentinel's Gaze.

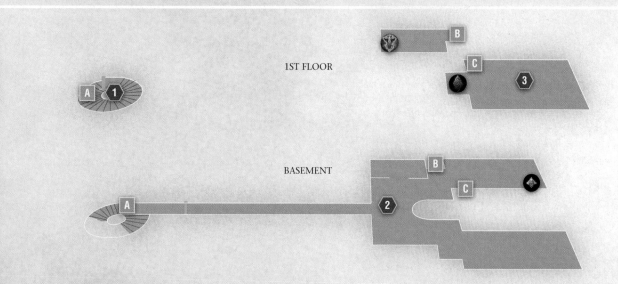

1ST FLOOR

BASEMENT

Area 1: Entry Stairwell

The winding stairwell that leads down into Sentinel's Gaze is broken. Wall-run to a post where the stairs have collapsed, and then slide down. Wall-run to the left to crack open a chest, return to the post, and wall-run to the right to reach the bottom of the stairs.

Area 2: Keep Grounds

Skeletons and Skeletal Warriors roam the grounds surrounding Sentinel's Gaze. Slay them all, and then run to the northeast corner of the area to find a Boatman Coin hidden inside a crate.

BOATMAN COIN
56

Backtrack a bit and scale the low wall near an alcove that's blocked by Corruption crystals. Climb up to a ledge where a Shadowbomb pod grows. Collect the Relic that's hidden behind the nearby torch, and then grab a bomb. Drop down from the ledge and use the bomb to obliterate the alcove's Corruption crystals so that you may access the weapon racks and chest within.

RELIC OF ETU-GOTH
5

Stand near the front of the main structure and split Death's soul. Climb the main structure and wall-run around its curved front wall. Keep going until you're able to climb up to a higher ledge, where more Corruption crystals block your progress.

Switch souls and return to the Shadowbomb pod. Enter aiming mode and toss a bomb over to the soul that's standing near the crystals. Switch souls, destroy the obstacles, and then scale the hand holds they were covering.

Area 3: Keep Roof

The hand holds lead up to the keep's roof. Shoot the Stonebite on the back of the tall statue, and then stand on the roof's northeast corner.

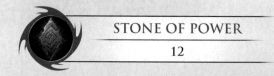

STONE OF POWER
12

Switch souls again and hurl another Shadowbomb up to the soul on the roof. Use this bomb to obliterate the crystals inside the roof's alcove, exposing a large chest. Claim your plunder, and then optionally drop down into the hole behind the chest to visit another side dungeon called Boneriven.

BONERIVEN

This shadowy side dungeon is filled with vicious fiends. Plenty of treasure awaits those daring enough to brave Boneriven's forgotten halls. You can't enter this dark place without the aid of the Soul Splitter. Its entrance lies at the top of Sentinel's Gaze.

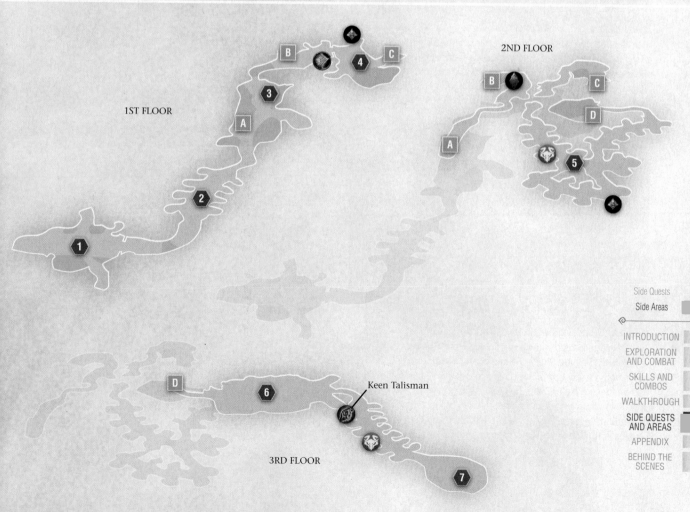

2ND FLOOR

1ST FLOOR

Keen Talisman

3RD FLOOR

Side Quests
Side Areas

INTRODUCTION

EXPLORATION
AND COMBAT

SKILLS AND
COMBOS

WALKTHROUGH

**SIDE QUESTS
AND AREAS**

APPENDIX

BEHIND THE
SCENES

Area 1: Stalker Lair I

Death's foray into Boneriven starts off with a bang: a menacing Undead Stalker and several Undead Prowlers must be dealt with in the very first room. Stay mobile and unleash Death's best skills as you combat these dangerous foes. Beware the Stalker's ability to unleash long, vicious attack combos when it nears death.

Stand on the central pressure plate after the battle and wait for the east gate to slowly rise. Sprint toward the gate after it locks into place, evading as you run to roll forward and pick up speed. Make haste, for you have only seconds to pass through the gate before it slams shut again.

Area 2: Coffin Corridor

This passage is filled with Corruption crystals, Shadowbomb pods, and coffins. Slay the Skeletons and Skeletal Warriors, and then use a bomb to destroy the crystals in two places, exposing a chest and a pressure plate. Stand before the north gate and split Death's soul. Then, have one soul stand atop each of the two nearby pressure plates. Wait for the gate to fully rise, and then revert to physical form and dart through before it slams shut again.

Area 3: Two Routes

The path forks beyond the second gate, offering a choice of routes. Slay a few Skeletons and raid the chest in the east nook, and then backtrack and take the high trail. Cut down more Skeletons as you follow the curve of the trail, and blast the Stonebite atop one of the stone pillars on the inside of the curve.

STONE OF MYSTICS
24

Secure the area by defeating the Skeletal Warriors and Undead Prowlers that storm up to attack. Collect a Shadowbomb from the pod in the east nook afterward, and then follow the trail around the curve, carrying the bomb down to the first floor. Destroy the east Corruption crystals to open a nook that houses an ornate chest and a pressure plate. Open the chest to acquire the Dungeon Map.

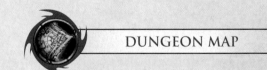

DUNGEON MAP

Split Death's soul before the east gate and use the souls to trigger the two nearby pressure plates. Return to physical form and dart past the gate after it's fully raised.

Area 4: Stalker Lair II

Claim the Boatman Coin in the north nook that lies just beyond the third gate. Backtrack out, and then battle another Undead Stalker, using evasive maneuvers and powerful skills to bring down the beast. Follow the path as it winds up to the second floor, plundering a chest along the way.

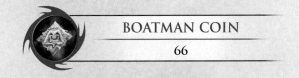

BOATMAN COIN
66

Area 5: Burial Passages I

Deathgrip a hoop to clear a gap and reach these bone-filled passages. Slice up the Scarabs that lurk up here, and claim a Soul Arbiter's Sacred Scroll from the third nook on your right as you advance.

SOUL ARBITER'S SACRED
SCROLL 6

Ignore the pressure plate at the end of the first passage and enter the next passage to the south. Loop around to find a Scarab Mound and a second pressure plate at the passage's end. Wipe out the mound to stem the tide of Scarabs, and then loot the two nearby chests. Backtrack a bit and claim a Boatman Coin from the south nook.

BOATMAN COIN
67

Split Death's soul while standing atop the pressure plate near the north gate. Send one soul back through the burial passages to trigger the pressure plate you noticed a moment ago. With both plates depressed, the north gate begins to open. Revert to physical form and hurry through. Slaughter more Scarabs on your way up to Boneriven's third floor.

Area 6: Scarab Hulk Lair

This spacious chamber is home to multiple Scarab Mounds. Three formidable Undead Scarab Hulks also combat you here. Stay mobile and focus on slaying the Hulks first, and then wipe out the Scarab Mounds. Crack open the southeast chest after the battle, and then stand before the east gate and split Death's soul. Move each soul onto the two nearby pressure plates before racing past the gate as you've done before.

Area 7: Burial Passages II

This final stretch of burial passages is devoid of hostiles and houses a number of prizes. The time has come to claim your just rewards. Find a unique talisman in the first nook on the right, and a Soul Arbiter's Sacred Scroll farther ahead, inside another nook on the right. Three other nooks house chests that beg to be looted.

KEEN TALISMAN

SOUL ARBITER'S SACRED SCROLL 7

Area 8: Treasure Chamber

A large chest rises from the floor when Death strolls into this final cavern. Rip open the chest to claim even more precious loot, and then fast-travel out of this forsaken place.

SOUL ARBITER'S MAZE

An ancient maze lies at the north end of the Spine's west valley. Normally, you'd have little hope of solving this labyrinth until you discover all of the Soul Arbiter's Scrolls that are scattered throughout the realms. However, because you've wisely purchased this guide, you don't really need those scrolls at all—we reveal exactly how to solve the maze right here.

Maze Entry

The Soul Arbiter's Maze features a small entry area that must be navigated in order to reach the maze proper. Smash the crates in the southeast corner to obtain a Boatman Coin, and then scale the north wall to reach a hand hold. Deathgrip across the overhead hoops to reach a southern ledge with a switch.

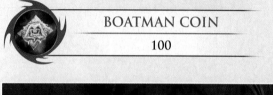

BOATMAN COIN

100

Before pushing the switch, aim west and blast the Stonebite on the wall. Push the switch afterward to make a row of pegs appear on the west wall. Drop down and quickly scale the west wall before the pegs retract. Deathgrip the overhead hoops to swing over to the east ledge.

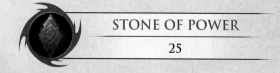

STONE OF POWER

25

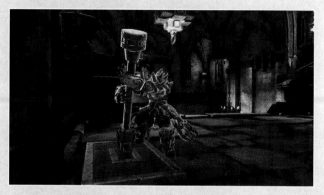

Pull the east ledge's lever to permanently lock the west wall's pegs in place. Open the nearby chest, and then proceed through the north door. Follow a short passage to discover the unassuming entrance to the Soul Arbiter's Maze.

Read the mysterious book that sits on the table to learn the basics of the maze, which we'll cover in the next section. Collect the scroll that hovers near the maze's entry portal, and then step onto the portal and travel into the maze.

SOUL ARBITER'S SCROLL

10

Solving the Maze

There are ten levels to the Soul Arbiter's Maze. Each level features multiple rooms, and each room presents you with a choice of four directions: north (N), south (S), east (E), or west (W). Simply defeat the enemies that attack you in each room, and then choose your direction. Keep searching until you find the stairs that lead down to the next level.

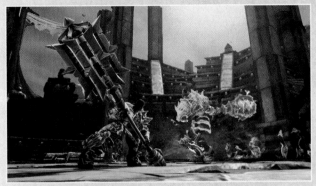

SOUL ARBITER'S MAZE SOLUTIONS

LEVEL	SECRET DIRECTIONS	NEXT LEVEL DIRECTIONS
1 – Declination	S, E	N, W
2 – Apprehension	N, N	E, S, N
3 – Opposition	N, S, E	W, E, N, N
4 – Separation	W, E, N	E, W, N, S
5 – Deception	W, N, S	W, W, N, E
6 – Isolation	E, E, E, S	S, E, E, N, N
7 – Revulsion	S, S, W, N, N	S, W, E, E, E
8 – Inversion	N, S, S, E, N	N, W, N, W, E
9 – Benediction	S, W, E, E, N	E, N, E, N, S
10 – Ascension	N, S, E, W	W, E, N, S, W

Each level of the maze presents you with progressively stronger enemies. When you reach the end of the maze, you'll need to contend with the nefarious Soul Arbiter himself. Defeat this worthy adversary to obtain the Soul Arbiter's Crown, which the Chancellor at the *Eternal Throne* seeks as part of his "The Chancellor's Quarry" side quest. See the previous "Side Quests" section of this chapter for further details.

You could get lost forever on a single floor of the maze if you don't know the correct route to take. Normally, the only way to solve the maze involves collecting the Soul Arbiter's Scrolls that are scattered across the realms. However, you can easily see exactly how to complete the maze by referencing the following table.

> **TIP**
>
> If you're determined to find all of the Soul Arbiter's Scrolls and solve the maze in the traditional fashion, you might consider referencing the "Appendix" chapter for a quick-reference table that reveals the locations of every scroll.

Every level of the maze also holds a secret treasure trove. You'd normally only know to find these by collecting the Soul Arbiter's Sacred Scrolls that are also hidden throughout the realms—but these, too, are revealed in the following table.

Maze Collectibles

In addition to the Soul Arbiter's Maze's secret treasure troves, there are a few items of special interest hidden within the maze. When you reach the fifth level (Deception), access the secret treasure trove to discover unique scythes called the Black Demise. Also, as you approach the portal the leads down to the maze's eight level (Inversion), look for a Stonebite on the on the wall behind it. You'll also earn a special secondary weapon for killing the Soul Arbiter: The Executioner's Hooks.

> **TIP**
>
> Smash breakable objects within the maze to potentially score potions. If your supply is dangerously low, consider leaving the maze to restock. You can return to the start of the lowest level you've reached by inspecting the Mysterious Book on the table near the maze's entrance.

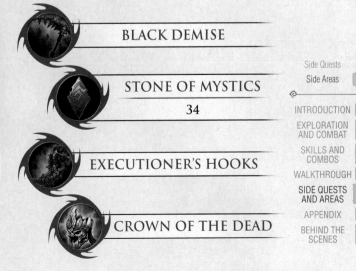

BLACK DEMISE

STONE OF MYSTICS

34

EXECUTIONER'S HOOKS

CROWN OF THE DEAD

On the eleventh level of this twisted labyrinth, the Rider arrives at an ancient arena.
Here, the Arbiter himself will attempt to test Death's mettle.

Beware of the Soul Arbiter's speed, as he will attempt to deliver furious combo attacks that can make short work of the Rider. Wait for his attacks, then evade and quickly counter with a combo of your own.

When unleashing Death's fury upon the Arbiter, be wary when he begins to levitate higher. Quickly move away from the Arbiter, as he is about to drive his mace into the ground and deliver a massive area attack.

TIP

Unstoppable is an extremely helpful skill to use during this battle. The boost of strength aids when delivering punishment in the brief moments you have to strike the Arbiter.

After the Arbiter loses a quarter of his health, he calls upon his undead legions and envelops himself in a protective barrier. When in this state, he is impervious to any attack. When in this state, the Arbiter will not engage in combat. Use this time to focus on dispatching the undead soldiers that the Arbiter has called forth. Once his horde has been laid to waste, the Arbiter leaves the safety of his barrier and resumes his assault. Continue to evade his blows and counter with swift attacks.

Now it is time to finish this. Weakened and nearing his end, the Arbiter begins to unleash rapid combination attacks. Evade his violent swings and continue to counter with combos. Make effective use of your counter attacks and soon the Arbiter will lock blades with Death.

Once the Arbiter's health has fallen to half its capacity, he returns to the safety of his barrier and calls forth more soldiers from beyond the grave. Dispatch these minions and the Arbiter returns to the fray once again.

Death does not stay his blade and slays the Arbiter, reclaiming the Crown of the Dead in the process. Take a moment to relish in your victory over the diabolical labyrinth and it's keeper.

When the Arbiter's health has been depleted to one quarter, he calls upon the aid of an Undead General. With a behemoth like this by his side, the Arbiter is not content to sit out the fight from the safety of his barrier. Still impervious to attack, the Arbiter will attempt to bludgeon Death. Keep your distance from the Dead Lord and focus your attacks on the Undead General. Soon the Undead General will fall, as will the Arbiter's defensive shield.

Before exiting through the portal, make your way downstairs and crack open the large chest found in this basement. After claiming the spoils, you can now exit the maze through the portal upstairs.

Appendix

These final pages of the guide expose every item of interest in *Darksiders II*. Use the provided checklists to monitor your progress in tracking down the many items of value that are scattered throughout the realms.

LEGENDARY ITEMS

The following weapons and pieces of gear are one-of-a-kind, making them highly prized.

LEGENDARY ITEMS—SCYTHES

OBTAINED	ICON	NAME	LEVEL	STATS	LOCATION	DETAILS
☐		Barbed Defilers	22	Damage: 187-215 Special Ability: Defile	The Crucible	Complete Stage 3 of the Crucible (Waves 51-75).
☐		Bheithir's Talons	15	Damage: 64-84 Critical Damage: +150% Special Ability: Bheithir's Fire	The Nook	Defeat Bheithir in the basement of the Nook. (Requires the Deathgrip.)
☐		Black Demise	15	Damage: 131-151 Healing Bonus: 50 Health Steal: +10% Special Ability: Black Heart	Soul Arbiter's Maze	Find the secret area on Level 5 of the maze.
☐		Chaos Fang	1	Damage: 48-56 Critical Chance: +20% Critical Damage: +200%	Tri-Stone	Muria will give this to you if you've beaten Darksiders I.
☐		Demonflame Renders	19	Damage: 161-185 Critical Chance: +40% Critical Damage: -50% Special Ability: Demonfire	The Black Stone - Area 5: East Wing (Past)	Drop to the cylindrical pit's lowest hand hold and shimmy around to the secret passage. Scale the passage's north wall to reach a secret room containing the scythes.
☐		GnoMAD Scythes	21	Damage: 140-166 Special Ability: You Mad?	—	Sent to you through the Tome system after you collect the fourth and final GnoMAD Gnome.
☐		Goldbringer	17	Damage: 142-164 Special Ability: Midas Touch	The Ivory Citadel - Area 4: South Courtyard	After solving the Soul Splitter puzzle to advance past the aqueduct, destroy the nearby corruption crystals to expose a lever. Pull the lever to open the aqueduct's other gate, then go through to find the scythes.
☐		Guillotine	19	Damage: 161-185 Critical Damage: +300% Special Ability: Fate	The Fjord	Speak with Blackroot and return the final Stonebite to him.
☐		Lifebane	21	Damage: 174-200 Special Ability: Lifebane	The Veil	Awarded on defeat of the Icebound Guardian. (Second playthrough only.)
☐		Static Blades	25	Damage: 213-245 Critical Chance: +10% Arcane Critical Chance: +15% Special Ability: Static Shock	The Eternal Throne	Awarded after returning the Bloodless Talisman to Draven. (Gamestop pre-order only. Second playthrough only.)

LEGENDARY ITEMS—SECONDARY WEAPONS

OBTAINED	ICON	NAME	LEVEL	STATS	LOCATION	DETAILS
☐		Absolution	20	Damage (Slow): 527-597 Strength: 43 Special Ability: Absolution	The Well of Souls	Awarded on defeat of Absalom.
☐		Achidna's Fangs	14	Damage (Fast): 126-144 Critical Chance: +16% Special Ability: Searing Venom	The Psychameron - Area 7: Path of Shadows	Awarded on defeat of Achidna.
☐		Aftermath	30	Damage (Slow): 713-821 Strength: 106 Wrath Per Hit: 767	The Crucible	Complete All 100 Waves in one sitting.
☐		Dark Avenger	5	Damage (Fast): 60-72 Defense: 36 Knockback Power: +25%	The Cauldron - Area 13: Gharn Showdown	Awarded on defeat of Gharn.
☐		Executioner's Hooks	18	Damage (Fast): 120-136 Special Ability: Execution	Soul Arbiter's Maze	Awarded on defeat of the Soul Arbiter.
☐		Fists of Elhazar	16	Damage (Fast): 144-166 Critical Chance: +16% Special Ability: Elhazar's Glare Special Ability: Elhazar's Might	Earth - Area 17: Hotel	In the room with the debris slope, leap to the nook in the wall that contains the weapon.
☐		Gauntlets of Savagery	8	Damage (Fast): 78-90 Wrath Cost: -25% Special Ability: Bloodlust	Tri-Stone (The Maker's Forge)	Speak with Karn after returning the third and final lost item to him. (Gamestop pre-order only.)
☐		Gorewood Maul	10	Damage (Slow): 254-292 Knockback Power: +50% Strength Bonus: +100%	The Weeping Crag - Area 9: Gorewood's Lair	Awarded on defeat of Gorewood.

STONEBITES

A construct named Blackroot resides within the Fjord and asks Death to bring him the energy of special stones that are scattered about the realms. Here's where to find them all.

STONES OF MYSTICS

NO.	OBTAINED	LOCATION	DETAILS
1	☐	Forge Lands (Overworld) - Fjord	Close to Blackroot, on the cliff.
2	☐	Forge Lands (Overworld) - Stonefather's Vale	On a cliff near the Book of the Dead page.
3	☐	Forge Lands (Overworld) - Baneswood (NW Ruin)	Climb the ruin; Stonebite is across from the chest.
4	☐	Forge Lands (Overworld) - Baneswood	On the cliff in the north nook between the northwest and northeast ruins.
5	☐	Forge Lands (Overworld) - East Trail	On the ruined stone shrine atop the side trail.
6	☐	Forge Lands (Overworld) - East Trail (Enclosed Shrine)	High on the wall behind the enclosed shrine's statue.
7	☐	Forge Lands (Overworld) - Charred Pass	Heading toward Cauldron, take the left trail toward the Scar. It's on an overhead rock.
8	☐	Forge Lands (Overworld) - Charred Pass (Southwest Ruin)	In the southwest ruin, in the room to the right of the treasure chest at the top.
9	☐	Forge Lands (Overworld) - Shadow Gorge	On the outside wall to the right of the entrance to the Shattered Forge.
10	☐	Forge Lands (Overworld) - Path to Drenchfort	Inside the cave as you leave the Fjord en route to the Drenchfort.
11	☐	Drenchfort - Area 3: Great Aqueduct	Above the south water canal.
12	☐	Tri-Stone	On the back (south) side of the Maker's Forge.
13	☐	Nook - Area 5: Elevator Chamber	On the wall near the north elevator (ride up and shoot).
14	☐	Lost Temple - Area 3: Great Hall (Revisited)	After returning with the Custodian, drop into the south pit and shoot.
15	☐	Weeping Crag - Area 1: Entry and Drawbridge	On a tall stone pillar beyond the drawbridge (east side of the bridge).
16	☐	Kingdom of the Dead (Overworld) - Serpent's Peak	On the ceiling of the cave, near the path to Vulgrim.
17	☐	Gilded Arena - Area 2: Stairwell	At the very top of the long, spiral staircase leading to the arena, on the sword hilt of a statue.
18	☐	Gilded Arena - Area 7: Room of Death	Up near the ceiling.
19	☐	Gilded Arena - Area 9: Animus Stone Chamber I	Affixed to a hanging cage.
20	☐	Kingdom of the Dead (Overworld) - Maw (South Gate)	West exterior side of the Maw's south gate, in a high window.
21	☐	Phariseer's Tomb - Area 3: Elevator Chamber	Fourth floor, on the high wall.
22	☐	Judicator's Tomb - Area 13: Room of Wax	After slaying the Bone Giant, look up and shoot the Stonebite on the ceiling.
23	☐	Psychameron - Area 7: Path of Shadows	Above the area's entry door (turn around after you enter).
24	☐	Boneriven - Area 3: Two Routes	On a stone pillar (stalagmite) where the upper route curves downward.
25	☐	Lostlight (Overworld) - Path to Crystal Spire	Above the door to Death Tomb III.
26	☐	Lostlight (Overworld) - Crystal Spire Grounds	On the sword of the kneeling angel statue to the right of the Crystal Spire's entry.
27	☐	Lostlight (Overworld) - Crystal Spire Grounds	On the sword of the kneeling angel statue to the left of the Crystal Spire's entry.
28	☐	Earth - Area 1: Courtyard	On the corner of a north building.
29	☐	Earth - Area 4: Subway Station	On the station's ceiling near the center of the station. Easily visible from the north walkway.
30	☐	Earth - Area 5: Southern Streets	On the side of a building near the overpass.
31	☐	Earth - Area 15: Lower Bridge	After passing the first broken section of bridge, turn around and shoot the low Stonebite on the support column.

STONES OF MYSTICS, CONT.

NO.	OBTAINED	LOCATION	DETAILS
32	☐	Ivory Citadel - Area 3: East Courtyard	Scale the south stairs and enter a narrow passage. After climbing up to the passage's upper level, wall-run to a chest. Turn around and shoot the nearby Stonebite.
33	☐	Ivory Citadel - Area 8: East Tower	Atop the arch at the bottom of the tower's stairs.
34	☐	Soul Arbiter's Maze	Visible behind the portal that leads down to the maze's eighth floor.

STONES OF POWER

NO.	OBTAINED	LOCATION	DETAILS
1	☐	Forge Lands (Overworld) - Charred Pass	Dive into the well in the marsh area and swim into a small cave. The stone is on the wall.
2	☐	Forge Lands (Overworld) - Fjord (East Keep)	Inside the east keep, above the entry door.
3	☐	Lost Temple - Area 12: Orb Junction	High on the east wall.
4	☐	Weeping Crag - Area 9: Gorewood's Lair	Near some high branches in the final area where Gorewood lurks.
5	☐	Lair of the Deposed King - Area 1: Death Tomb Access	All the way downstairs, atop the door of Death Tomb II.
6	☐	Kingdom of the Dead (Overworld) - The Maw—West Valley (NW Ruin)	In the room with the portals, high on the west wall.
7	☐	Gilded Arena - Area 10: East Passage	In a side nook as you navigate the passage.
8	☐	Phariseer's Tomb - Area 7: Pillar Pit	On the hilt of the statue's sword at the top of the room.
9	☐	Kingdom of the Dead (Overworld) - Spine	After exiting the south gate, turn around and climb its exterior wall to reach a chest. Face south and shoot the stone.
10	☐	Kingdom of the Dead (Overworld) - Spine (East Tower)	Scale the east tower and shoot the Stonebite on the high interior wall.
11	☐	Judicator's Tomb - Area 2: Dungeon	On a hanging cage over the central pit.
12	☐	Kingdom of the Dead (Overworld) - Sentinel's Gaze	On the back of the statue atop the main structure. Soul Splitter is needed to destroy the Corruption crystals and reach.
13	☐	City of the Dead - Area 9: Wraith Gates	After lowering the east gate, go south and find the Stonebite on a wall near a chest.
14	☐	Lostlight (Overworld) - Crystal Spire Grounds	On the tower's first floor balcony, on the wall above a statue.
15	☐	Scar (BEFORE EARTH)	After reaching the Scar's entry balcony, look up and shoot the Stonebite in the broken overhead pipe.
16	☐	Earth - Area 7: Car Tunnel—West	Loop around to a dead end with a chest. The Stonebite is on the tunnel's roof above the chest.
17	☐	Earth - Area 17: Hotel	On the north wall in the room with the slope of debris.
18	☐	Ivory Citadel - Area 15: Corruption Pool - Third Floor	On the chest of the tall north statue.
19	☐	Ivory Citadel - Area 17: North Courtyard	On the rocks to the southwest of the second (southern) crank and rotating wall.
20	☐	The Black Stone - Area 4: Great Foyer (Past), Revisited	When reentering the Great Foyer from the East Wing, look to the right and shoot the Stonebite on the belly of the north statue.
21	☐	The Black Stone - Area 6: West Wing (Present), Revisited	High on the north wall.
22	☐	The Black Stone - Area 7: West Wing (Past), Revisited	On the south exterior wall, easily visible from the area's central walkway.
23	☐	Shadow's Edge (Overworld) - Death Tomb IV	Found within Death Tomb IV.

INTRODUCTION

EXPLORATION AND COMBAT

SKILLS AND COMBOS

WALKTHROUGH

SIDE QUESTS AND AREAS

APPENDIX

BEHIND THE SCENES

STONES OF POWER, CONT.

NO.	OBTAINED	LOCATION	DETAILS
24	☐	Shadow's Edge (Overworld) - Death Tomb IV	Found within Death Tomb IV.
25	☐	Kingdom of the Dead (Overworld) - Soul Arbiter's Maze (Entry)	After using the Deathgrip to swing to the high switch, turn and shoot the Stonebite on the west wall.

◆ STONES OF RESISTANCE

NO.	OBTAINED	LOCATION	DETAILS
1	☐	Foundry - Area 1: Foundry Entrance	Stand near the north door and wait for the hanging cauldrons to pass by. The stone will be on the north side of the fourth cauldron.
2	☐	Eternal Throne	On a support pillar in the lower cargo hold, partially obscured by a hanging tarp (near the Tome).
3	☐	Breach Rooftop	Atop the Breach's roof. You can only get this after rotating the lantern statue atop the Maw's northwest ruin.
4	☐	Kingdom of the Dead (Overworld) - Leviathan's Gorge (Underbelly)	Navigate the hoops beneath Leviathan's Gorge's southern valley, then use the Soul Splitter to access a chest. Before leaving the chest ledge, look up to notice the Stone.
5	☐	City of the Dead - Area 13: Exterior Walkways	High on the north tower.
6	☐	Earth - Area 6: Noss Ambush	On the north building of the plaza where the Noss attacks you.
7	☐	Ivory Citadel - Area 13: West Tower	Inside the West Tower, top floor, above the doorway.
8	☐	Ivory Citadel - Area 19: Portal Platforms	Travel through the portals to reach the high chest nook. Look up after looting the chest and find the Stonebite on the broken wall near the portal.
9	☐	Forge Lands (Overworld) - Fjord (Vulgrim's Area)	In a small room after you destroy Corruption crystals by throwing a Shadowbomb through a portal.
10	☐	The Black Stone - Area 5: East Wing (Past)	In the secret second floor chamber, visible on the high ceiling.

RELICS

A mysterious merchant named Ostegoth asks Death to bring him a number of lost Relics that have been scattered around the realms. Here's where each Relic is found.

◆ RELICS OF ETU-GOTH

NO.	OBTAINED	LOCATION	DETAILS
1	☐	Kingdom of the Dead (Overworld) - Leviathan's Gorge	Just northeast of the bridge, near the edge of the cliff.
2	☐	Lair of the Deposed King - Area 3: Main Ruin	Drop from the end of the broken stairs, then turn around to discover the relic beneath the stairs.
3	☐	Gilded Arena - Area 13: Broken Stairwell II	Hidden on the third section of the stairs. Backtrack up the stairs after landing to discover.
4	☐	Eternal Throne	Behind the Dead King's throne.
5	☐	Kingdom of the Dead (Overworld) - Sentinel's Gaze	Climb up to the Shadowbomb pod and find the Relic near the nearby torch.
6	☐	Phariseer's Tomb - Area 6: Room of Pillars	Inside a crate to the northwest.
7	☐	Kingdom of the Dead (Overworld) - Spine	South of the Soul Arbiter's Maze, near the edge of the east cliff.

RELICS OF ETU-GOTH, CONT.

NO.	OBTAINED	LOCATION	DETAILS
8	☐	Judicator's Tomb - Area 8: East Wing	After pulling the lever, scale the nearby wall to the right and drop from the final hand hold to reach a passage that contains the Relic.
9	☐	Psychameron - Area 7: Path of Shadows	On the landing as you cross the bridge.
10	☐	City of the Dead - Area 9: Wraith Gates	Near the south wall, across from the lever.
11	☐	Lostlight (Overworld) - Path to Crystal Spire	In the brush near Vulgrim.
12	☐	Earth - Area 17: Hotel	In the hotel's entry hallways, in the hole in the wall across from the chest.
13	☐	Ivory Citadel - Area 13: West Tower	After purifying the water, follow the north aqueduct. After dropping down to the lower channel, turn around and find the Relic behind the waterfall.
14	☐	Ivory Citadel - Area 19: Portal Platforms	Behind a statue as you enter the room.
15	☐	The Black Stone - Area 7: West Wing (Past), Revisited	In the side room with the Shadowbomb pod, hidden in the southeast corner.

◆ RELICS OF RENAGOTH

NO.	OBTAINED	LOCATION	DETAILS
1	☐	Gilded Arena - Area 5: Arena	Scale the arena's east walls to reach the upper most balcony on the east side, then Deathgrip a hoop and make your way to the northeast Relic.
2	☐	Leviathan's Gorge—West Valley	Near the edge of the west cliff, behind a rock and gnarled vine.
3	☐	Kingdom of the Dead (Overworld) - Spine	East of the Judicator's Tomb, on the edge of the cliff near the east tower.
4	☐	Psychameron - Area 5: Puzzling Passages—West	After claiming the Skeleton Key, Deathgrip a high hoop as you return to the upper passages. The Relic sits atop the high ledge.
5	☐	City of the Dead - Area 3: Central Plaza	Near the sealed north door, which leads to the final battle.
6	☐	Lostlight (Overworld) - Crystal Spire Grounds	In the far east nook (circle around the Crystal Spire).
7	☐	Earth - Area 4: Subway Station	North of the first demonic growth containing the Staff of Arafel, behind the red Corruption crystals.
8	☐	Earth - Area 5: Southern Streets	At the northwest dead end, behind a car.
9	☐	Ivory Citadel - Area 10: East Aqueduct	After purifying the water atop the East Tower, follow the aqueduct. After dropping twice, turn around and look through the waterfall.
10	☐	Ivory Citadel - Area 13: West Tower	Near the two cranks and portal puzzle, across from the switch.

◆ RELICS OF KHAGOTH

NO.	OBTAINED	LOCATION	DETAILS
1	☐	Kingdom of the Dead (Overworld) - The Maw—West Valley (South Ruin)	Atop the ruin. Press the switch, then quickly scale the wall.
2	☐	Judicator's Tomb - Area 6: West Tower	Search underwater to discover.
3	☐	Ivory Citadel - Area 17: North Courtyard	Near the black Corruption pool, hidden behind a web of Corruption.
4	☐	Shadow's Edge (Overworld) - Outer Keep	On the way to Black Stone, take the left passage through the keep and climb the wall to reach a pressure plate. Split Death's soul there, then backtrack to the right passage and find the Relic.
5	☐	Shadow's Edge (Overworld) - Death Tomb IV	Found within Death Tomb IV.

SOUL ARBITER'S SCROLLS

The Soul Arbiter's Maze is nearly impossible to solve without the aid of several scrolls that are scattered across the realms. Some scrolls are collected like items; others are obtained by inspecting bloody scrawls hidden in certain areas. Ten Soul Arbiter's Scrolls reveal how to solve the maze, while ten Soul Arbiter's Sacred Scrolls reveal how to access a secret treasure cache on each of the maze's ten floors. See the "Side Quests and Areas" chapter for aid in mastering the Soul Arbiter's Maze.

NO.	OBTAINED	LOCATION	DETAILS
		SOUL ARBITER'S SCROLLS	
1	☐	Gilded Arena - Area 10: East Passage	Scrawl on the wall of the nook with the Stone of Power.
2	☐	Gilded Arena - Area 12: West Wing; West Statue	In the southwest alcove. Obtainable after rotating the lantern statue to the south.
3	☐	Kingdom of the Dead (Overworld) - Maw (South Gate)	In an interior nook as you exit the south gate, heading into the Spine.
4	☐	Judicator's Tomb - Area 2: Dungeon	After crossing the pit, search behind the pillar on the right.
5	☐	Judicator's Tomb - Area 7: Prison	After slaying the Tormentor, search the cells to discover the scrawl.
6	☐	City of the Dead - Area 7: Rotating Bridge	Scrawl on the wall on the wall to the south.
7	☐	Earth - Area 1: Courtyard	In the pit at the northwest end of the road.
8	☐	The Black Stone - Area 3: Great Foyer (Present), Revisited	After traveling through the East Wing, use the northeast portal to return to the present, then find the scroll nearby.
9	☐	The Black Stone - Area 6: West Wing (Present), Revisited	While attempting to obtain the Skeleton Key in the past, destroy the Corruption crystals near the Shadowbomb pod. Return to the Shadowbomb pod area in the future and find the scrawl on the wall where the crystals formerly stood.
10	☐	Soul Arbiter's Maze	The scroll hovers near the entrance to the maze.

NO.	OBTAINED	LOCATION	DETAILS
		SOUL ARBITER'S SACRED SCROLLS	
1	☐	Lair of the Deposed King - Area 3: Main Ruin	After descending the entry stairs, turn right and scale the wall. Round the corner and find the scroll on the ledge above.
2	☐	Lair of the Deposed King - Area 6: The Deposed King's Court	Before approaching the Deposed King, search the south side cavern to discover scrawl on the wall in the southwest corner.
3	☐	Kingdom of the Dead (Overworld) - Maw (NW Ruin)	On the ruin's upper balcony, in an alcove near a switch.
4	☐	Phariseer's Tomb - Area 6: Room of Pillars (Exit Passage)	In the north passage, search behind the cage in the east nook to discover.
5	☐	Phariseer's Tomb - Area 9: Phariseer's Hoard	Scrawl on the wall in the dark northeast corner of the lower room with the three chests.
6	☐	Boneriven - Area 5: Burial Passages I	Hidden in the third alcove on the right in the Scarab-filled passage.
7	☐	Boneriven - Area 7: Burial Passages II	In a nook near the end of Boneriven.
8	☐	City of the Dead - Area 19: Burial Passages	Scrawl on the wall near the moveable platform.
9	☐	Earth - Area 11: Car Tunnel—North	In the southwest alcove, scrawl on the wall near the doorway.
10	☐	Ivory Citadel - Area 17: North Courtyard	On the low ledge near the second (southern) crank.

GNOMAD GNOMES

Four creepy-looking Gnomes are cleverly hidden in Darksiders II. Find all four and you'll receive a special weapon: the GnoMAD Scythes.

NO.	OBTAINED	LOCATION	DETAILS
1	☐	City of the Dead - Area 16: Northwest Balcony	Hidden in a secret passage in the wall behind the rotating hand hold.
2	☐	Ivory Citadel - Area 13: West Tower	In the north passage that's filled with Corruption ooze. You can't get it until you've purified the pool atop the West Tower.
3	☐	The Weeping Crag - Area 5: Forgotten Treasury	In a secret underwater cave. Dive into the treasure room's northern waters to locate.
4	☐	The Black Stone - Area 6: West Wing (Present), Third Visit	After opening the locked door in the past and returning to the Great Foyer, descend the north wall's hand holds to reach a lower walkway. Go through the portal to return to the present, then scale the north wall again and go through the west door to find the Gnome in the passage beyond.

ACHIEVEMENTS

Satisfy the following achievements in order to consider yourself the ultimate Horseman.

OBTAINED	NAME	ACHIEVEMENT	DETAILS	XBOX/PC	PS3	AVATAR LOOT
☐	Crow Carrion	Defeat the Crowfather	Any difficulty. Defeat the Crowfather.	20	Bronze	Darksiders Logo Cap
☐	Dust to Dust	Defeat the Guardian	Any difficulty. Defeat the Guardian.	20	Bronze	—
☐	Clipped Wings	Defeat Archon	Any difficulty. Defeat the Archon.	20	Bronze	—
☐	It's Not Over	Defeat Samael	Any difficulty. Defeat Samael.	20	Bronze	—
☐	Soul Crushing	Defeat the Wailing Host	Any difficulty. Defeat the Wailing Host	20	Bronze	—
☐	The Big Boss	Defeat Absalom	Any difficulty. Defeat the Avatar of Chaos.	20	Bronze	—
☐	A Stroll In The Demonic Park	Complete the game on any difficulty setting.	Any difficulty. Defeat the Avatar of Chaos.	30	Silver	Darksiders Art Shirt
☐	Four My Brother	Complete the game on NORMAL	Normal Difficulty. Defeat the Avatar of Chaos.	90	Gold	—
☐	A True Horseman	Complete the game on APOCALYPTIC	Apocalyptic Difficulty. Defeat the Avatar of Chaos.	90	Gold	—
☐	Pathfinder	On first use of Fast Travel	Any Difficulty. Unlocks when Death arrives after using fast travel for the first time.	10	Bronze	—
☐	The Spectral Touch	Collect Deathgrip	Any difficulty. Upon collecting the Deathgrip gear item.	10	Bronze	—
☐	I Can Has Cake?	Collect the Voidwalker	Any difficulty. Upon collecting the Voidwalker gear item.	10	Bronze	—
☐	Tearing Time A New One	Collect the Phasewalker	Any difficulty. Upon collecting the Phasewalker gear item.	10	Bronze	—
☐	Looks Familiar	Collect Redemption	Any difficulty. Upon collecting the Redemption gear item.	10	Bronze	—
☐	Death Will Tear Us Apart	Collect the Soul Splitter	Any difficulty. Upon collecting the Soul Splitter gear item.	10	Bronze	—
☐	By Your Command	Collect the Interdictor Stone	Any difficulty. Upon collecting the Interdiction gear item.	10	Bronze	—
☐	The Triple Lindy	Complete three different high dives in The Foundry	Any difficulty. Jump off the three different high points of The Foundry; the area with the Water Wheels, water and crushing machine. (Area 16: Foundry Plaza.)	10	Bronze	—
☐	Fire of the Mountain	Complete Fire of the Mountain	Any difficulty. Upon completing the Fire of the Mountain quest.	10	Bronze	—
☐	Tears of the Mountain	Complete Tears of the Mountain	Any difficulty. Upon completing the Tears of the Mountain quest.	10	Bronze	—
☐	GnoMAD	Find all the Gnomes	Any difficulty. Unlocked upon finding all four GnoMAD Gnomes.	40	Silver	—
☐	To Move A Mountain	Complete To Move a Mountain	Any difficulty. Upon completing the To Move a Mountain quest.	10	Bronze	—
☐	Heart of the Mountain	Complete Heart of the Mountain	Any difficulty. Upon completing the Heart of the Mountain quest.	10	Bronze	—
☐	Tree of Life	Complete Tree of Life	Any difficulty. Upon completing the Tree of Life quest.	10	Bronze	—
☐	The Lord of Bones	Complete The Lord of Bones	Any difficulty. Upon completing the Lord of Bones quest.	10	Bronze	—
☐	The Toll of Kings	Complete The Toll of Kings	Any difficulty. Upon completing the Toll of Kings quest.	10	Bronze	—
☐	The Court of Bones	Defeat Basileus	Any difficulty. Upon defeating Basileus.	10	Bronze	—
☐	The Book of the Dead	Complete The Book of the Dead	Any difficulty. Unlocked after the fourth and final Chapter of the Dead is given to Vulgrim. (Collect all forty Book of the Dead pages to create the four chapters.)	10	Bronze	—
☐	City of the Dead	Complete City of the Dead	Any difficulty. Unlocked upon defeating the Wailing Host.	10	Bronze	—
☐	The Root Of Corruption	Opening The Well Of Souls	Any difficulty. Unlocked when Death opens the Well of Souls.	10	Bronze	—

OBTAINED	NAME	ACHIEVEMENT	DETAILS	XBOX/PC	TROPHIES	AVATAR LOOT
☐	The Rod of Arafel	Complete The Rod of Arafel	Any difficulty. Unlocked upon the completion of the Rod of Arafel. Triggered by collecting the third and final rod piece.	10	Bronze	—
☐	Diamond Geezertron	Unlock the Final Skill in Either Skill Tree	Any difficulty. Unlocked upon purchasing either Bone Storm (Harbinger Skill Tree) or Frenzy (Necromancer Skill Tree).	10	Bronze	—
☐	Mass Ruckus	Equip Elite items to all slots	Any difficulty. Unlocked when Elite level items (purple menu font) are equipped to all available slots: gauntlets, boots, body, shoulder and talisman.	10	Bronze	—
☐	Stains of Heresy	Complete Stains of Heresy	Any difficulty. Upon completing the Stains of Heresy quest.	10	Bronze	—
☐	The Mad Queen	Complete The Mad Queen	Any difficulty. Upon completing the Mad Queen quest.	10	Bronze	—
☐	Lord of the Black Stone	Complete Lord of the Black Stone	Any difficulty. Upon completing the Lord of the Black Stone quest.	10	Bronze	—
☐	The Secondary Adventure	Complete all Secondary Quests	Any difficulty. Unlocked upon completing all of the side quests.	50	Silver	—
☐	Grim Reaping	Unlock Reaper Form	Any difficulty. Unlocked upon obtaining the Reaper Form ability. Reaper Form is unlocked upon reaching experience Level 10.	10	Bronze	—
☐	Bravo Old Chap	Defeat Wicked Killington	New Game+. Any difficulty. Complete all 100 Waves of the Crucible in one sitting, then defeat Wicked K. Unlocked upon defeat of Wicked K.	30	Bronze	—
☐	Respect Yourself	Your First Respec	Any difficulty. Unlocked upon the player using their first "Respec" item from the demonic merchant, Vulgrim.	20	Silver	—
☐	Is There Anyone Else?	Complete the Crucible	New Game+. Any difficulty. Complete the 100th Wave of the Crucible.	30	Silver	Death Mask
☐	Like a Noss	Defeat the FOUR creatures named by Thane.	Any difficulty. Unlocked after defeating all these four creatures: Karkinos, Achidna, Gorewood & Bheithir	30	Bronze	—
☐	Abracadabra	Open all Death Tombs	Any difficulty. Unlock all four Death Tombs. Unlocked when the fourth and final Death Tomb is opened by Death.	30	Silver	—
☐	Antiquing	Collect all Ostegoth's Relics	Any difficulty. Unlocked when all 30 lost Relics (15 Etu-Goth, 10 Renagoth and 5 Khagoth) are returned to Ostegoth.	30	Bronze	—
☐	I've Brought You A Gift	Complete the Arbiter's Maze	Any difficulty. Upon defeating the Soul Arbiter (on the final level of the Arbiter's Maze)	30	Bronze	—
☐	Feeding Time	Level Up your First Possessed Weapon	Any difficulty. Find a possessed weapon. Continue to sacrifice items to the possessed weapon, until it reaches it's first level increase.	30	Bronze	—
☐	Epic!	Death Reaches Level 30	New Game+. Any difficulty. Unlocked upon Death reaching an experience level of 30.	10	Bronze	—
☐	Pay It Forward	Gift an Item to a Friend	Any difficulty. Unlocked after successfully sending your first gift to a friend, via the Tome system.	10	Bronze	—
☐	All You Can Eat Buffet	Feed Blackroot all His Enchantment Stones	Any difficulty. Collect and return all of the Stonebites to Blackroot. Unlocked upon the giving the final Stonebite to him.	30	Bronze	—
☐	Full Potential	Unlock all Combat Moves and Upgrades	Any difficulty. Purchase all the combat moves/upgrades from Thane & Draven. Unlocked upon purchasing the final move from either character.	30	Bronze	—
☐	BFA	Unlock Everything	Various Difficulties. Unlocked when all other achievements/trophies are unlocked.	10	Silver	—

INTRODUCTION

EXPLORATION AND COMBAT

SKILLS AND COMBOS

WALKTHROUGH

SIDE QUESTS AND AREAS

APPENDIX

BEHIND THE SCENES

Vigil Games founders Marvin Donald, David Adams, Ryan Stefanelli, and Joe Madureira.

DARKSIDERS® II

BEHIND THE SCENES

DAVID ADAMS
STUDIO GENERAL MANAGER

PRIMA: Could you introduce yourself and explain your role in the development of *Darksiders II*?

DAVID: My name is David Adams. I'm the General Manager of the studio, and I guess I'm involved in pretty much everything. I spend most of the time just reviewing stuff. You know, going to meetings, looking at levels, playing, and giving feedback. Working with the artists, giving them feedback on their work, and just whatever I can do to help people get their job done better.

PRIMA: Could you explain how the Tome system works, and how you came up with the idea?

DAVID: Even though *Darksiders* is a single-player game, we wanted there to be a lot of interaction between players. Especially if you're playing the game at the same time one of your friends is. The original idea is that you could go out in the game and put a treasure chest down, put stuff in it, and tell your friend, "Hey, dude, I left you a treasure chest, let's go figure out where it is." For various reasons, we simplified that down to just a mailbox system. You can send items and equipment and all that kind of stuff. If you find a cool scythe and you know your friend's a little lower level, you can throw them the scythe through the tomes, and then when they get on they'll get that item. So, there's just a little bit of interaction even though it's a single-player game.

PRIMA: What would you say is your favorite area in the game?

DAVID: I think one of my favorite areas overall is the undead area, just because I like skeletons. Any game where there are skeletons, I'm in. Within that area, there's a guy called the Dead King, and I like him because most of the characters in the game fear Death—they're like, "Oh no, the Reaper's come to take our souls, run away, blah-blah-blah, whatever."—but he actually doesn't care because he's already dead. So they have a lot more interesting interactions. They talk almost as equals in the game, even though the Grim Reaper is there in the realm of the dead, so I just think their interactions are a lot more interesting and cool than some of the other NPC's.

PRIMA: Could you tell us a little bit about the Crucible, and how you came up with the idea?

DAVID: The crucible is an optional mini-game in the game which we actually generated from our internal mini-game challenge. One of the designers came up with the idea. Essentially, it's a good way to test your weapons, your skills, all your different stuff… and it's meant to get progressively harder and harder to the point where it's nearly impossible at the end. Unless you're super awesome, you're probably not going to get to the 100th wave of the crucible, but at every checkpoint along the way you'll get different awards and you can kind of gamble your award to continue forward, or you can take it and leave the crucible. You also get little codes so that you can continue at certain levels of the crucible and you don't have to start from square one if you don't want to. It's really meant for the hardcore combat guys to test their awesomeness.

PRIMA: Could you explain how you came up with the way secondary weapons would work in *Darksiders II*?

DAVID: In *Darksiders I*, we've always had X as your primary weapon, and we always imagined that as the character's iconic weapon. War's was a sword, and Death's was a scythe. Y was always secondary weapon, which we thought was kind of cool because in most games, X is light attack and Y is heavy attack. When we went into *Darksiders II*, we knew it was going to be an RPG and that we were going to want a lot more variety in that regard, so we came with a bunch of different secondary weapon ideas. Initially there were fast and slow, which is light and heavy, and then thrown weapons like shuriken and blades and darts and stuff. We ended up converting the thrown weapons to the pistol but we kept the light and heavy. The heavies are axes and maces and pole arms and that sort of thing. The lights are hand blades and gauntlets and that sort of thing. But it really is just to give you the full spectrum of combat choices. With the scythe, it's sort of medium speed and range. The small weapons are short range but fast, and the heavy weapons are long range but heavy.

HAN RANDHAWA
ART DIRECTOR

PRIMA: Could you please introduce yourself and describe your role in the creation of *Darksiders II*?

HAN: I'm Han Randhawa, and I'm the Art Director for *Darksiders II*. My day-to-day role has a lot to do with making sure that the concepts and models and game assets that we made on *Darksiders II* ended up being very faithful and consistent to Joe Mad's visionary style. When there's a high-level concept from Joe, and let's say we have to make sure that it gets turned into a production drawing that the characters guys or modelers can understand… Once it goes to the modelers, they start building, and I'm on-hand on a daily basis to paint over and correct wherever possible to make sure that the end result is faithful to that style.

PRIMA: What have you done to evolve the art of *Darksiders II* from the first game?

HAN: To evolve the style from *Darksiders I*, what you guys saw there and in *Darksiders II*, we really wanted to push a lot more of the fantasy element. That's the biggest thing that we've done. It's also a much more open world. The actual style itself is way more fantasy. In *Darksiders I* you saw a post-apocalyptic city, relatively realistic looking buildings, and demons. Now, the setting is far more fantastic. We've got demon citadels; we've got angelic fortresses. A lot more of the environment is akin to the characters that Joe makes, so there's a lot more coherence there.

PRIMA: The game has a wide variety of colors; areas can look very different from each other. What were some of the things that inspired each area?

HAN: We have a much more colorful pallet on *Darksiders II* now. For some of the thematic that we were using for the color, we built out a color script to ensure that the player had a different experience every time he went to a different level. So if he went to a very blue looking area, he went to a green area next. There were reasons beyond just picking arbitrary colors. The Makers' area, for example, is green and lush, but there's a kind of toned down sensibility to them because this is a dying race and they've seen the best of their years. They're in their twilight years and it's time for their race to end. There's only a few of them about. So you can see there's kind of a sad beauty. I know that sounds a little farfetched, but that's basically what it is. You go to the demonic area, and naturally we're going to do oranges and reds, but there are actually two aspects to the demonic area. We know that throughout the game, there's corruption wherever you go, and the corruption has a kind of yellow-y twinge, so we'll see a part of the demonic area that has a yellow-y kind of feel. But you'll also travel back at one point in the demonic realm, and you'll see it as it was, all fiery brimstone red as you traditionally would see demonic realm. And then, to hop back to *Darksiders I*, Eden was the only angelic area we actually saw. That was kind of a Fall; beautiful oranges and burnt sienna. We kind of mimic that in the angelic area, but of course it's got the corruption aspects. Again, you'll see a place that was once beautiful, but which is overshadowed by this horrendous corruption.

PRIMA: Is there any part of the game that turned out so well that you are particularly proud of it?

HAN: The one aspect that I'm really proud and happy of is the combining of the fantasy environment and the stylization of the environment that allows those characters to really feel like they're in the right place and that it's all coherent. I think the colors and the lighting are something which I was pretty happy with because we really wanted to make sure that we didn't end up with some next gen kind of gray or brown-y feel. For me, colors aren't just about your base mother color. It's about the complementary colors and the triadic colors that go along with that. And I think where there are areas in which we got some beautiful sort of optical color going on. I don't know if anybody's familiar with impressionists and stuff like that, but they use optical color a lot, so that kind of coloring is actually very interesting and exciting for me. I was pretty happy with that.

PRIMA: Death has some pretty awesome looking weapons. Which one is your favorite, and why?

HAN: Death's weapons, if you really knew how many there were… there were just so many we created concepts for: everything from scythes, to hammers, to axes, to melee weapons. My favorite ones are probably going to be the scythes, and of those, the possessed scythes because you can feed other weapons into them. There are so many designs that I like of those scythes. There's an angelic one and a Maker one, which are probably my two favorites. I like the scythes, especially because it's Death and, you know, it just wouldn't be the ideal Death without a scythe. So that's the perfect weapon for me, playing that character.

PRIMA: So what comes after *Darksiders II*?

HAN: Right now I'm focusing on DLC, which is also very exciting. We're looking at some of the DLC and wondering, "Wait, why wasn't this in the main game? This is so awesome." There's some really good stuff there because we've all been working very, very hard on this and putting in some long hours. To get the game as best you can, that's what it takes.

HAYDN DALTON
LEAD DESIGNER

PRIMA: Could you please introduce yourself and tell us what a Lead Designer does?

HAYDN: Hi, my name is Haydn Dalton, and I'm the Lead Designer for *Darksiders II*. The Lead Designer role encompasses many different disciplines. I'm usually the person at the start of the project that gets everyone together to figure out what we want to do as a team, and I'll go in and try to put a framework to that and split it up into all the different components of what we think we need in order to make the game that we want to make. What would the Lead Environment guy do? What would the combat encounter people do? I work with the programmers on implementing new gear items, and see that through with the designers who are also implementing that. Once we get all of the main systems in it, it's just about taking care of all of those features until completion.

PRIMA: Where did you pull inspiration from for *Darksiders II*?

HAYDN: A lot of the inspiration for *Darksiders* came from Joe Mad's mind, essentially. I mean, he came up with the initial idea of setting a game around the four horsemen and the apocalypse. It was a toss-up between Death and War on the first game, and we decided to go with War. It was a natural progression to, "Who are we doing next?" He's all, "Okay, well, Death is the most popular horseman, it's the one that we nearly did for the first game." Based on the concepts that Joe did, Death was a lot sleeker, a lot more athletic looking than War was. So we needed to fit that into the character; the look of his character. Let's make him more agile, more fluid in combat. Joe had done the pictures of him holding two scythes, and he's like, "Well, why don't we make it so it's a singular scythe that can split and morph?" That's where all of that came from. Then it just developed with me and Dave Adams. Dave Adams did a lot of work on the story side to flesh out the world and everything, and it just grew from that.

PRIMA: What inspired you to institute a randomized loot system in *Darksiders II*?

HAYDN: The reason we went with the randomized loot system in *Darksiders II* is because we wanted to give the player a slightly different experience depending on how they play the game. Also, we had a lot of ambient encounters in the first game where you saw a creature off in the distance and thought, "Well, I don't really get anything from that creature other than an extra fight. I could just move on." But now there's always that smart machine tout type of feel for the player, where if he goes and kills that guy, he might get that one piece of rare loot that he's looking for, or that item with the specific stat that he's looking for, whatever it might be. Once you add that sort of jackpot-type of randomized element, there's always that way of giving randomization through gameplay. The loot really helped draw people to go and kill things and smash things open to try and find things in the world. I think, since we've been testing it, that it's definitely been a great draw for the game. In *Darksiders I*, you barely went into the inventory, right? You played the game, you killed things, and you picked up some odd items. A lot of that stuff had just continued off the flow of the gameplay. Now, with loot, there are a lot of times when you might want to go into the inventory to compare and switch things out. You're spending a lot of time fracturing the gameplay experience. That's one of the reasons why we placed a comparison window right in the game, so you can see how a piece of loot goes up against the piece of loot that you currently have equipped, and so you don't have to always go into the inventory. I can see how people could see that as a downside to the flow of the game, but I think that once you get used to the fact that you can either auto-equip or you can manual equip the items straight from the scene, I don't think it fractures it as badly as it could have. Plus, the loot gives so much depth, allowing players to really focus on certain attributes of their character stats. If you just want to focus on strength to make sure that your melee attacks do a lot of damage, you can do that. If you really want to just go all out on critical chance, or if you want every critical hit to do double or three times the amount of damage, you can do that. But you have to take a hit somewhere else. Maybe you have to lose a bit of defense to get the stat you want, or maybe you have to lose some strength to get a bigger buff on your arcane. It might just do more damage. These are all choices that players are going to have to do on the fly, and I feel like it's going to be its own little ecosystem of a game in itself. I think that's the one thing that we spent a lot of time on, so I'm hoping people like it and that they don't think that it fractures the gameplay too much, and it doesn't deter too much from the original *Darksiders*.

PRIMA: Where did the idea for the Crucible come from?

HAYDN: Dave, the GM of the company, basically threw down the gauntlet to the entire company. "Let's come up with an idea that we can put in the game, and if we think it's good enough and we can draw on resources that we already have for the game and plan to do, and we can use those things to create a new component, we'll put it in the game." So essentially, it was like anyone on the project could come up with an idea and have a whole chunk of the game dedicated to it, which I thought was kind of cool. Our Combat Designer, Ben Cureton, came up with the idea of doing a crucible which is a bloody palace-type thing where you progress through levels of combat and it gets harder and harder and the prizes get more and more high level. The difficulty is based on how far you can gamble without dying. We thought, well that's great, because we're going to be bringing in creatures from the game that we've already done. The mechanics of the creatures would already be there. We just need to create a new environment, and then basically do a ton of waves that our character's got to get through. Then, we test in layers, and in how far the player can go. When you get to the crucible, the creatures are usually a few levels higher than the player, so to actually get through a whole section of the crucible is going to be pretty hard. Plus, it's entirely new loot that players can get, inside, and it's the only place that you can get it. I think people are going to find some cool stuff, including some pieces of the newer bits of armor that Death has.

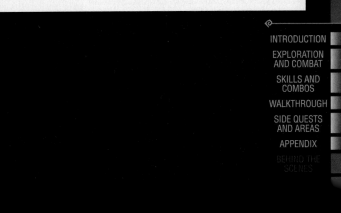

JOE MADUREIRA
CREATIVE DIRECTOR

PRIMA: Could you please introduce yourself and tell us what it is you do at Vigil Games?

JOE: I'm Joe Madureira, the Creative Director at Vigil Games. As the Creative Director, I oversee the character creation and story, and early on I was involved in pretty much every aspect, creatively, that you could be. Nowadays we have a grown team. We have a lot of leads in various departments, and I communicate with them directly.

PRIMA: How did you first become involved with the *Darksiders* franchise?

JOE: *Darksiders* started as the kind of game we wanted to make before there was even a Vigil Games. Myself, David Adams, Ryan Stefanelli, and Marvin Donald; we knew we wanted to make a 3D action adventure game, but we had no idea about a theme. We ran through a bunch of ideas that we hated, and then one day I had this idea of a post-apocalyptic theme—not after a nuclear holocaust, but after an angelic and demonic invasion. Who would fight these guys? There were the four horsemen, these mythical, biblical superheroes, sort of. There's so little known about them that it was like a blank slate. We got really excited because everyone's heard of the four horsemen. Even if you don't know a thing about them, you've heard of them. You know they are somehow involved in the destruction of earth. I felt like there was less that we had to explain to people; they got the premise right away. After that, we were all excited about it and we didn't really feel like exploring any other opportunities.

PRIMA: Where did your inspiration for the character design in the *Darksiders* universe come from?

JOE: I come from a comic book background, and a lot of the style of the game and of the character design is grounded in a comic book, larger-than-life style. We created a lot of stylized art at the studio. That means we don't make a lot of photo real games, like many studios do. We are very art heavy, and a lot of the people that we hired on were already familiar with my work from comic books, and people we would meet with were excited about that aspect of it and how the art was looking so we just pushed it more in that direction. It gives our games a pretty distinct look, I think. Keeps it from getting too dark and keeps it out of the horror genre; it's not scary horror, it's cool. We just try to make sure everything looks cool, and the weapons are huge so that all the dudes are ripped, and all the women are really pretty. It's just like what you'd find in comics.

PRIMA: *Darksiders II* seems much bigger in scale when compared to the first game. Did this present any challenges for the team?

JOE: It was pretty challenging this time around because the game world is so much bigger and we have so many more characters. Just creating content that's new and cool when we had so much in the first game as it is… It definitely presented a couple of challenges, but at the same time, our team was much more experienced, and we did have some outside help as well. We were smart enough to get help because we knew the game was really big. I think it came together really well, though.

PRIMA: What are you hoping to work on once *Darksiders II* is all done? Any comic related projects coming up?

JOE: After *Darksiders II*, we're obviously already planning the next title; whether it will or won't be a *Darksiders* title, we're not saying just yet. But we are in the early stages of that project, and I do still do comics outside of Vigil. I have a project for Marvel that's coming out early next year, I think, but that hasn't been announced either. It'll be cool.

PRIMA: Who is your favorite character, and why?

JOE: My favorite character in *Darksiders II* is, strangely enough, probably one of the first characters that you encounter early on. He's called the Crowfather, and he's the keeper of secrets. I didn't quite know how he was going to translate into 3D. He's this gnarly old guy with huge feathers and wizard robes and stuff, and he's probably one of the more stylized characters that we have. I think that the way he came together and his role in the game is really cool. It surprised me. I just didn't think it was going to come together as well as it did. We had already done tons of demons and cool monsters in the first game. I think the ones that I wasn't expecting to be cool always end up being my favorites.

Marvin Donald

Game Director

PRIMA: Could you introduce yourself and explain your role in the creation of *Darksiders II*?

MARVIN: My name is Marvin Donald, and I'm the Game Director for *Darksiders II*. I spent most of my time focusing on the story, the key moments, the quests, all of the voiceovers in the game, and anything else that was quest related because that was probably the biggest feature that was added to the *Darksiders* experience.

PRIMA: The original *Darksiders* was well-received by the gaming community. What did you hope to accomplish in *Darksiders II*?

MARVIN: We made the experience more RPG driven, with character progression, and limited your skill points so that you had to make choices on how your character was going to develop rather than just acquiring every single upgrade. You're going to have to make some sacrifices, so there's some meaning behind what you do. Deciding what to focus on as a major strength in regards to your gear, whether you're going to be focusing on strength or arcane, makes a big difference regarding the wrath abilities that you're going to use. You're choosing one avenue over another; one way of kicking ass in the game and getting through some of the boss fights and tougher encounters, as opposed to another. People are going to have debates over what's best, and I think that's really good.

PRIMA: What has been your favorite part of creating *Darksiders II*?

MARVIN: Getting involved with the items system, and just being excited in general about the ability to equip things that were dropped by monsters or that you find in chests, and watching your character change. Working on the random item generation and giving players the experience where they're going to feel like their character's unique because the same loot won't be dropped every single time you play through the game—I thought that was really pivotal to making the *Darksiders II* experience more personal, and watching that system develop was really cool.

PRIMA: What would you say is your favorite location in *Darksiders II*?

MARVIN: I really like the second zone, overall. I like the kingdom of the dead because the dark atmosphere is something that Death fits in well. When you look at the way the character is designed, his cool skull mask and his emo rock and roll look, I think it all jives really well. And I really like some of the ambient music; it's really cool and a little bit different. Not what you'd expect. It's got a nice modern touch to it, while still staying within a fantasy realm of music. It was definitely nice and unexpected, and there's just something about smashing skeletons that is totally rewarding. You'll have the opportunity to do that over and over again, and it's a lot of fun.

RYAN STEFANELLI
PRODUCER

PRIMA: Could you please introduce yourself and describe what you did during the development for *Darksiders II*?

RYAN: My name is Ryan Stefenalli and I was the Producer for *Darksiders II*. My role ultimately ended up being filling in the cracks wherever we needed it. I was the Lead Level Designer on *Darksiders I*, so I ended up working very intimately with the level team on *Darksiders II*. There was some of the boring producer stuff, interfacing with corporate, but most of what I did was building levels and helping our Lead Designer lead the Level Design Team.

PRIMA: What was an average day like for you during the production of *Darksiders II*?

RYAN: The average day varied. I mean, early on it was pretty relaxed and we were having a lot of fun. And of course, you get toward the end of the project and the intensity ramps up on the attention to detail; it becomes much finer. We work a lot of hours in this industry. It's definitely a labor of love, but I think that love is going to show. There's a lot to *Darksiders II*. It was a huge game. It was very ambitious, and there are so many facets to it that required a lot of focus, but the team pulled it off despite the difficult hours.

PRIMA: What would you say is the most difficult area in *Darksiders II*?

RYAN: We try to make games for gamers. It's sort of an old cliché, but games now are becoming so cinematic and story-driven, so driven by the visuals and the events that are occurring that there are fewer and fewer games that are driven specifically by the gameplay. But that's the studio as a whole—we are a gameplay-driven studio. I think that shows with a game like *Darksiders*, which offers players so much. There's so much you can play with between the traversing and the puzzle solving, and we hope that players can really appreciate that sort of old-school mentality to game development.

PRIMA: Do you have any funny stories to share about things that happened during production?

RYAN: The people who work here all get along so well, and there's such good chemistry. Whether it's getting in food fights where we're throwing tortillas at each other, or pushing each other down the hallway as fast as we can on office chairs only to have somebody inevitably tumble out of the chair and hit the wall and put a hole in it or break something... if you come into our leads row and look up, there are thumbtacks stuck in the ceiling. Old *Darksiders I* disks are thrown all over the place. Whoever was the last person to make a mistake with a build gets this giant pink Tasmanian Devil that has to sit behind their monitor until somebody else screws something up. There are so many examples of those types of pranks and jokes being played on people that it's almost hard to remember one that stands out because there are a lot.

PRIMA: What is your favorite part of *Darksiders II*?

RYAN: I, personally, am attached to some of the smaller areas. Designing the smaller areas is always a little more interesting because they're sort of freed from stories, so you can just do whatever you want. I had the luxury of designing some of the smaller side dungeons that are in the Makers' realm. I don't even remember what they're called because we have our own internal names for them and they don't translate into the real game. The one that I would probably go back to the most as being personally fulfilling was the Foundry. The General Manager, David Adams, and I, that's the dungeon that we laid out. It was a big challenge, and there's a lot going on in it, but the team that helped us and worked on it with us really pulled it off. I think it's going be one of the more memorable and epic dungeons. It will be interesting to see how players fare when they get into some of the later dungeons, when they have a lot of gear items to play with. People who've played *Darksiders I* know that one of our most important formulas is the alchemy between all the gameplay, once we're throwing the player between combat, traversing, and puzzle solving. You get into some of the later dungeons when you have a lot at your disposal, and there are some pretty mind bending puzzles in there. I think when people reach the angel citadel and start getting to mess with the Voidwalker, I think it's really going to be a challenge, but there's a great feeling of fulfillment once you make it through some of those puzzles because they're real brain benders.

PRIMA: What was something that you were very happy to get into the game?

RYAN: The thing that we were the most amped up to get into the game was the loot. I think that's something that is really going to start to set *Darksiders* apart as a franchise, from the steps that we took in *Darksiders I*—the depth of the character development and how the loot plays with the skills trees that are now available. Because exploration is such a big part, because it's so intrinsic to the franchise, having something like loot is a great way to give people incentive to explore every little nook and cranny out there in the world. We like to explore, so being able to put in the type of mechanic that gives players the incentive to do it and really care about it, it becomes a lot of fun every time you kill a creature, break a barrel or open a chest. You just don't know what you're going to get. We're all loot whores; we love it, and we can't wait for it to get into players' hands.

INTRODUCTION

EXPLORATION
AND COMBAT

SKILLS AND
COMBOS

WALKTHROUGH

SIDE QUESTS
AND AREAS

APPENDIX

BEHIND THE
SCENES

TIM DONLEY
DEVELOPMENT DIRECTOR

Could you please introduce yourself and explain what you do and what you enjoy about working at Vigil Games?

TIM: My name is Tim Donley and I'm the Development Director for *Darksiders II*. What did I enjoy about working on *Darksiders II*, and what was exciting to me? It was the team. The team is great; a very fun group of guys. We had a great management group and a very invested team. What did that mean to me? It made it easy to come into work. It made it exciting. It made me excited to see the game each day. It made me happy to work with this great group of guys. Most of the team loved the game. They just wanted to be there. They wanted to work on stuff. And yeah, we had our ups and downs, and we had our moments where maybe things didn't go exactly as planned. But a lot of times, it went better than we'd hoped.

PRIMA: So, just how big is *Darksiders II*?

TIM: I worked on *Darksiders I*, so I know how big that was. I'd say *Darksiders II* is maybe three or four times as big, and to keep that quality level, to go that much bigger and have that much more quality to basically hit—it's hard. We had a great team to do it. We had a really good, strong vision at the top, and we had a really strong crew in the middle and down through the ranks, and everybody was always trying to hit that bar. And it was tough. I mean, it was really tough. But, you know, we worked really hard. Sure, we had late nights, but overall, the game's great. I've been playing it, now that it's all wrapped up; I've been playing it and I've just been amazed. You know, it's one of those things that, now that it's finished, going back and playing it… it just seems even more amazing now. Because it's one thing to see people develop the game, to see people working on stuff, and then another thing to go back and play it and go, "Oh, these guys are related to that. Oh, I didn't know that was connected to there." I mean, we've got so much stuff in the game.

PRIMA: Can you tell us about the loot, abilities, and any other interesting information fans might want to know about?

TIM: We have loot; didn't have that in *Darksiders I*, or at least not to this extent. You've got pretty much a custom character you can create. You know—tons of different weapons and armor. One of the things I'm excited about is the possessed weapons, which are basically custom weapons. You can find weapons and feed other weapons into them to make your own weapon. So you can, let's say, have a weapon that's a possessed hammer and feed it another weapon. It could be armor; it could be another type of weapon. Doesn't matter. Let's say it's got some attribute like fire or healing or whatever. If you feed that to the possessed weapon, the possessed weapon takes on the qualities of the weapon you fed it. And you can feed it different kinds of weapons. So you can have a possessed weapon that does fire, healing, maybe even does ice damage or some sort of critical or piercing damage—something that you wouldn't have had before. I mean, it's just one of those things that it makes it super exciting to me because you wouldn't normally have that kind of stuff. So instead of buying a custom weapon that's maybe like, you know, a volcano hammer that does all this damage, you can make your own hammer. What makes it cool is that once you realize what you have to do, you just start saving up your weapons. It's almost like the game takes on a whole different life. Everything you pick up is suddenly way more important than before. You're always looking at items, like, "Oh, what are the stats on this?" You're checking them out in the menus and trying to figure it out. It's made the game a lot more fun to me. I want to go everywhere and do everything now. I want to open every chest. I want to go to every corner of the world because I want to make sure I get all the treasure I possibly can so that I can make the best weapon possible. And really, the only way to do it is to go and explore. It's fun to just run around and fight the creatures and everything. Not only is the combat much more extensive because all of the weapons have their own abilities and moves and special moves, but you can buy tons of moves, too, which is another big thing. The game has a level of customization that *Darksiders I* didn't have. I mean, now you have trainers; you have people you can buy moves from; you have people who give you moves. You have tons of abilities that are related to the Reaper Form. You've got your alter ego. In *Darksiders I* you had your Wrath Form, which was the big fiery demon that came out, and in *Darksiders II* you've got the Reaper Form, and he can do all sorts of damage. Beyond that, you have a magic system and you can buy attributes and skills that allow you to cast out crows, or summon all these ghouls that come out of coffins, and do all this damage. You've got combat abilities to buy there, too. You'll probably see teleport slash; I'm sure you guys will notice all that stuff. But there's just so many things, and it really is one of those things we always said: the name of the game is customize your own Death. And this is one of those games where you really do get to customize whatever you want. By the end of the game, it really is your Death, and it really is the way you like to play. The game lets you do the things you want to do. If you enjoy a certain type of game play, if you're an aggressive player, you can play an aggressive game; you can buy a bunch of stuff that makes the game fun for you. If you're someone that likes to stand back and be defensive and cast spells and deal damage from a distance, you can do that, too. You can do pretty much whatever you want, and it's fun. The game is bigger and better. I've enjoyed it, I think it's great, and I hope the people who play it enjoy it as much as I did. It's fun, and I'm not just saying that because I worked on it. I'm saying it because I'm a gamer and I play a lot of games and I don't get excited about too many of them unless they're really, really fun. I've been playing this and looking forward to getting my real gamer score instead of my gamer score here. I'm tired of that.

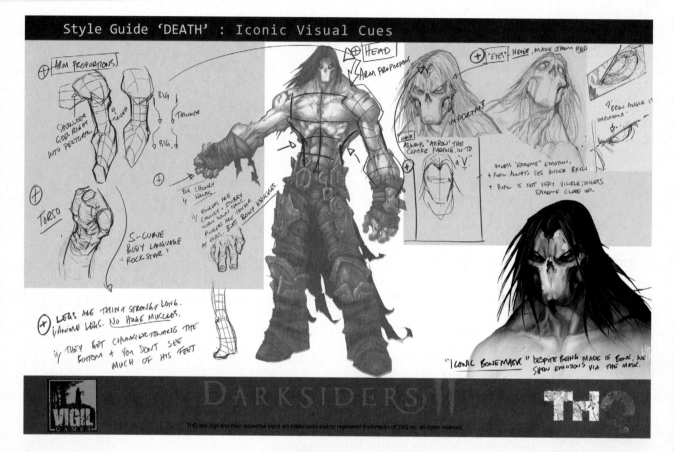

By Han Randhawa

Style Guide 'DEATH' : Iconic Visual Cues

DARKSIDERS II

PRIMA: How do you get from an original Joe Mad drawing to the final 3D model or character environment, whatever it may be?

HAN: There's a process to it. I've spent quite a lot of time looking at Joe's stuff and then breaking it down for the uninitiated to understand what's going on underneath that 2D image. If we have a Joe sketch of Death, you can see his basic physique structure and some common elements of Joe's style. He never does very rounded silhouettes or anything like that. It's always usually pretty edgy, and that goes for not only the silhouette but actually the surface treatment as well. You can see that it stems from his influences in anime, manga, movies, and all kinds of awesome artwork. You can see the structure, the body language that Death has. You can see that he's got rather big shoulders and slightly skinnier arms, and bigger forearms and hands. This is a key character trait. Also, I've broken down the faceted style, and you'll see that the character from the base is a lot larger wider in his stance and narrowest to the top. This gives him weight, gives him a kind of a presence and really firm rooting as he's standing and posing and looking awesome.

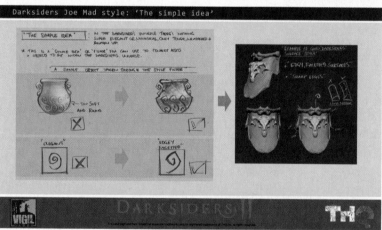

Darksiders Joe Mad style: 'The simple idea'

Early BlueRooms : Paintover exploration

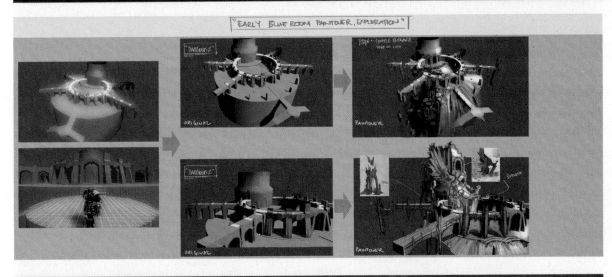

Maker Shaman : 'Concept To Ingame model'

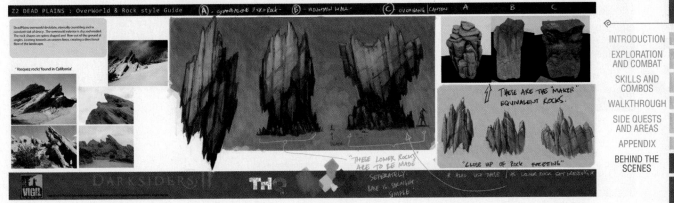

Those ideas can be translated exactly into a doorway entrance, or even something as simple as a pot. I did a re-simplified drawing just to get all of those ideas into one image; to say, "How do we take one asset and sort of Joe-Mad-ify it?" In this drawing, you can see that we have a perfectly usable and serviceable pot; it's round, it's got details, it's got a nice flat surface. Now, take that through the *Darksiders* machine, and what we get on the other side is something which is a little bit different. It's got facets to it, the surface is a little bit uneven, it's not perfectly symmetrical, and it's got edgier breaks that are going onto it as well. So, in a nutshell, you should be able to translate this sort of idea to any asset or character in the game. For us, that's a key drawing that you can take away and memorize easily. That's why I wanted to make sure that we didn't have pages and pages and pages of rules and rules and this. It's hard to retain that when you're working on like any asset, so you need a simple idea that you can apply at any point. That's why this drawing exists. This, what we have here, is a really good asset; a 3D asset that uses those rules to get it into the Darksider style. If you want to see one end result of that, this is a sidepiece to Death's armor that conforms to all those rules. You can see it's got fasted edges where the planes meet, and it feels like if you ran your hand across it you'd hurt your hand or something. It's not all perfectly smooth, and that gives us that kind of edgy style.

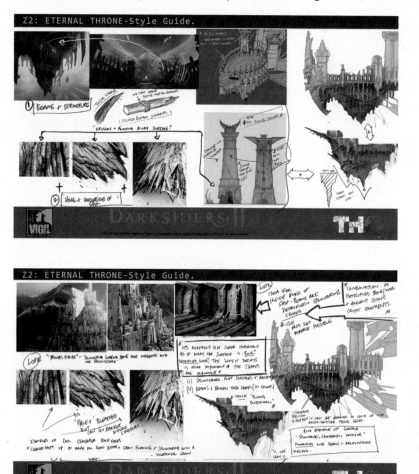

This is more Death feedback, focusing mostly on his iconic faceplate. So, one of the big things that we've been pushing is Death's mask. It was very important to make sure that certain key things about his mask were understood exactly by whichever artist, external or internal, had to build something from there. They needed to know what the key iconic shapes were, and what could not be messed with, especially around his eyes. It's like a V shape, the way his eyes are spaced, the spacing of where his nose is, and the way his cheeks cut in—these are all key things that cannot be messed with. Otherwise, it ceases to become Death's mask.

So these are examples of an asset in Zone 2, and this is where the dead king is flying about. You get to go and speak to him about the next quest you're going to do. This is his bone ship, so it's made of encrusted bones and all kinds of other cartilage matter. We had to break that down. We looked at material, stone-type material. The artists need to know what the surface is going to be made out of in real terms because they have to sculpt it and texture it, and it's got to work in the lighting. Then, there's also the architecture. You can see that it's got a rib cage kind of feel; it almost looks like it's a big gutted whale, which is pretty awesome. These show how we take a simple idea and break it down a little bit more. Obviously, if you gave someone just that simple idea, they might still be lost.

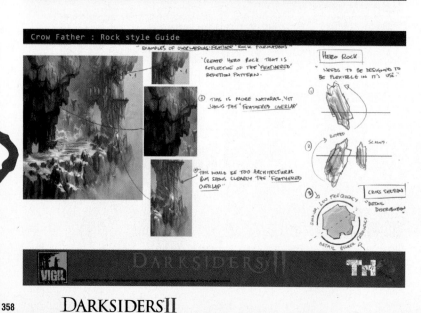

I also do paint-overs. Take this character, for example. This is where our modeler started to do the Reaper Form, and you can see what he's doing—he's pushing the style—you can see he's putting the curvature in there, but it's still very computer generated and still relatively smooth. He's still allowing the computer to do all the talking, and it basically looks like it could be a generated image. So I've gone in there, painted over it, and really offset some of the bones and broken down some of the angles so that nothing is aligning perfectly. So things are offset and you get that sense of uneasiness which ties into the supernatural feel of *Darksiders II*. This is the way we do course correction. We've got our high level concept, the concept they're working from, and style sheets. Then, they build a model out, and I'm on-hand on a daily basis. We look at our work in progress every day, and if there's something that needs course directing, I'll grab that image and paint over it. Of course, Joe and all of our leads are looking at this because all of those WIPs go company-wide. Everybody gets to see how the art on the game is progressing, and everyone gets excited about where we're going with this. That's a very, very condensed version of what happens when you take a 2D concept drawing and try and convert it into a 3D element.

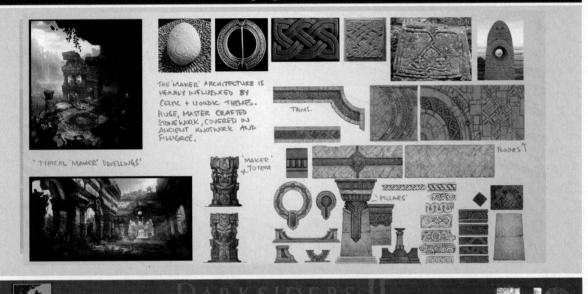

INTRODUCTION

EXPLORATION AND COMBAT

SKILLS AND COMBOS

WALKTHROUGH

SIDE QUESTS AND AREAS

APPENDIX

BEHIND THE SCENES

A CLOSER LOOK AT DEATH WITH CREATIVE DIRECTOR JOE MADUREIRA

Designing Death was pretty interesting because everyone has these preconceived images of what Death is—the Angel of Death, the horseman called Death, the Grim Reaper—and we had a very specific plan for how this character would be. We wanted him to be a lot different than War, who was a big, tough fighter. With all of the horsemen, we wanted it to be very clear that they are not human. It's not a guy in a costume. It's not a human person. You'll see pieces of bone coming through the skin. He'll stand a little more hunched, and we see how far we can push it from the direction of playing like a human creature without losing people's ability to empathize with him and relate to him. He definitely strikes a lot of cool poses, and he's always hunched over. The way he climbs is a little more like scurrying, and he's very acrobatic, but in a sort of scary way. We definitely wanted him to be imposing and not just like a hero; not like Batman or Captain America or a traditional hero. It's almost more like playing a villain. That's one of the things that I love about Death more than any other character that we've done. Our version of Death would be more of an assassin—still a killer, but a different type of killer. You know, light weapons, light armor, and very agile. He can climb walls, and he can do a lot of stuff that War couldn't do. But we didn't want to give him a face; we wanted to leave a little mystery. That's why he has the mask. There are certain things we kept as the character evolved, and we tried different looks. Whenever we took those things away, like the mask or the scythes, it just felt wrong.

Despair Color Study
WIP

When we decided to give Death the mask no matter what, we did realize that in a lot of the cut scenes, because there are so many cut scenes nowadays, that you really rely on expression a lot. Subtle like lip twitches, or eyes narrowing, or whatever it takes to make a snarl. You kind of need a face, and you need facial features, so we were worried that because there's a mask, it's all hidden from you. How were we going to convey all this drama? We had to play around with that quite a bit, and I think what we ended up with was really cool, partly due to the fact that Michael Wincott's voice is just so awesome—he could be behind a paper bag and he would still sound pretty awesome.

DARKSIDERS II

THQ

In trying to build this very recognizable character that is obviously Death, we were faced with the additional challenge of wanting players to be able to customize them so that my version and your version might look different, and that presented challenges as well. When you start mixing and matching the pieces, they could look strange, and usually when you create an iconic character, you don't change anything about them. We had to have this character that was iconic within our world and still be able to dress him up however we wanted. We developed these archetypes that never stray too far from that version of death we were trying to create. It still looks like the character, but it has the flavor of a rogue, or as we call it, the wanderer. And we have increments, and they're just different aspects of the character. In addition to that, we did feel like we were gypping people if they didn't get to see the Grim Reaper in all his glory, so we do have a Reaper Form that manifests itself in subtle ways throughout the game. Ghostly hands slam a door open in front of Death to let him into a room, or sometimes you actually do turn into him, and he is the robed skeletal nightmare with a giant scythe and everything. It's more like what people expect, sort of like the idealized version of Death.

BRACERS
(BUCKLER)

TOP
VIEW

ARM
BLADE
(TONFA)

POLEARM
(NAGINATA)

BOMB

THROWING
BLADE

All of the horsemen have a pretty awesome steed that they ride. Ruin was War's mount in the first game, and for Death we created Despair. Not surprisingly, Despair is skeletal, and he's got this brimstone and—I don't even know what it is—unholy fire coming off of him. It's really awesome to summon him and ride around on him. In the first game, Mark Hammel played a character called the Watcher, who basically directed War around the game world. We decided that because we don't have a guide in this game like we did in the first game, we would give Death a raven companion called Dust.

He follows you around and he does act as a guide, but it's in a more subtle way. He might fly down a hallway or just circle around important areas that you should explore, but he never speaks to you or hits you over the head with knowledge. You just hear him cawing, and he lands on your shoulder. It gives a lot of character to Death, and we felt like whenever we tried to remove it, the overall character wasn't as cool because this bird wasn't around, so Dust ended up becoming a pretty important character in this game, as well.

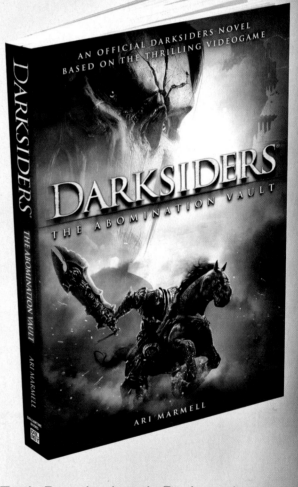

DARKSIDERS® II

PRIMA Official Game Guide
WRITTEN BY: STEVE STRATTON

Prima Games
An Imprint of Random House, Inc.
3000 Lava Ridge Court, Suite 100
Roseville, CA 95661
www.primagames.com

 The Prima Games logo is a registered trademark of Random House, Inc., registered in the United States and other countries. Primagames.com is a registered trademark of Random House, Inc., registered in the United States. Prima Games is an imprint of Random House, Inc.

Product Manager: **Jesse Anderson**

Design & Layout: **In Color Design**

Copyedit: **Joanie Chew**

Maps: **Philip Roes**

Technical Editor: **Paul Bernardo**

Photographs: **Andrea Hill**

Prima Games would like to thank Jay Fitzloff, Tyler Johnston, Jeramy Bergerson, Ben Cureton, Ben Gabbard, Steve Massey, Han Randhawa, Haydn Dalton, Joe Madureira, Mathew Everett, Simon Watts, and Jon Bailey for their help and support.

Important:

Prima Games has made every effort to determine that the information contained in this book is accurate. However, the publisher makes no warranty, either expressed or implied, as to the accuracy, effectiveness, or completeness of the material in this book; nor does the publisher assume liability for damages, either incidental or consequential, that may result from using the information in this book. The publisher cannot provide any additional information or support regarding gameplay, hints and strategies, or problems with hardware or software. Such questions should be directed to the support numbers provided by the game and/or device manufacturers as set forth in their documentation. Some game tricks require precise timing and may require repeated attempts before the desired result is achieved.

ISBN: 978-0-307-89477-9   Printed in the United States of America   12 13 14 15 LL 10 9 8 7 6 5 4 3 2 1